Blind over Cuba

NUMBER ELEVEN: FOREIGN RELATIONS AND THE PRESIDENCY

BLIND
OVER
CUBA

The Photo Gap
and the Missile Crisis

David M. Barrett
& Max Holland

Texas A&M University Press
College Station

This paper meets the requirements of
ANSI/NISO Z39.48-1992 (Permanence of Paper).
Binding materials have been chosen for durability.

Library of Congress Cataloging-in-Publication Data

Barrett, David M., 1951–
    Blind over Cuba / David M. Barrett and Max Holland. — 1st ed.
        p. cm. — (Foreign relations and the presidency ; no. 11)
    Includes bibliographical references and index.
    ISBN 978-1-60344-768-3 (cloth : alk. paper) —
    ISBN 1-60344-768-7 (cloth : alk. paper) —
    ISBN 978-1-60344-772-0 (e-book) —
    ISBN 1-60344-772-5 (e-book)
    1. Cuban Missile Crisis, 1962.   2. Intelligence service—Political aspects—
United States.   3. Executive-legislative relations—United States.
4. United States—Politics and government—1961–1963.
5. National security—Political aspects—United States.
I. Holland, Max.   II. Title.   III. Series: Foreign relations
and the presidency ; no. 11.
    E841.B36   2012
    973.922—dc23
    2012004754

In memory of Stephen S. Barrett and Cynthia Hernandez Kolski
and
to Sam Halpern, for his patient tutelage

Contents

Introduction

A nother book on the Cuban Missile Crisis? Yes and no. Other than outright wars, probably no US foreign policy crisis of the twentieth century has been the subject of more books than this crisis. So, as researchers and writers, our interest has not been in writing another general history of the event. Instead, we tell a heretofore mostly unknown story of intelligence and politics during John F. Kennedy's presidency, both before and after the crisis. We believe there are at least five reasons that justify this endeavor.

Surprising as it might seem, some papers of the people and agencies that were crucially involved in the crisis are still being declassified. The slowness of this effort is regrettable and perhaps indefensible, seeing as how it occurred a half century ago, but such are the ways of the US government and the vagaries governing access to private papers. And a good rule of thumb is that until the paper trail is exhausted, the history of any event is subject to revision.

Second, scholars have mostly neglected the papers of members of the US Congress, some of whom predicted, weeks or months before the crisis, that the Soviet Union would deploy missiles and nuclear warheads in Cuba. As formerly secret tape recordings made at the White House indicate, President Kennedy worried that Congress might investigate not only the performance of intelligence agencies during the lead-up to the crisis but also his own performance. His concerns were more than warranted. This book, drawing on papers of senators and representatives, documents the questions that were asked in the wake of the crisis, and the one investigation that was conducted, by a Senate subcommittee. It is not a gratifying story. The Kennedy administration repeatedly misled legislators who were groping to ask the right—and hard—questions.

Third, while the famous thirteen days of the crisis have been widely chronicled, the days, weeks, and months preceding mid-October 1962 have been relatively understudied and insufficiently chronicled. Meanwhile, the months following the crisis have been all but ignored in the history books with a few exceptions. As we show here, a tense, behind-the-scenes domestic political drama occurred from November 1962 through the following May. While the Kennedy White House ultimately succeeded—perhaps too well—in shaping the predominant narrative of the Cuban Missile Crisis, it took considerable and highly stressful political work by President Kennedy and his associates to make that occur.

Fourth, although many authors have written about the CIA and other intelligence agencies in relation to the crisis, they have barely described the distinctly political interactions between CIA leaders, who pushed for more aggressive intelligence collection before the acute phase of the crisis in October, and President Kennedy and his subordinates, who either resisted those CIA efforts or tried to cover up most evidence of pre-crisis "intelligence failures" after the crisis had subsided. While perhaps not agreeing with JFK's private description of McCone as "a bastard," a "horse's ass," and "stupid," readers will (we hope) understand the source of the president's resentment.

Finally, in showing that the "story" of the Cuban Missile Crisis was substantially shaped by Kennedy administration leaders, our book is a sobering reminder that "spin" and "stonewall" are words that can be applied to the behavior of many a president in American history, including one of its most celebrated.

Blind over Cuba

The Making of a "Photo Gap"

O
n October 28, 1962, President Kennedy triumphed in the most fearsome and direct clash with Moscow since the 1948 Berlin airlift. Without seeming to have made any meaningful concessions, he both avoided nuclear war and forced Soviet premier Nikita Khrushchev into a humiliating retreat. On November 5, the Soviets, as promised, began withdrawing the first of forty-two nuclear-tipped offensive missiles they had shipped to Cuba that September.[1]

During and after the crisis, however, the administration harbored three secrets that would have substantially altered public and international perceptions of events. The first was Operation MONGOOSE, an ongoing effort to subvert Fidel Castro's regime that had been launched six months after the unsuccessful Bay of Pigs invasion in April 1961. Washington's hostility to Havana, of course, was hardly a secret. But the existence of a government-wide operation, overseen by Attorney General Robert F. Kennedy and including plans to assassinate Castro, was not known outside of the president's national security apparatus, and the direct plots against Castro were even more tightly held than that.[2] Operation MONGOOSE became public knowledge in 1975 as a result of congressional investigations conducted by the so-called Church committee.[3] Many historians since have pointed out the ways in which it helped foment the missile crisis: Castro's fears of further US intervention, it turned out, had not been wholly unfounded.[4]

The second secret was equally sensitive: the quid pro quo that ended the acute phase of the crisis. In exchange for the prompt, very public, and verified withdrawal of the Soviet missiles, President Kennedy publicly pledged not to invade Cuba. At the same time, he privately committed to quietly dismantle the US Jupiter missile sites in Turkey the following year. No more than eight of Kennedy's advisers knew about this agreement at the time, and they went to great lengths to protect the information, such that the quid pro quo remained a lively but unconfirmed rumor for nearly three decades.[5] Not until 1989, when the former Soviet ambassador Anatoly Dobrynin publicly disclosed the secret agreement, did they stop denying its existence.[6]

The third secret concerned why it took Washington a full month to spot the offensive missiles. This secret proved to be the most durable and hardest to unpack. The US government had been regularly sending U-2 surveillance flights over Cuba since October 1960 in advance of the Bay of Pigs invasion.[7] However, lulled somewhat by extensive Soviet and Cuban efforts to disguise the missile deployment, the administration decided to limit those overflights for five crucial weeks in the late summer and early fall of 1962—precisely when the offensive missiles were being moved into place.[8]

The "photo gap," as Republicans dubbed it at the time, was rightly seen by administration officials as more problematic even than the secret quid pro quo.[9] They labored mightily to obfuscate it—and largely succeeded. Only after the declassification in 2003 of certain key primary records, including investigations held immediately after the crisis, could this aspect of the crisis be fully documented and understood.

These records alter the conventional narrative in important respects. The handling of events did not epitomize a "wonderfully coordinated and error-free 'crisis management'" between policy makers and the intelligence community, as Bundy would later have it.[10] It was largely the opposite: a close call stemming directly from decisions made in a climate of deep distrust between key administration officials and the intelligence community. Almost every standard account of the crisis has essentially ignored the tension and rampant uncertainty between these entities and within the CIA itself, to the detriment of depicting the full complexity of what actually occurred.

The New Leader at Langley

At the time of the missile crisis, and for the first time in its short history, the CIA was led by a man whose political affiliation and ideology were widely viewed as being at direct odds with the administration he served.

As part of the reshuffling of officials after the Bay of Pigs operation, President Kennedy had appointed John McCone the acting CIA director in September 1961, subject to Senate confirmation. Liberals in the administration were appalled. For starters, McCone, a California engineer-turned-tycoon, was the embodiment of the wealthy, conservative Republican businessmen who had overwhelmingly populated Dwight D. Eisenhower's administration (although McCone had also served as Truman's undersecretary of the air force). More important, while chairman of the Atomic Energy Commission during Eisenhower's last term, he had earned a reputation as a "militant" anticommunist and "real [bureaucratic] alley fighter."[11] Many Democrats and administration officials were specifically concerned that his stiff-necked anticommunism might distort the intelligence produced by a demoralized CIA still reeling from the Bay of Pigs failure. His relations with the scientific community, which generally supported arms control and disarmament efforts, had also been problematic, and he seemed out of sync with the Kennedy administration's dominant ethos, which, while ill-defined, was supposed to be distinct from the brinksmanship that characterized the 1950s.[12] In fact, McCone would probably have been the leading candidate for secretary of defense had Richard Nixon won the 1960 election.[13]

The opposition to McCone's permanent appointment badly unnerved him. When his wife suddenly died, he seriously contemplated declining the nomination. In January 1962, he asked associates at the CIA to consult with the White House about the possibility of withdrawing his name; however, administration aides assured him this was "unnecessary and undesirable" from the president's point of view. His credentials, and good ties to Eisenhower, were considered important in protecting Kennedy's right flank. It was hoped that McCone's involvement would temper the former president's criticism, which was considered very problematic given Eisenhower's popularity and reputation.[14]

Apprehension inside the CIA was nearly as great as among liberals. The agency had enjoyed a period of enormous growth in the 1950s, the consequence of having been run by a director—Allen Dulles—who had a patron in the form of his brother, John Foster Dulles, who just happened to be the secretary of state for most of the decade. Allen Dulles's forced retirement after the Bay of Pigs marked a decided end to this privileged position and the beginning of a more uncertain future for what still was, after all, a relative newcomer vis-à-vis the State and Defense Departments.[15]

In addition, of course, McCone was virtually a novice with regard to the craft of intelligence, his experience limited largely to being a consumer of intelligence while undersecretary of the air force and, later, chairman of the Atomic Energy Commission. Inflicting an outsider on the agency was considered even worse than saddling it with a dogmatic man known for his "slide-rule mind" and molten temper. And early on, McCone appeared imperious to staffers, overly interested in bureaucratic status symbols. On October 31, 1961—just after McCone started working at the CIA, in advance of his confirmation—Deputy Director of Support Lincoln "Red" White recorded a discussion with two staff members about "renting a Cadillac limousine for Mr.

McCone," noting that he had "instructed them to put as much pressure on General Motors as they could to get this done." A few weeks later White was confronted by an unhappy McCone. The "Command Post at his home" had been furnished with fixtures "supplied by Logistics [which were] surplus and added nothing to the décor."[16]

The Senate approved McCone's nomination on January 31, 1962, with only twelve members voting no. However, the unease over his appointment was deeper and more widespread than this number suggests; by comparison, all three of the CIA's previous directors had been unanimously confirmed. It was against this backdrop of doubt and distrust that the untested McCone faced his first real crisis late in the summer of 1962.[17]

Cuba Heats Up

Starting in February 1962, U-2 surveillance of Cuba had followed a regular schedule of two overflights a month.[18] The first of the two August 1962 overflights occurred on the fifth—too early, by a matter of days, to capture any telling evidence about the Soviet military build-up to come. Nonetheless, reports from other sources prompted McCone, during a Special Group Augmented (SGA) meeting on August 10, to raise the specter of offensive missiles being placed on the island.[19]

McCone sounded the alarm again on August 21, in Secretary of State Dean Rusk's office, and yet again on August 22 and 23, while meeting with President Kennedy. The Soviet Union was "in the red [behind in terms of nuclear missiles] and knew it," he declared, arguing that Khrushchev was likely to try to redress the imbalance via Cuba.[20] But he did little to improve his persuasiveness, and much to enhance his Manichean reputation, by going on to suggest that the United States stage a phony provocation against its base at Guantánamo, so that Washington would have a pretext for overthrowing Castro.[21] McCone came across as "too hard-line and suspicious," as Undersecretary of State George Ball later put it, and was too cavalier about the connection between Cuba and the East-West face-off in Berlin.[22]

Right after his August 23 meeting with the president, McCone left for the West Coast. A sixty-year-old widower, he was about to be married for the second time and planned to honeymoon on the French Riviera until late September. Kennedy's advisers would later criticize McCone for not warning the president before leaving for the Mediterranean and for being absent during what turned out to be such a critical period.[23]

The first charge was demonstrably false, as the president well knew, and McCone had also expressly sought Kennedy's consent for his absence. But

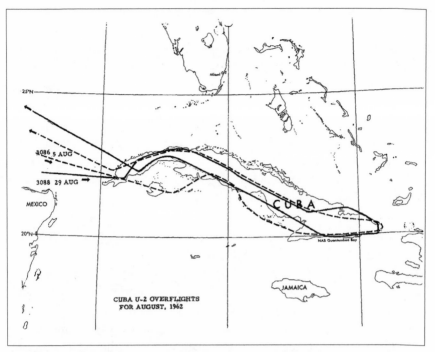

U-2 flight paths over Cuba, August 1962. Both missions traversed the entire island, following the surveillance pattern in place since February. *Courtesy Central Intelligence Agency.*

whether his physical presence in Washington would have made a marked difference during those crucial weeks in September is an open question. McCone was able to exert some influence via the so-called honeymoon cables that went between Langley and Cap Ferrat. Yet as Sherman Kent, the chairman of the CIA's Board of National Estimates, later observed, even if McCone "had been in Washington and made a federal case of his intuitive guess," he would have been opposed by "(1) the members of [the] US Intelligence Board [USIB, i.e., the intelligence community]; and (2) most presidential advisers including the four most important ones [those who were experts on the Soviet Union]—[former ambassadors Charles] Bohlen, [Llewellyn] Thompson, [George] Kennan, and [serving ambassador] Foy [Kohler]."[24] The president would have been far more apt to trust the USIB and these esteemed Kremlinologists than a "robber-baron Republican."[25]

On August 29, after several delays because of bad weather, the second August overflight took place. "I've got a SAM [surface-to-air missile] site,"

an analyst shouted minutes after the film was placed on a light table at the National Photographic Interpretation Center (NPIC), the specialized facility in Suitland, Maryland, where U-2 film was taken for processing and examination.[26] The SAM proved to be the SA-2 model—the same type of antiaircraft missile that had forced down Francis Gary Powers's U-2 over the Soviet Union in May 1960. Analysis of the August 29 film revealed at least eight SA-2 sites in the western half of Cuba.[27] Soon, it appeared, the CIA would not be able to overfly the island with impunity, its regimen restricted only by weather forecasts. As McCone reportedly observed after being informed about the SAMs, "They're not putting them in to protect the cane cutters. They're putting them in to blind our reconnaissance eye."[28]

For virtually every other senior official and analyst, however, the SA-2 deployment came "as a problem to be dealt with deliberately," as one later recalled.[29] After all, the same SAMs had been sent previously to other Soviet client states in the Third World. President Kennedy was inclined toward the view held by the overwhelming majority of senior officials in his administration: that the Soviet military aid, though unprecedented in the hemisphere, was for the purpose of ostentatiously defending Cuba while setting up the island as a model of socialist development and bridgehead for subversive activities in the region.[30] By this reasoning, the SA-2 deployment did not signal a foreign policy crisis as much as a domestic political one. With a midterm election fast approaching, pressure to "do something" about Cuba was bound to mount and would have to be managed carefully.[31]

On September 1, the president told the CIA's deputy director, Lt. Gen. Marshall "Pat" Carter, that he wanted the SA-2 information "nailed right back into the box" until the White House decided to make it public (which it did on September 4).[32] He also pressed the Pentagon for an assurance from the Joint Chiefs of Staff that US military flights would not be conducted in a provocative manner.[33] These precautions left the vexing issue of the intrusive bimonthly U-2 surveillance unaddressed, though not for long.

"Growing Danger to the Birds"

On its own initiative, the CIA's Office of Special Activities (OSA), which carried operational responsibility for the U-2 missions, made incremental changes in early September to lessen the planes' vulnerability to the SA-2s. First, the base of operations was shifted from Laughlin Air Force Base in Del Rio, Texas, to McCoy Air Force Base in Orlando, Florida. This would enable the U-2s to reach a higher altitude over Cuba and reduce pilot fatigue and the stress placed on fragile mechanical equipment, including the plane

itself.[34] The OSA also made changes to the "mission profile." Lightening the fuel load and refueling in midair (a delicate task) immediately after the U-2s left Cuban airspace would help the aircraft attain its maximum altitude during the critical minutes. Finally, the OSA adjusted the flight path of the next scheduled U-2 mission to limit the plane's exposure to western Cuba. This marked the first time since U-2 surveillance had been instituted over Cuba that an overflight did not attempt to traverse the entire island. Still, the next flight, on September 5, detected several additional SAM sites on the western part of the island, along with other signs of a military build-up.[35]

Completely by coincidence, the "growing danger to the birds" over Cuba, as Pat Carter put it in a cable to McCone, was underscored by two distant events—bookends, in effect, to the September 5 flight.[36] On August 30, a Strategic Air Command U-2 on an air-sampling reconnaissance mission had accidentally violated Soviet airspace for nine minutes, resulting in a public protest by Moscow. Then, on September 8, a U-2 manned by a Taiwan-based pilot was lost over mainland China.[37] These events provided new ammunition to critics of U-2 surveillance, of which there were more than a few. One of long standing was the State Department, which for years had looked askance at U-2 missions over sovereign airspace. And suddenly the department had a powerful new ally: the White House.

On Monday, September 10, the first business day after the loss of the U-2 over China, the matter came to a head. At 10:00 A.M., national security adviser McGeorge Bundy made an "out-of-channel" request to James Reber, the chairman of the Committee on Overhead Reconnaissance (COMOR), the interagency committee charged with developing surveillance requirements for the U-2. Within thirty minutes, Bundy wanted answers to three questions:

How important is it to our intelligence objectives that we overfly Cuban soil?

How much would our intelligence suffer if we limited our reconnaissance to peripheral activity utilizing oblique photography?

Is there anyone in the planning of these missions who might want to provoke an incident?[38]

The COMOR members found the third question so bizarre that they wondered if they were really expected to answer it.[39] Just weeks before, the issue of U-2 reconnaissance over Cuba was regarded as so routine that the COMOR wasn't even bothering to submit specific flight plans to the Special Group for approval. Yet Bundy's pointed questions reflected resentments that had been festering in the administration, particularly at State and the White House, since the Bay of Pigs fiasco. Corresponding with the president's own jaundiced view, Bundy and Dean Rusk believed the CIA and the Pentagon had put Kennedy in an unforgivable bind in the spring of 1961. The two men, moreover, had been criticized severely after the debacle for their own passivity. They were thus hypervigilant about protecting the president from anything that could turn into a similar debacle, especially because several high-ranking military and intelligence officials had voiced their determination to force Kennedy "to atone for his restraint" during the bungled invasion.[40]

Reber pleaded for more time to prepare his answers, and a high-level meeting was scheduled for 5:45 P.M. in Bundy's office, after a previously scheduled meeting on other matters related to Cuba was to occur. Shortly before 3:00 P.M., Bundy abruptly rescinded presidential approval of the remaining September overflight. He presumably wanted to demonstrate beforehand that he was dead serious about avoiding any provocative surveillance.[41]

To be sure, Special Group debates about U-2 overflights over "denied areas" (e.g., regions under Communist control) were nothing new—at least not since May 1960. The shootdown of Francis Gary Powers had been traumatic for the US government, both at home and abroad, and the after-effects were still tangible even years later. Indeed, when the first U-2 overflights of Cuba were inaugurated during the waning days of the Eisenhower administration, in October 1960, they were carried out despite a distinct sense of trepidation, even though the airplane then faced no known threat over Cuban airspace. Livingston T. Merchant, then the undersecretary of state for political affairs, had argued before the Special Group that "it will always be easy [to find a reason] not to run such a mission" but that the need for the best intelligence in advance of the Bay of Pigs operation outweighed any reservations about using the plane.[42] Two years later, however, no one would be making that argument as forcefully.

Rusk tried to open the 5:45 meeting with a bit of levity. Nodding to Carter, whom he had known since World War II, he asked, "Pat, don't you ever let up? How do you expect me to negotiate on Berlin with all these [U-2] incidents?" As he typically did when Rusk advocated caution, Robert Kennedy immediately pushed back. "What's the matter, Dean, no guts?" he snapped.[43] The tension between the two almost overshadowed the substance of the meeting. "Let's sustain the overflights, and the hell with the international issues," Kennedy said.[44]

As the meeting progressed, Reber displayed a map showing the route of the next overflight—the one for which Bundy had just rescinded approval. Rusk objected to the planned path, which involved extensive violation of Cuban airspace and overflight of known SAM sites.[45] He worried openly about the possibility of another U-2 incident, which could provoke two simultaneous, if opposing, uproars: a domestic outcry for an invasion of Cuba and an international condemnation of the United States. Soviet propaganda after the downing of Powers's aircraft had "turn[ed] U-2 into a kind of dirty word," as one columnist later put it.[46] International opinion regarded the overflights as "illegal and immoral," and even Washington's staunchest allies found them unpalatable.[47] Rusk argued that losing a U-2 over Cuba would compromise Washington's now-unquestioned right to fly the planes over international waters along Cuba's periphery. Given the island's narrowness, he postulated, offshore flights might be sufficient in any case.[48] COMOR experts said that such a plan would likely leave interior areas of Cuba uncovered. "Well, let's just give it a try," Rusk replied. One participant remarked after the meeting, "After all this time and the many photographs that had been shown to Secretary Rusk, I was surprised to see how stupid he was on reconnaissance."[49]

The COMOR members at the meeting were at a double disadvantage. Not only were they in the uncomfortable position of dealing with officials who far outranked them, but the CIA was represented by its number two man, Pat Carter, who lacked McCone's stature and fearlessness.[50] Once administration officials began drawing up flight paths that avoided known SAM sites, they retreated. "When men of such rank involve themselves in planning mission tracks, good intelligence officers just listen," Reber later observed.[51] In the end, facing Bundy's steadfast support and Robert Kennedy's eventual acquiescence, Carter reluctantly agreed to a plan proposed by Rusk. The remaining September overflight would be reinstated but reconstituted as four separate missions: two flights that would overfly international waters and two that would go "in-and-out" over small portions of central and eastern Cuba. Western Cuba, the known location of the Soviet SAMs, would be left unsurveilled.[52] Carter voiced his dissatisfaction: "I want to put you people on notice that it remains our intention to fly right up over those SAMs to see what is there." But there was no response to his declaration, either positive or negative—just silence and the shuffling of papers.[53]

This decision—to degrade the surveillance regime—was the primary reason for the photo gap. As Cynthia M. Grabo, an experienced intelligence analyst and scholar of strategic warning, would later write, "It really did not matter what intelligence 'thought' about it [the likelihood of a deployment in Cuba]. But it did matter, imperatively, that [the intelligence community] collect the data which would permit a firm judgment whether or not the missiles were there, and hence provide the basis on which the president could confront the Soviet Union and justify his actions to the people of the United States and the rest of the world."[54] Yet the next morning, September 11, President Kennedy approved the schedule of what would soon misleadingly be called "additional" flights.[55] The decision would prove especially crippling because of an uncontrollable (yet highly foreseeable) factor—the vagaries of Caribbean weather from September to November, when the region is beset by tropical storms. Because approval for overflights was hard to come by, the CIA was conservative with its U-2 missions, aborting them whenever the weather forecast predicted cloud cover of 25 percent or more.[56] Thus, the plan made on September 10 not only limited the photographic "take" from future overflights but also drastically stretched out the mission schedule, creating a compromised surveillance regime at a time of dangerously changing conditions in Cuba.[57]

The first offensive missiles, we now know, arrived in Cuban ports about a week later; surface-to-surface missile (SSM) equipment reached the vicinity of San Cristóbal, a town sixty miles west of Havana, on September 17–18.[58] Reports of such activity flowed almost constantly into the CIA from Cuban assets and refugees, and in some cases from members of Congress who had been approached by people in or connected to the Cuban exile community, especially in the Miami area. Virtually all the analysts working on the problem, however, tended to discount the reports, as did officials higher up. As Dr. Albert "Bud" Wheelon, head of the CIA's Office of Scientific Intelligence, later explained, "I was sensitive to the fact that you had to worry about fabrications. I was also sensitive to the fact that Keating was making a big fuss [Kenneth Keating, a Republican senator from New York and one of the administration's most vocal critics, had been loudly warning about Soviet offensive missiles in Cuba]. . . . I was also sensitive to the fact that Cubans in Miami would just love to have us invade Cuba so they could get their property back."[59]

Wheelon chaired the GMAIC (pronounced "gimmick"), the USIB's Guided Missile and Astronautics Intelligence Committee. Because he was relatively new, having joined the CIA in June, and had never dealt with raw intelligence before, by early September he decided to familiarize himself with the flood of intelligence reports being provided by CIA agents in Cuba and from debriefings of refugees.[60] One made a particularly strong impact on him because of its details: the agent described a caravan of "very long trucks and trailers" proceeding through a small town and having to "make a turn in the central square"; the agent even spoke of seeing a mailbox removed by

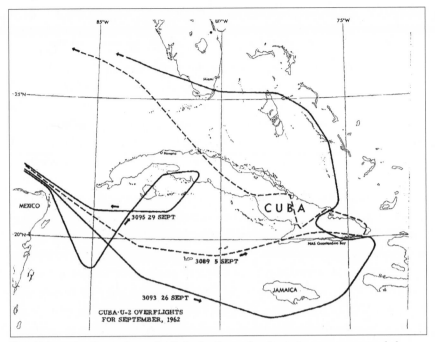

U-2 flight paths, September 1962. Only the September 5 mission spent an extended amount of time in Cuban airspace. The paths of the two flights that occurred after September 10 meeting in the White House effectively precluded coverage of western Cuba and interior areas. *Courtesy Central Intelligence Agency.*

an acetylene torch in order to make room for the convoy to pass. Wheelon thus became the second CIA official (besides McCone) to be convinced that "there really were missiles down there." He made his case to Sherman Kent just before issuance of a Special National Intelligence Estimate (SNIE) on the probability of Soviet offensive missiles being deployed in Cuba. After a long conversation, Kent told him, "I appreciate your view, I have a lot of respect for you, but this is the way we're going."[61]

"Quicksand Hardening into Concrete"

"We cannot put a stop to collection," Carter fumed during a USIB meeting on September 19. "Otherwise, the president would never know when the point of decision was reached."[62] He spoke of the need to "fly the hell out of that sacred Cuban airspace."[63] Carter, nonetheless, was unable to reverse the decision to attenuate surveillance, and the SNIE, released the same day, was a key element that worked against his efforts.[64] The report reaffirmed the conventional wisdom: even if the Soviets dared to introduce SSMs, an action the authors deemed highly unlikely, they would do so only after the SA-2 defense system was complete, which seemed weeks away.[65] An agency officer later observed, perhaps unfairly, that Carter was "standing in quicksand, which was hardening into concrete, but . . . was too dumb to realize it."[66]

Exactly when McCone learned about the changes in surveillance is hard to pinpoint even today. The cable traffic between Langley and Cap Ferrat was so torrential that one officer in the cable section commented, "I have some doubts that the old man knows what to do on a honeymoon."[67] But the abrupt alteration in the U-2 regime was never mentioned in the cables, and McCone apparently did not realize the extent of the attenuation until after his return to Washington on September 24.[68] Even before then, though, he was sufficiently concerned about the administration's lassitude to button-hole McGeorge Bundy in Paris while the national security adviser was en route to a September 27 NATO meeting in Copenhagen. During a morning walk, McCone contested the SNIE's presumption that Moscow would not provoke Washington by placing offensive missiles in Cuba. Yet Bundy, who believed that McCone was too fixated on a single element of the geopolitical struggle—the thermonuclear balance—was unmovable.[69] He remained more worried about provoking an unnecessary showdown and was determined not to let McCone persuade the president to sanction overflights with impunity. Any shootdown of a U-2, Bundy feared, would become a casus belli for those itching to invade the island.

Once back in Washington, McCone made no secret of his irritation with Pat Carter. McCone felt his deputy hadn't fought hard enough to get McCone's views, as laid out in the "honeymoon cables," accepted; worse, Carter had acceded to a curtailment in collection.[70] Yet when McCone met privately with President Kennedy and the attorney general on September 26, the DCI proved unable to reverse the administration's "near-crippling caution," as Richard Helms, then the CIA's deputy director of plans, later termed it.[71] The attenuated overflight schedule stood. Indeed, the photographic "take," limited though it was, was seen as proof that the military build-up did not include offensive missiles (as predicted) and was being relied upon to rebut the administration's arch critics.[72] For example, on September 17, at a closed joint hearing of the Senate Foreign Relations and Armed Services Commit-tees, Dean Rusk assured the senators of the administration's vigilance con-cerning Soviet missile sites, notwithstanding Keating's allegations. "We do have very firm information indeed, and of a most reliable sort," he testified, just seven days after he had helped to degrade that information.[73]

Publicly, too, the administration sounded a reassuring note. The Cuban build-up "is a configuration of defensive capability," Rusk confidently asserted during a rare nationally televised interview on September 29.[74] Simultaneously, the White House sought to influence opinion leaders like Walter Lippmann and James Reston, with some success. In early October, drawing on public statements and private conversations with administration officials, these columnists characterized the surveillance of Cuba as "elaborate" or "total."[75]

By then, McCone had become determined to remove the strictures on U-2 surveillance as a matter of principle. He believed the CIA had been "remiss" in settling for such incomplete coverage, and he did not want overflights to be contingent on human intelligence reports from the field either.[76] Rather, he wanted a return to the pre-September overflight paths that photographed the entire island in one mission.[77] Coincidentally, the National Photographic Interpretation Center's chief, Arthur Lundahl, had asked his staff to develop a visual representation of the limited photo surveillance of Cuba since early September, which he showed to McCone shortly after the DCI's return to Washington on September 24. The map demonstrated at a glance that large portions of Cuba had not been photographed at all since late August. McCone "nearly came out of his chair when he saw the map," Lundahl recalled. "I'll take this," McCone said, apparently intending to make the map Exhibit A at the October 4 SGA meeting.[78]

The SGA meeting was chaired by the attorney general. He and McCone were generally of like mind about Cuba: both were adamant about the urgent need to eliminate Castro and replace his regime with one friendly to the United States. But when McCone suggested there was an element of hesitancy on the part of the administration, he was echoing, in effect, what several Republicans, especially Kenneth Keating, were now asserting virtually every day in Congress, and Kennedy bristled.[79] When the subject became the self-imposed reconnaissance restrictions, McCone stressed that they were ill-advised, particularly since the SAMs were "almost certainly not operational."[80] Presumably with Lundahl's map visible to everyone in the room, McCone "noted to the Special Group that there had been no coverage of the center of Cuba and more particularly, the entire western end of the Island for over a month, and all flights since 5 September had been either peripheral or limited and therefore CIA did not know, nor could advise, whether an offensive capability was being created. DCI objected strenuously to the limitations which had been placed on overflights and there arose a considerable discussion (with some heat) as to whether limitations had or had not been placed on CIA by the Special Group."[81]

Now that the gaping hole in coverage had been made obvious, no one wanted to take responsibility for it. The SGA as a body, of course, had never issued a written edict against intrusive overflights. Rather, under duress from Rusk and Bundy—neither of whom was in attendance now—the CIA and COMOR had refrained from submitting requests for additional overflights because they had effectively been told that any requests would be denied.[82] Indeed, the White House could technically claim—and Bundy later would—that the president had approved every overflight request submitted to him after the SA-2s were discovered in late August.[83]

Making Headway

Although it was almost imperceptible at first, the October 4 SGA meeting began to turn the tide in McCone's favor. "It was the consensus that we could not accept restrictions which would foreclose gaining all reasonable knowledge of military installations in Cuba," he recorded in a memo.[84] But the State Department, for one, was not going to yield ground easily. During the same meeting, Deputy Undersecretary of State U. Alexis Johnson—Rusk's alter ego—managed to win agreement for the drafting of a National Reconnaissance Office (NRO) report on an overall surveillance program for Cuba, to be presented at the next SGA meeting on October 9.[85] That meant several more days lost while the NRO pondered whether there might be a substitute for the U-2 sweeps of the island. This was not an insignificant delay. As those involved at the operational level well knew, surveillance opportunities could be hard to come by this time of year because of the weather. It turned out that the October 7 forecast for all of Cuba was "good"—less than 25 percent cloud cover—but that day's U-2 flight did not pass over the western half of the island, the area cordoned off since September 10.[86]

And it was far from clear, moreover, that the White House would ultimately agree to end the hiatus on overflying western Cuba. On October 5, the day after the SGA meeting, McCone met with Bundy privately to discuss Soviet policy in Cuba. It was obvious to the DCI that the White House still viewed the military build-up as primarily a domestic, not a foreign policy, crisis. Remarkably, Bundy "seemed relaxed" about the lack of hard information, McCone thought.[87] From Bundy's perspective, no doubt the national security adviser thought he was expertly steering the president clear of a needless crisis that might prove as politically damaging as the Bay of Pigs invasion had been.

Meanwhile, and independent of McCone's efforts, CIA officers at the operational level were correlating new human intelligence reports about alleged missiles in Cuba. One report, dated September 7, had attracted the attention of Ted Shackley, the chief of the CIA's station in Miami, and of officers in Task Force W (TFW), the MONGOOSE component at CIA head-quarters. The report came from a Cuban observer agent—the lowest rank in the intelligence pecking order—who had been recruited under MONGOOSE.[88] It described a mountainous area near San Cristóbal where "very secret and important work," which the agent believed to involve missiles, was in prog-ress. The report was intriguing in that it gave coordinates for a specific area and coincided with two separate refugee reports about large missiles heading west from Havana to that general vicinity.[89]

Under normal circumstances, TFW officers would simply have dissemi-nated the intelligence community-wide, and CIA would have made a case to the COMOR for coverage of the area in question. But since the Septem-ber 10 meeting, considerable uncertainty and even a degree of defensiveness had developed within the agency over the U-2 flights. Sam Halpern, TFW's executive officer, wanted to avoid having only the CIA's fingerprints on the intelligence. It was the "damndest thing," Halpern thought, to have to worry about whether the request would be immediately discounted as the product of a politicized, unruly, or overly aggressive agency. Indeed, a comment had been placed in the report already, denigrating the information as just another sighting that would in all likelihood turn out to be false. Thus, it seemed "better for someone else to make the proposal to the COMOR," Halpern recalled. The newly formed Defense Intelligence Agency (DIA), in existence barely a year, was a good candidate for the task, although such a maneuver was almost unheard of. Normally, the various components that made up the intel-ligence community were fiercely, almost comically, competitive and credit-conscious.[90]

Consequently, on September 27, Col. John R. Wright Jr., the head of the DIA's MONGOOSE component, was invited to a briefing in Task Force W's war room. He was a logical choice, and not only because he was the most knowl-edgeable person in DIA on Cuba. Unlike many other analysts, he took new information seriously, though it contradicted presumptions, and had an open mind about the scope of the Soviet build-up. Several weeks earlier, Wright had pushed NPIC photo interpreters to redirect their attention to some spe-cific locations described in refugee reports as places where Soviet military equipment was being deployed. The initial NPIC readout of the August 5 U-2 overflight of these areas had reported nothing of special interest, but when Wright saw the photos, he became convinced that the "long and slim objects" being concealed were SA-2 missiles. Although the photo interpreters refused to confirm his hunch, the subsequent August 29 overflight proved that Wright had been correct.[91]

Now the colonel would be asked to engage in an even bolder prodding of the intelligence bureaucracy. Based on the coordinates provided by the MONGOOSE agent, CIA officers in TFW had delineated a trapezoid-shaped area on a map of Cuba. They showed it to Wright and asked him to push a request for U-2 surveillance of the area up *his* chain of command. Wright, who harbored his own suspicions about this trapezoidal area, quickly agreed, fully recognizing that he would be sticking his neck out by pushing for something that might well result in the loss of a U-2. On October 1, Wright's "hypothesis" was presented to Secretary of Defense Robert McNamara, who sanctioned the submission of a DIA request to the COMOR on October 3.[92] This maneuver "got us out of the line of fire and let DIA take the lead" during the "days of fighting" about an overflight in early October, Halpern recalled.[93] There was, of course, a potential downside: If an overflight was finally approved and anything was found, Wright and the DIA would be forever credited with exploiting the crucial human intelligence.[94]

By the time of the October 9 SGA meeting, the last two missions authorized on September 10 had flown, on October 5 and 7, without finding any evidence of offensive missiles. (For good reason, of course: neither flight went across the western end of Cuba, where the missile sites were most advanced.)[95] The warnings from Capitol Hill had gone unabated in the meantime. Although Keating gained most of the nationwide press attention, other legislators had also raised questions. On October 6, for example, Bob Dole, a World War II veteran and first-term Republican representative from Kansas, inserted this notation in the *Congressional Record:* "Today, just 90 miles from the United States, anti-aircraft missiles are being installed by the Soviet technicians . . . it becomes increasingly apparent that the Soviet Union is establishing a base in the Western Hemisphere from which an attack might one day be mounted against the United States. Who can say that the next step will not be the installation of short- and intermediate-range ballistic missiles which could be launched against the United States?"[96]

McCone came to the October 9 SGA meeting armed with a paper hastily prepared by the Office of National Estimates on the consequences of a presidential declaration that the Soviet build-up necessitated regular and invasive reconnaissance of Cuba.[97] He also invited along a colonel, Jack Ledford, head of the air force's Office of Special Activities, to speak about the odds facing a U-2 that made an intrusive sweep of Cuba. Ledford was fully conscious of the stakes: any decision to loosen the self-imposed limits might well turn on his study.[98] Admittedly, the SA-2 sites were now fully equipped from a US perspective, Ledford observed; however, they were not yet functioning

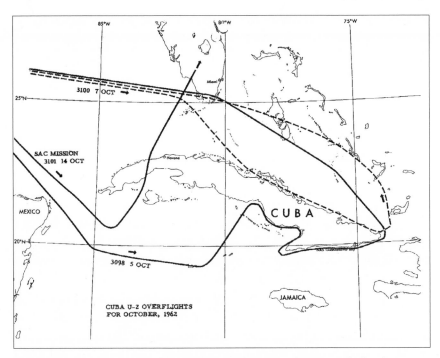

U-2 flight paths, October 1962. The first two U-2 missions, flown in early October, skirted the island entirely under the restrictions established on September 10. A U-2 finally ventured over western Cuba on October 14, based on intelligence provided by a CIA-recruited observer agent. It was the first time this region had been subject to aerial surveillance since August 29. *Courtesy Central Intelligence Agency.*

as an integrated SAM system, thus lessening their effectiveness.[99] Ledford presented a "vulnerability analysis" that estimated the chances of losing a U-2 over Cuba at just one in six.[100]

No one else at the meeting, however, insisted that the September 10 restrictions had to be lifted on principle, which was what McCone wanted, and his stance remained a lonely one.[101] There would be no whole-island surveillance. Instead, the meeting turned on what to do about the deficit in coverage of western Cuba. After receiving the DIA's urgent recommendation, the COMOR had merely put the San Cristóbal trapezoidal area at the top of its list of targets *if* overflights of western Cuba were approved.[102] And, for much of the meeting, Ledford took the brunt of harsh questioning about the dangers of a U-2 incident and whether some alternate flight path to "cover" Cuba's western end would not suffice. Couldn't something be done to trim the flight down? Couldn't we maybe go over there, or maybe avoid the SA-2 sites?

Finally, Robert Kennedy asked Ledford's interrogators to "stop badgering the colonel." Ledford later told a close friend and colleague, Bud Wheelon, that Kennedy's intervention, which cut through all the temporizing, shifted the tone of the meeting. As Ledford recalled it, the attorney general then suggested, "Let's have an up or down vote." Although no one (save McCone) had been insistent about the need for an overflight of western Cuba, no one was willing to vote against it, either. Wheelon later observed that although Kennedy was sometimes, in his opinion, "a little fast off the mark . . . he saved the day, and the mission, as far as Ledford was concerned."[103]

The SGA's resulting recommendation to the president eased the restrictions on overflights, but by the most incremental margin imaginable: it sanctioned only one "in-and-out" flight over western Cuba, plotted to include the San Cristóbal trapezoid.[104] If the single approved mission "did not provoke an SA-2 reaction," additional in-and-out flights over western Cuba would be proposed and presumably sanctioned until a full mosaic of the region was obtained.[105] President Kennedy promptly approved the recommendation, but no one expected very much. After all, it was not much of a flight—Ledford termed it akin to a "bologna slice"—and nowhere close to the previous full sweeps of the island from west to east.[106] Even so, the White House's anxiety would be manifest down the chain of command. "This is the most over-controlled operation I've ever been in," Gen. William McKee observed to Deputy Director Pat Carter three days later, on October 12. McKee, the vice chief of staff under Gen. Curtis LeMay, commander of the Strategic Air Command, was responsible for supplying air force pilots who would be flying the more powerful U-2s normally operated by the CIA.[107]

Knowing that the one U-2 flight over western Cuba had been authorized, but not knowing, of course, what might be found, McCone did not shy from expressing his concerns before a subcommittee of the House Appropriations Committee on October 10. Records do not indicate the attendees, but such sessions were usually scheduled to permit attendance by Appropriations chair Clarence Cannon (D-MO), the CIA subcommittee chair George Mahon (D-TX), as well as Gerald Ford (R-MI) and a few others. According to an unsigned memo by one of the DCI's aides (probably legislative liaison John Warner, who regularly attended such meetings), "You [McCone] showed pictures of IL-28 crates and made it clear that intelligence could not determine if the build-up is defensive or offensive. You told the group that the Soviets could move in MRBMs, probably indicating Soviet control of them and the warheads. Once they were in it would be extremely difficult for the US to do anything about it. You told the group there were many experts who did not

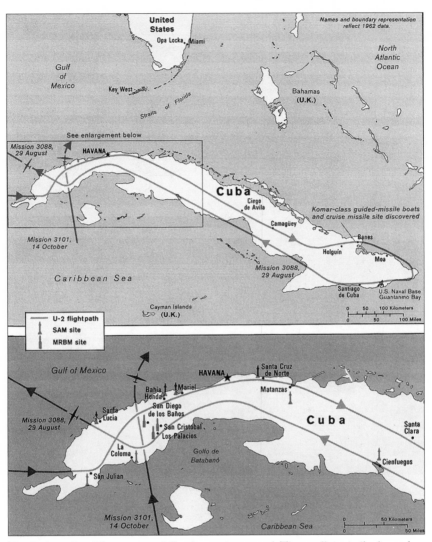

U-2 flight paths of August 29 and October 14, juxtaposed. The smaller missiles located along the coast represent SAM-2 emplacements, the larger missiles approximate locations of SSM sites. *Courtesy Central Intelligence Agency.*

believe the Soviets would make such a move, but you differed with them. You said if you were Khrushchev, this is precisely what you would do."[108]

Very likely McCone or his deputy, Pat Carter, also shared these fears with other congressional leaders who were supposed to monitor the CIA, such as Senator Richard Russell (D-GA). He chaired the full Armed Services Committee and its tiny informal subcommittee on the CIA. Between August 1

MRBM site as seen from the intrusive U-2 overflight of western Cuba on October 14. *Courtesy Central Intelligence Agency.*

and October 9, Russell had a dozen interactions with agency heads, either in person or by telephone.[109]

In the end, the approved overflight of western Cuba did not occur until October 14, five days after it was sanctioned, owing partly to inclement weather forecasts and partly to a decision to train an air force pilot to fly the CIA's more powerful U-2s. The administration wanted to preserve "plausible deniability" in case of an incident, and a cover story involving an air force pilot rather than a CIA pilot was deemed marginally more credible.[110] Clearly, dread of another U-2 incident was still greater than concern about reports of missiles with the potential of striking the United States.[111] But finally, on the morning of October 14, Maj. Richard Heyser piloted a U-2 that took 928 photographs of western Cuba in six minutes—the first surveillance of this critical area in forty-five days.[112] After what Heyser termed a "milk run," the film was rushed to the National Photographic Interpretation Center, arriving on the morning of October 15. Shortly before 4:00 P.M., a CIA photo inter-preter announced, "We've got MRBMs [medium-range ballistic missiles] in Cuba."[113] It was a "moment of splendor," as Sherman Kent put it—splendor for the U-2, its cameras and film, the photo interpreters, and perhaps the CIA's finest hour of the Cold War.[114]

Almost everyone involved, with the possible exception of John McCone, had anticipated that any adverse news from the October 14 overflight would take the form of another downed or lost U-2. Thus, the photo interpret-ers' conclusion came as an unexpected jolt.[115] Informed of the results on the morning of October 16, President Kennedy immediately issued a blanket authority for U-2s to traverse the island. And the showdown that would be known domestically as the Cuban Missile Crisis began in earnest.[116]

Obscuring the Photo Gap

From Washington's perspective, the missile crisis began with the detection of the Soviet weaponry on October 15. But its underlying origins dated back to at least the 1960 presidential campaign, and, perhaps more accurately, the 1959 Cuban revolution, which saw the rise to power of a pro-Communist regime—the first in the Western Hemisphere.

As the Democratic nominee, Kennedy had run to the right of Republican Richard Nixon on a number of national security issues, ranging from Formosa (as Taiwan was then called) to the alleged missile gap between the United States and Soviet Union (which was, in fact, nonexistent). On no issue, however, was Kennedy's rightward drift more apparent than with respect to Cuba. Although Nixon was privy to President Eisenhower's March 1960 decision to overthrow the Fidel Castro regime by covert means, in public the Republican nominee took a surprisingly moderate stance. That allowed Kennedy (who also knew about CIA training of a Cuban-exile invasion force) to attack Nixon for being "soft on Cuba." It turned the tables on the Republicans, who had invariably mounted such attacks against the Democrats since the start of the Cold War. If anyone was going to be tarred with "losing" a country to world Communism in 1960, in other words, it was going to be the GOP's standard-bearer. This stance also gave Kennedy political protection in the event of an "October surprise"—that is, if President Eisenhower launched the effort to topple Castro just before the election.

Prominent liberals in the Democratic Party, such as Chester Bowles, who was Kennedy's chief foreign policy adviser during the campaign (at least in name), had been appalled by this position. Kennedy took the militant stances volitionally, often during the famed televised debates. It ran counter to what Bowles thought was the superior alternative: isolating Cuba in the hemisphere and promoting social democracy all around it. Bowles feared that with such rhetoric Kennedy was causing a huge problem for himself should he become president.[1]

Bowles's fears were realized in early 1961, when President Kennedy approved Operation ZAPATA, the CIA-sponsored operation to liberate Cuba. Having painted himself into a corner rhetorically, the new president had little choice. He could hardly call off the operation without sparking a huge uproar. Yet he had reservations, especially about maintaining "plausible deniability" that Washington wasn't involved with the invasion. Kennedy thus insisted upon pruning several elements of the scheme, most importantly, the part that called for domination of the skies over the landing site. He thought scaling the effort back would help preserve Washington's deniability in case things went awry. But the result was the worst of both worlds: the fig leaf of US noninvolvement was quickly stripped away by a skeptical media; and simultaneously the limits imposed on the no-longer-covert operation eliminated whatever slim chance it had of being successful.

The Bay of Pigs was a demoralizing and inauspicious beginning for Kennedy, although his approval ratings briefly rose as Americans rallied around their chief executive. After the debacle, getting rid of Castro before the 1964 election became an obsession within the administration, leading to what was then the largest covert action ever mounted by the CIA: Operation MONGOOSE, with Attorney General Robert F. Kennedy acting as the president's executive officer.

Regardless of the exact reasons for the surprise emplacement of Soviet missiles in Cuba—whether to protect the nascent socialist state from a US invasion or to redress the nuclear imbalance—once the missiles were detected, it was instantly recognized that the crisis threatened to make or break the Kennedy presidency. There was a widely held perception that the president simply could not withstand another shattering defeat that involved Cuba. Either the missiles would be removed, or Kennedy would be removed from office a year hence.

Nonetheless, the president, from the outset, was unenthusiastic about what many others (particularly in the US military) perceived as a golden opportunity to remove Castro's regime once and for all. By this time Kennedy had begun to see the issue of occupied Berlin, not Cuba, as his central foreign policy problem in the geopolitical contest with the Soviet Union. Any US move against Cuba would invite Soviet retaliation against Berlin, and in the end, the strategic position of the United States would be worse off—and that was assuming no escalation to an all-out nuclear exchange between the two superpowers. The fate of Berlin was of paramount concern to Kennedy, even though many hard-liners refused to make the connection to Cuba, and was one of the key factors that guided the president's decision making throughout: initially, in trying to prevent the Soviet build-up from becoming a full-blown crisis and then, after the detection of the offensive missiles on October 15, in trying to find a way out short of a US attack to destroy the missiles.[2]

October 16 to October 22: ExComm Deliberations

Initially an ad hoc body, the Executive Committee (ExComm) of the National Security Council came into existence to help the president plan a response to the unexpected Soviet deployment of missiles; midway through the crisis, ExComm's existence was codified. It consisted of all the high-ranking officials normally associated with the formulation of US foreign policy, such as the secretaries of state, defense, and treasury, the national security adviser, and the director of central intelligence. But it also included a several actors who did not ordinarily sit in on such high-level meetings, such as presidential speech-writer Theodore Sorensen, chief of staff Kenneth O'Donnell, and Kremlin-ologist Llewellyn E. Thompson, an ambassador-at-large.[3]

ExComm would meet at least once a day but sometimes more often over the next seven days. The reasons for the Soviet move were not discussed at great length.[4] What mattered was that the president had warned, beginning in August, that the United States would not tolerate "offensive" weapons in Cuba as part of the Soviet build-up. Yet Khrushchev, despite statements or implications to the contrary, had gone ahead and done precisely that. Although views differed on how much the MRBMs and IRBMs actually altered the strategic balance—the United States still enjoyed a marked superiority in numbers—the overwhelming consensus was that having drawn a clear line, Kennedy could not now do nothing. The prestige, credibility, and power of the United States were on the line, not to mention the president's political standing domestically. The fundamental question was, what was the "least dangerous strategy likely to be successful?"[5]

Throughout the six days of secret deliberations, ExComm members met, usually without the president in attendance. Positions shifted from day to day and sometimes within the same day. Militant position became dovish, and vice versa. Robert Kennedy, contrary to his posthumously published memoir, *Thirteen Days*, was among the most hawkish advisers initially and suggested finding a pretext to take out the missiles—a sink-the-*Maine* scenario for the 1960s. Positions were also not predictable merely on the basis of what agency an official represented—the "you stand where you sit" thesis later advanced by political scientist Graham Allison. Secretary of Defense Robert McNamara, who represented an institution brimming with military officers itching for a conflict, was actually one of the most consistently dovish ExComm members. Even John McCone, perhaps the most reflexive hard-liner in the group, would come around to supporting the idea of a quarantine (the word "blockade" was carefully avoided) and eventually a swap of the US missiles in Turkey for the Soviet missiles in Cuba.

With McCone participating in ExComm meetings, he assumed more of a policy role, in accord with the president's wishes, and consciously—and to some observers, ostentatiously—removed himself from presiding over USIB meetings, leaving his deputy, Gen. Marshall "Pat" Carter in charge. This became one of the forums in which the military openly expressed irritation over the president's policy to desist from an immediate invasion. At one meeting Carter distributed a memo urging an immediate attack, noting, "Maybe if we get a Republican Congress we could declare war." The representatives of the military intelligence services, meanwhile, "regularly snorted over the delay" in what they believed was "an inevitable invasion."[6]

After a nearly a week of ExComm deliberations, on October 22, during a nationwide radio and television address, President Kennedy publicly announced that the government had detected the presence of Soviet MRBMs in Cuba and uncompleted IRBM sites.[7] Declaring that these missiles represented "offensive weapons," Kennedy suggested they threatened the United States and said that use of the missiles against any state in the hemisphere would be considered by Washington as an attack on the United States. The missiles had to be withdrawn promptly, and to back up his words Kennedy announced that he was immediately ordering a "strict quarantine" of Cuba by US naval forces to block further shipments of military matériel.

In the tense, six-day period following Kennedy's nationwide address, the general reaction of Americans was to rally around the flag with little dissent. There was some grumbling on the right that the quarantine was too little, too late, and did nothing to force the removal of the missiles menacing the United States. But by and large, public criticism was muted.

ExComm meetings continued apace, while Robert Kennedy met privately with Soviet Ambassador Anatoly Dobrynin to facilitate communication between the two sides. These discussions, along with Dobrynin's messages back to Moscow, would prove crucial in reaching a settlement. The day of greatest tension—the so-called blackest day of the crisis—was Saturday, October 27. After feelers that suggested a resolution was near, Khrushchev publicly issued a letter demanding that Washington remove the Jupiter missiles from Turkey as part of any settlement. Although the president seemed inclined to agree, most of the ExComm members were against such a explicit quid pro quo. A pall was cast over the deliberations when news arrived that one of the U-2s now overflying Cuba with regularity had been shot down and the pilot killed. That report underscored a growing sense that with the superpowers' daggers drawn, events might soon to take on a life of their own and that the crisis might escalate uncontrollably. Indeed, Gen. Maxwell Taylor argued for a proportionate military response in reaction to the U-2 shoot-down, a proposal the president rejected.

Instead, the president instructed Robert Kennedy to meet secretly with Dobrynin again and offer to trade the Turkish missiles for the Cuban ones as part of any deal—with one stipulation. The quid pro quo could not be acknowledged publicly. In his message back to Moscow, Dobrynin stressed that time was short and the danger of a US attack high if a settlement was not reached promptly. The next day, October 28, Radio Moscow announced that a settlement had been achieved. Khrushchev agreed to remove the missiles labeled as "offensive" by the United States and accepted on-site verification by United Nations inspectors. In return, Khrushchev said he had received a pledge by Washington not to invade Cuba, which he claimed was the reason the missiles had been dispatched in the first place. As agreed, Khrushchev did not publicize the secret codicil, under which Kennedy had promised to remove the fifteen Jupiter missiles that had been emplaced in Turkey in 1961–62.

Although the missile crisis was largely viewed as having peaked, the settlement almost came undone in the days that followed. Castro, angry at what he regarded as the Soviets' capitulation and lack of consultation, refused to grant on-site inspection. At the same time, Washington upped the ante by also demanding that the Soviets remove forty-two IL-28 light bombers from Cuba. Tense negotiations lasted until November 20, when the Soviets yielded on the issue of the bombers. The superpowers also arranged for inspections on the high seas to work around Castro's refusal to allow inspections. While Kennedy refused to make the no-invasion pledge explicit because of Castro's recalcitrance, Khrushchev nonetheless conveyed to the Cuban premier that the final terms protected the island from a US-led invasion.

In the meantime, the peaceful resolution of the crisis was hailed by America's Cold War allies, in addition to being popular by an overwhelming margin at home. It undoubtedly contributed to the Democrats' good showing in the midterm election: they lost only four seats in the House and had a net gain in the Senate of two seats. At least as significant was the about-face the successful resolution meant for the president's political standing. His handling of foreign policy, once feared as a major vulnerability in 1964, was suddenly viewed as a strong suit. His actions, as historian Barton J. Bernstein later wrote, "seemed a wonderful blend of toughness, shrewdness, and reasonableness: a willingness to go near the brink on the missiles, the ability to push Khrushchev and the Soviets to accede, and a capacity to end the crisis without pressing for excessive Soviet concessions or the overthrow of Castro."[8] Kennedy's Republican critics were left sputtering; the president could no longer be accused of pursuing a "spineless" policy in Cuba.

Success or Failure?

In the weeks after the crisis, the performance of the intelligence community was largely deemed a success in public. The SSMs had been detected before any were operational, and this fact was vital to the resolution that followed.[9] It had given President Kennedy "breathing space"—precious days in which to deliberate, discuss options with his advisers, and orchestrate a reaction short of an instant military attack.[10] Ultimately he had decided to impose a naval quarantine on Cuba, which shifted the onus of using force onto the Soviets—a responsibility both sides were almost desperately eager to avoid, since neither truly wanted a war. And once having seized the initiative, Kennedy never lost the upper hand. Correspondingly, because Soviet premier Nikita Khrushchev was denied the fait accompli he had sought, he was forced to improvise in a situation for which he had not planned sufficiently, if at all.[11]

Some weeks after the crisis ended, Ray Cline, the CIA's deputy director of intelligence, asked McGeorge Bundy and Robert Kennedy how much "that single evaluated piece of photographic evidence [from October 14] was worth." Both said that it fully justified every penny the CIA had cost the nation since its inception in 1947.[12]

But once someone with access to all the facts fitted them together, an entirely different assessment was also possible: the episode could actually be regarded "as a near-failure of American intelligence" of the first magnitude, as one scholar later put it.[13] The Kennedy administration had degraded the one intelligence-gathering tool capable of delivering precisely the kind of dispositive information about missiles that the president had been insisting on all along. Together with delays caused by predictably inclement weather, the net result had been a dysfunctional collection regime in a dynamic situation. Moreover, if some combination of the administration's caution, more active Soviet radars, mechanical problems with the U-2 or its cameras, or longer stretches of cloud cover had delayed discovery of the missiles by even another week to ten days, at least some of the SSMs, according to CIA analysts, would have been capable of being launched before they were detected.[14]

It was the administration's restraint in the face of a blatant Soviet provocation that had quickly won allied support for, and world opinion over to, the US posture. But that restraint might not have existed without the relative luxury of time to weigh the alternatives. In addition, the impending midterm election had helped define what the administration saw as its window of opportunity for a negotiated settlement: had the crisis still been unresolved during the November 6 voting, the Republicans would probably have gained seats in the Senate and the House.[15] Assuming that Kennedy's determination to avoid an armed conflict remained fixed, the president might have had to settle the crisis on much less politically advantageous terms, such as the explicit exchange of the Soviet missiles in Cuba for the US Jupiter missiles in Turkey, ostensibly proposed by UN secretary-general U Thant.[16]

The narrow margin of success was not entirely due to failures in intelligence gathering, of course; two other intelligence deficits had also played a role. The first was estimative, namely, the months-long miscalculation of Moscow's intentions, culminating in the spectacularly incorrect Special National Intelligence Estimate (SNIE) of September 19. The second was analytical: the failure to grasp indications that something other than a defensive build-up by the Soviets was taking place in Cuba. But these errors paled beside the delay in acquiring hard evidence of the missile deployment.

Virtually every official, scholarly, and journalistic postmortem of the intelligence community's performance would address one or more of these failures. There was, however, a dramatic difference in the political consequences attached to each one. With respect to the misestimates and analytical shortcomings, unless it could be shown that the White House had tried to influence the process or had ignored stark evidence presented to it, only the intelligence community, and not the administration, stood to be criticized.[17] When it came to the photo gap, however, the situation was reversed. Now that the once-villainous U-2 had been transformed, virtually overnight, into a heroic instrument, it would be more than awkward for the administration to admit that the CIA had been "enjoined to stay well away from what we called the business [western] end of the island," as Richard Helms later wrote.[18] The intelligence community might be criticized for acceding too easily to the administration's cautious overflight policy. But most of the onus from the fact that "American intelligence . . . went blind for five crucial weeks" would be on President Kennedy and his top advisers, especially Dean Rusk and McGeorge

Bundy.[19] While demanding absolute proof of the missiles' presence, on behalf of the president, they had simultaneously acted, albeit inadvertently, to prevent that very evidence from being gathered.

The photo gap thus constituted an enormous political problem for the administration. President Kennedy faced the uncomfortable prospect of having to explain why his administration had degraded its best intelligence-gathering tool until it was almost too late. There was a whole host of statements by administration officials, including ones by the president, prior to and immediately after October 14, that suggested US surveillance of the build-up had been the most rigorous imaginable, if not stepped up.[20] But the record of what happened actually showed the opposite insofar as U-2 overflights were concerned, and the fragile airplane had become symbolic of all intelligence gathering. The photo gap also left the president vulnerable to charges that he had been taken in by the Soviets' deception to the point where he had tried to foist a false sense of security over the nation.[21]

Disguising the Facts

The problem represented by the photo gap became evident in the midst of the crisis and at the highest level, as revealed by surreptitious ExComm tape recordings, made at the president's behest. Kennedy himself was the first to raise the delicate issue, alluding to it during an ExComm meeting on the morning of Monday, October 22, seven days after the missiles' discovery. The administration was about to go public with news of the deployment; that evening President Kennedy was scheduled to make a televised address to the nation and finally reveal the missiles' presence in Cuba.

Kennedy raised the issue as ExComm members were discussing procedures for briefing the congressional leadership, the diplomatic corps, and the press prior to the president's televised speech. Kenneth Keating, who had been thundering about a Soviet build-up for weeks on the Senate floor, had specifically alleged on October 10 that construction of offensive missile sites had begun.[22] Everyone at the meeting understood that the press was sure to seize on that speech and wonder about the administration's seemingly belated discovery: Was Keating's "intelligence service" superior to the administration's?[23] Even worse, had the administration known of the missiles all along but withheld the information until Keating's speech forced a disclosure? Was the White House hoping to time the revelation to influence the November elections? "You don't want them to make like there's been work for two months here that, ah, our fellas knew about," Kennedy observed. "I'd make sure that it doesn't look like it's been going on for months."[24] In fact, the CIA would later calculate that construction of the Guanajay IRBM site had commenced seven weeks earlier, during the first week in September, and work at the San Cristóbal and Remedios MRBM sites had begun sometime between September 15 and 20.[25]

Attorney General Robert Kennedy, in his constant role as his brother's protector, immediately followed up by asking Roger Hilsman, director of the Bureau of Intelligence and Research (INR) at the State Department, for a persuasive rebuttal to the questions that were sure to be raised once the media had absorbed the explosive news. "Why didn't we detect them a month ago? What is your answer?" Kennedy demanded—though he knew full well that U-2 surveillance had been degraded. "My answer to this," Hilsman exclaimed somewhat defensively, "is that Mr. Keating is *wrong!*"[26] Hilsman went on to argue that Keating's informants had clearly misidentified SAM sites as being SSM sites (which was not necessarily true in every case). He also suggested that photographs illustrating the rapid pace of construction at the sites might be skillfully, if misleadingly, used to undercut Keating. "Mr. President," Hilsman said, "there are some *lovely* photographs, one taken on Sunday [October 14], one on Monday [October 15], and [of] the *enormous* change between Sunday and Monday, in twenty-four hours!"[27] Both Kennedys agreed that it would be useful to show these photos, which were normally highly classified. The president added, "But I do think we ought to be thinking of all the unpleasant questions" that might soon come up.[28]

At an afternoon meeting of the full National Security Council, Robert Kennedy returned to the issue of the photo gap, possibly by prearrangement with his brother.[29] Initially, the president himself responded when RFK raised the matter. Without the kind of hard evidence available after the October 14 U-2 mission, he argued, the United States would never be able to obtain the backing of the Organization of American States, which Secretary Rusk was scheduled to address the next day in the hope of eliciting a supportive resolution. The president added that in the absence of irrefutable proof, Washington's allies in NATO would look askance at any action that risked a confrontation with the Soviets over Berlin, the logical arena for countervailing pressure from Moscow. In sum, the president argued, the United States would almost certainly find itself isolated if it did not have the dramatic surveillance pictures in hand to prove that its hard line on Cuba was wholly justified.[30]

All of this was true enough, but it was also beside the point. Few members of Congress or the press were likely to suggest the administration should have acted without firm evidence. The pivotal questions, as Robert Kennedy had succinctly put them to Hilsman that morning, were going to be (1) had the administration been as vigilant as advertised? and (2) had the intelligence community assiduously collected and correctly evaluated the evidence as soon as it was available?

The president went on to acknowledge that a missile deployment had long been rumored, mostly by refugees who had fled Cuba.[31] He referred to Hilsman as one of the officials "who's in charge" of sifting through such reports and evaluating their credibility, prompting a flustered reaction from the INR director, who probably did not know whether to be flattered or embarrassed by the attention. "Yes, sir. I . . . I wouldn't say I was in charge," he mumbled. "What?" the president asked. "I wouldn't say that I was in *charge* of the whole thing," Hilsman repeated, in obvious discomfort. "Well, whatever," Kennedy responded, causing soft laughter to ripple through the conference room.[32]

Hilsman then suggested that McCone might speak to the issue, but first he gave a brief review himself of the intelligence gathering since August 29, when the first SAM sites were detected. Hilsman spoke about INR's increasing concern as Soviet transport ships had continued to unload their cargoes, particularly some big crates in late September (which turned out to hold IL-28s, medium-range bombers). He then intimated that "cloud cover," as much as anything, had been responsible for the delay in discovering the first MRBM site. The September 10 decision to attenuate U-2 coverage was not part of his review.[33]

McCone "surely increased Hilsman's uneasiness," as one scholar of the tape recordings later wrote, because he failed to endorse Hilsman's sketchy explanation. "I think we have to be careful at this point," the CIA director said. "I wouldn't be *too* categoric that we had no information . . . there were some 15 refugee reports" indicating that "*something* was going on." Even more alarming to Hilsman must have been McCone's subsequent reference to the lack of "hard intelligence" for some five weeks owing to the restrictions placed on U-2 overflights, although McCone, too, did not specifically mention the September 10 decision.[34] At this juncture, Robert Kennedy weighed in with an attempt to forge a quick consensus on a plausible explanation for why the missiles had not been discovered until October 15. Even if the U-2s had overflown the relevant area in mid-September, he asserted, it would not have resulted in usable proof of the deployment. We would not have "been able to tell *up* until the last ten days or two weeks," he claimed.[35] With this pronouncement, the NSC members turned to other pressing issues.

The next day, Tuesday, October 23, when ExComm convened again, McCone gave a briefing on the latest intelligence. Right afterward, the discussion turned again to fashioning a plausible explanation for the delay in discovering the missiles. In the wake of the president's address, Congress and the media were focused on the immediate crisis at hand. But everyone recognized that charges of duplicity and/or incompetence would not be long in coming. "I don't think it's realized how quickly these mobile bases can be set up and how quickly they can be moved," the president observed.[36] He mentioned that Arthur Krock, a columnist for the *New York Times* (and generally a major irritant to the administration), was already beginning, however, to ask hard questions in print.[37]

Without a great deal of further discussion, the ExComm members agreed "that the rapidity with which the Medium-Range Ballistic Missile (MRBM) site construction took place, and other events [that] took place, accounted for the suddenness of the findings," according to McCone's memo on the meeting."[38] At the urging of Secretary McNamara and Vice President Lyndon Johnson, who was particularly attuned to the political rhythms in Congress, the president approved what amounted to a public relations offensive on Capitol Hill and among influential members of the press. The best way to nip damaging speculation in the bud would be to appear forthright about the reasons for the delay.[39] McNamara recommended special briefings for congressional leaders and reporters "who will be asking this kind of question," identifying Representative Gerald Ford (R-MI), one of the "Young Turks" among the House Republicans, and *New York Times* columnist James Reston as among the people who should be contacted. Meanwhile, Johnson suggested that McCone single out Senators Richard B. Russell (D-GA) and J. William Fulbright (D-AR) for special attention. Subsequently, Senators Everett Dirksen (R-IL) and Bourke Hickenlooper (R-IA) and Representatives Carl Vinson (D-GA) and Charles Halleck (R-IN) were added to McCone's list.[40]

Deflecting congressional curiosity promised to be a delicate problem in light of certain pre-crisis hearings on Capitol Hill. On September 5, Marshall Carter, in McCone's absence, had briefed the Senate Foreign Relations and Armed Services Committees about the newly discovered Soviet SA-2s. He had testified that these SAMs were not quite operational—meaning there was no reason yet to alter the surveillance regime—and then had added that the CIA was in no way "assuming" that SSMs would *not* be implanted in Cuba.[41] Dean Rusk had given similar assurances before the same committees in executive session on September 17, without mentioning, of course, the attenuation of U-2 overflights that had been ordered in the meantime. Richard Russell, perhaps the most influential member of the Senate, had been present at both hearings, and his memory for tiny but critical facts was legendary. Indeed, the day before, one of the first questions he had asked McCone, after the

DCI finished his briefing of the congressional leadership, was whether the SA-2s were operational; the thrust of his question was clearly whether the U-2s could operate with impunity. "I'm sure you're monitoring [electronic emissions]," Russell had said, and McCone had told him that SAM radars "have been latching onto our U-2s the last couple of days."[42]

For the time being, however, the need to manage press coverage was of equal if not greater moment.[43] Because of the stakes, politicians would be apt to close ranks behind the president and refrain from criticizing the commander-in-chief until some resolution of the crisis was achieved, if only out of caution and for reasons of political self-preservation.[44] Moreover, since Congress was out of session, prospective critics lacked the natural podium afforded by the Senate or House floor or a hearing room, and that limited the amount of attention they might command. Finally, many members of Congress were preoccupied with their races for the coming midterm election.

In contrast, some journalists were already sniffing around, as the president had noted, trying to find an unused angle to the unfolding story.[45] Consequently, a prepackaged answer for the administration's spokesmen was prepared in anticipation of questions from the press. It seemed candid and detailed on the surface. But it was also misleading, because it claimed that surveillance in September had been greater than normal—the four-flights-versus-two argument.[46]

In addition, President Kennedy urged McCone to talk privately to members of the press "who are of particular significance."[47] McCone's status as the titular head of the intelligence community made him the logical person to put forward the administration's version of events. Then, too, his reputation as a geopolitical hard-liner would work to the administration's advantage; no one was likely to accuse McCone of being party to a deception. In addition, of course, he enjoyed great credibility on this specific issue. It was well known in Congress that as early as August, McCone had predicted a Soviet deployment, a fact that seemed likely to become widely known in the media as well. His dissent from what had been the conventional wisdom was something of a double-edged sword, though—while it bolstered perceptions of his integrity and foresight, it also meant that he posed something of a risk to the cover story the president was hoping to uphold.[48]

The list of journalists who were to be "contacted privately"—in other words, who would receive selective leaks from ExComm members—turned out to be somewhat longer than the congressional leaders who were going to receive special briefings from McCone.[49] The list included columnists Reston and Krock from the *New York Times,* along with Hanson Baldwin, the

CHAPTER 2

newspaper's military affairs specialist; managing editor Alfred Friendly and publisher Philip Graham from the *Washington Post;* syndicated columnists Walter Lippmann, Stewart and/or Joseph Alsop, and William S. White; Ben McKelway, the editor of the *Washington Star;* and David Lawrence, the dean of syndicated columnists in the nation's capital, who wrote for the *Washington Star* and *U.S. News & World Report* (the latter of which he also edited).[50] Simultaneously the president ordered that all contact between senior administration officials and the media be cut off save for official channels. Eventually only the press secretaries at the White House and the Departments of State and Defense were officially authorized to discuss the crisis.[51]

Just as the administration anticipated, the delay in discovering the missiles soon began to emerge as a potent issue. On October 26 John Finney noted in the *New York Times,* "Questions are being asked in Washington about how and why the Cuban crisis developed with so little warning . . . [although] administration officials insist there was no 'intelligence gap.'"[52] James Reston addressed the issue the same day, writing that "there is considerable suspicion either that the official intelligence was not as good as maintained or that the administration withheld the facts."[53]

The CIA did not yet have in hand a precise accounting of exactly what had happened, especially during McCone's absence from Washington; the DCI had already requested an internal report, but it was still pending. Nonetheless, the agency needed to come up with a plausible answer and soon. So on October 29 McCone issued an internal press guidance.

It differed from Robert Kennedy's suggested explanation, namely, that the U-2s could not have detected anything useful "*up* until the last ten days or two weeks," even if missions had been flown. Apparently McCone believed that story could not withstand much scrutiny. "Our line therefore should be about as follows," he instructed: "The MRBM and IRBM areas were surveyed on August 29 and September 5 and there was no evidence of any construction activity or unusual movements of matériel, etc. Subsequent reconnaissance efforts in late September and early October were ineffective because of bad weather and the flights that were successful concentrated on developing essential information on known installations such as SAM sites."[54] This was true as far as it went, although it exaggerated the difficulties caused by weather.[55] More significantly, it elided altogether the decision to attenuate U-2 coverage.

McCone's press guidance was almost immediately put to the test. Once the acute phase of the crisis ended on October 28, with Khrushchev's radio announcement that the missiles Washington had deemed "offensive" would be withdrawn, articles about the collection deficit began to appear in earnest.

An October 31 piece by Hanson Baldwin in the *New York Times,* headlined "An Intelligence Gap," evoked great concern among the ExComm members, who met at 10:00 A.M. that day.[56] McCone made a point of raising the article with the president in front of the group. The DCI knew that Baldwin, the *Times*'s military affairs editor and winner of a Pulitzer Prize, was very influential; where he led, other reporters would soon follow.

Rebutting the administration's wilder critics—those who argued that the White House had cynically known about the deployment all along but had milked it for political advantage—was not terribly difficult. But thoughtful skeptics like Baldwin, who were asking how the Russians had managed to build so many missile sites so quickly without being noticed, were a knotty problem. *Something* in the intelligence-gathering process had clearly gone awry, Baldwin was arguing, notwithstanding the administration's explanations.[57] But he hadn't quite managed to put his finger on it.

The administration's effort to influence press coverage did bear some early fruit. Two of the columnists McCone had been asked to contact, Joseph Alsop and Arthur Krock, both wrote pieces praising the administration's vigilance and ruling out the existence of any photo gap. On November 2 Alsop noted that despite "pleas for caution in the air surveillance of Cuba . . . the schedule of U-2 missions was *stepped up* [emphasis added] in September to four each month."[58] He attributed subsequent delays in surveillance solely to bad weather. On October 28 Krock, the cause of so much anxiety, wrote that "two forming hurricanes in close succession impeded the intelligence required for absolute verification that the military build-up was offensive."[59] Around the same time, both the *New York Times* and the Associated Press published long news stories on how the Soviet deception had been found out. Neither was a close approximation of what had actually happened.[60]

Most other commentators, though, were not easily reconciled to the administration's version of events. James Burnham, writing in the *National Review* in late November, clearly recognized the signs of an administration-generated public relations offensive and issued a scathing critique, particularly of Alsop's article. Burnham wrote, "Intimate off-the-record klatches yield a harvest of inspired stories, editorials, and columns. On November 2, the volunteer Court Apologist, Joseph Alsop, gave out the approved version of the moment. (This sort of thing always sounds so particularly silly coming from Joe Alsop, who clearly knows better.)"[61] Although Burnham had no access to the facts, and apparently no hope of obtaining them, he perceived that the administration's "emergent apology" had all the clarity of a dark dye. Given the ongoing geopolitical struggle with the Soviet Union, he argued, "the factual side of intelligence, if it is to be sound and timely, must be kept independent of changing political moves and moods." This was almost the opposite of what happened, he asserted; intelligence operations had been subject to fleeting policy considerations, such as "how cozy we were with Khrushchev at the moment . . . and the supposed feelings of various governments and the UN."[62]

Burnham, a prominent conservative, was such a predictable critic of the administration that his commentary could be discounted. It was much more troubling when David Lawrence—one of the journalists handpicked to be given early information by McCone—refused to adopt the administration's line. Lawrence skewered McCone's explanation in two successive columns in the *Washington Star*.[63] "A case of sheer negligence, if not incompetence, can be made out," he wrote on November 6. He called for Congress to mount a vigorous investigation when it reconvened in January, similar to the investigation held by the Senate Foreign Relations Committee after the downing of Francis Gary Powers's U-2 in May 1960.[64]

In preparation for the president's news conference on November 20, his first since the Soviet withdrawal had been announced, White House staffers prepared an extensive answer in anticipation of a question from the press about the intelligence gap. This time around, there would be no talk of stepped-up surveillance—not when the president was talking directly about the matter—only "systematic continuation of intelligence collection activities." The planned answer called the effort in Cuba "not an intelligence failure, but a major intelligence triumph," and ended with a plea to bring the issue to a close. "I am sure you will agree with me," President Kennedy was advised to say, "that the public interest will not be served by detailed speculation concerning the internal operations of this intelligence effort."[65]

As it turned out, no one actually managed to get in a question about the photo gap at the press conference. But the media's persistent interest in the issue, and the need to contain and channel this curiosity, came under discussion again during an ExComm meeting nine days later. According to Bundy's notes, "The importance of limiting discussion of [postmortems of the crisis] with the press was re-emphasized, and the designation of authorized White House sources was reaffirmed."[66] This placid notation failed to capture the argument that erupted during that meeting, once McCone took on almost everyone else in the room by insisting that aerial surveillance of Cuba during the late summer of 1962 had been dangerously weak. The disagreement erupted after the president had expressed displeasure over negative coverage in *Look* and *Reader's Digest*. According to McCone's contemporaneous notes, "There followed a discussion of the overflight policies in Cuba and an emphatic denial was expressed by various members of the Executive Committee that any flight requested by CIA or NRO during September had been denied. DCI took issue with these statements, stating that it was his understanding that the administration wished Cuban overflights program to avoid the possibility of a 'U-2 incident.' This caused the CIA and COMOR to program September flights so that planes would not be engaged by operational SAM sites. McCone stated that this was, in his opinion, an error, as those responsible for planning reconnaissance should have insisted upon overflying areas protected by SAMs in order to determine what was going on." McCone went on to remind the president and other ExComm members that the October 14 flight had not been authorized until October 9. Furthermore, McCone said, he realized just how big a problem the whole issue was when he had "trouble defending our September program" to the President's Foreign Intelligence Advisory Board (PFIAB). Questioning by Clark Clifford, one of the board's members, "had brought out the difficulty of explaining the lapse of 40 days in programming an aerial photography which would produce a complete mosaic of Cuba," McCone reported.[67]

This dispute marked the first time that the tension now underlying the September 10 decision had been brought out in the open at an ExComm meeting. One result was that, as Bundy noted, the "designation of authorized White House sources was reaffirmed." McCone, in his memo for the record, was more specific: "It was decided that all press contact with feature writers should be confined to Mr. Bundy and the Attorney General"—in other words, two ExComm members who could be counted on to keep the true facts obscured. Once this issue was settled for the time being, the president left the meeting. Undoubtedly he did so wondering about the extent of McCone's loyalty to the administration.[68]

By chance, Senator Russell summoned McCone for a talk later that day on the very subject of the intelligence gap. The CIA's legislative counsel, John S. Warner, who sat in on the discussion, noted, "Mr. McCone stated that he personally had pushed his concern about missiles in Cuba since last August. He mentioned that the president had commented to him today . . . that 'no one would believe you or take you seriously.' However, Mr. McCone added that while possibly we could have learned about them [i.e., strategic missiles in Cuba] earlier, we would have had no positive proof earlier." Clearly, McCone was trying to split the difference, at least when asked about the photo gap by perhaps the single most influential member of Congress. The DCI was trying to downplay the importance of the photo gap while not flatly denying its existence.[69]

Subsequently, the administration continued its efforts to spin press coverage when it couldn't persuade reporters that there was no story to write. Most of the efforts were sufficiently discreet to be not easily recognizable, but one was so blatant that the resulting article immediately generated controversy. This was the story was written by Stewart Alsop and Charles Bartlett for the December 8, 1962, issue of the *Saturday Evening Post,* then one of the nation's leading magazines.[70]

The article was the product of a three-week investigation, which meant that Alsop and Bartlett had begun their research in early November, not long after Hanson Baldwin's worrisome analysis in the *Times*—a point when the administration's interest in fostering positive press pieces would have been especially strong.[71] When the article appeared, one fact raised eyebrows right away: coauthor Charles Bartlett was a close friend of President Kennedy's, the two having grown close when both lived in Georgetown in the 1950s. Even without this connection, though, the article was bound to create controversy because of its substance, not to mention its claims about being "exclusive" and "authoritative." Almost immediately, it was seen (and rightly so) as the administration's preferred version of events, a calculated leak that perhaps bore little resemblance to actual events.[72]

The literature on the crisis has invariably concentrated on the article's unflattering—and misleading—portrayal of Adlai Stevenson. Alsop and Bartlett described the US ambassador to the United Nations as having "wanted a Munich": eager to appease the Soviets by proposing to withdraw Jupiters from Turkey, Italy, and Britain if Moscow did likewise in Cuba. In fact, Stevenson, a steadfast advocate of "negotiation and sanity," had enunciated positions that would turn out to be as close to the president's true views as anyone's. In any case, it was patently unfair to single out Stevenson when many ExComm participants had changed their minds from day to day—and sometimes during the same meeting, as Bundy was wont to do.[73]

This Stevenson red herring was calculated to conceal the existence of the quid pro quo agreement, and in that sense, it succeeded: the false controversy directed attention away from the true terms of the settlement.[74] Lost in the uproar was the fact that the article also conveyed a patently disingenuous explanation for the delay in discovering the missile sites. Alsop and Bartlett's formulation vaguely resembled McCone's proposed press guidance but was even more muddled. According to the article, "U-2 flights continued over Cuba [in September and October], weather permitting, on a biweekly basis."[75] There was no photo gap, in other words, just delays caused by the forces of nature.

Very few observers noticed the latest twist in the official story of the U-2 reconnaissance. Indeed, because of what Bundy subsequently called the "gratuitous and anonymous [intra-administration] sniping that [would] become common in later years," the controversy over the article's depiction of Stevenson obliterated for a time the media's interest in whether the offensive missiles had been discovered at the earliest reasonable opportunity.[76]

Other factors, too, played a role in distracting attention away from this facet of the crisis. The misestimate of Moscow's intentions, once it became public knowledge after the settlement, immediately garnered attention. Finally and ironically, the administration also got an assist from its congressional nemesis, Kenneth Keating. The senator claimed that there had been no intelligence gap: it was simply a case of top officials being unwilling to believe what the intelligence community was coming up with.[77] The media's fixation on what was sometimes referred to as the "KIA"—Keating's supposedly superior Intelligence Agency—meant that Keating's ostensible "scoop," while undoubtedly a headache for the White House, also inadvertently suited the administration's purposes because it drew so much attention away from the real intelligence issues.[78]

By December, it appeared that the cover story (or some version of it) was holding insofar as public perceptions of the photo gap were concerned. Sometimes it seemed to disappear from the horizon altogether, for it was far from the only residual problem connected with the crisis. Despite the lifting of the blockade, diplomats were still wrangling over the contours of the Soviet military presence in Cuba, as Khrushchev tried to salvage something from his risky undertaking. Eventually the administration's severest critics would even claim that President Kennedy still had a missiles-in-Cuba problem.[79]

Nonetheless, in general, the White House kept a watchful eye on one of the few secrets that threatened its newly won reputation for shrewd leadership—or in the effusive words of Arthur Schlesinger Jr., "[a] combination of toughness . . . nerve and wisdom, so brilliantly controlled, so matchlessly calibrated that [it] dazzled the world."[80]

The Struggle over the Postmortems

W hile the administration was still busy influencing public perceptions of the crisis, the battle over its history began in earnest. For
the most part, it would be in the form of the efforts to influence
the secret postmortems conducted by various entities in the government. In
all, four intelligence investigations would be conducted in 1962 and 1963 at
various altitudes of the government. For the most part, these analyses, along
with the documentation necessary to evaluate them in context, have been
declassified only recently, some forty years after the event.[1]

The postmortems would be essentially unanimous in their praise of the
intelligence community's work *after* the discovery of the Soviet missiles on
October 15. But they would vary greatly in their findings regarding its performance in the run-up to the crisis. The postmortems were all subject to
extraneous influences that distorted their findings and even the presentation
of facts. Their key conclusions depended inordinately on *who* wrote the postmortem, *when* it was written, and for *whom*, and represented nothing less
than a struggle to control the history of the crisis.

The Lehman Report

Richard Lehman, a thirteen-year veteran of the CIA, was the assistant for
special projects in the Office of Current Intelligence (OCI) in 1962.[2] On
Saturday, October 27—the day that would be the turning point in the crisis—the OCI director, Russell Jack Smith, called Lehman into his office and
told him that McCone wanted an analysis of the agency's performance to
date. Although the end of the crisis was seemingly not yet in sight, "McCone
wanted to know how we had got[ten] there," Lehman later recalled, "what
we [had done] right, what we [had done] wrong, and so on." McCone was
likely anticipating the day, perhaps well in the future, when congressional
hearings on the Soviet missiles would begin, akin to the 1946 investigation

that Congress launched into Japan's surprise attack. Indeed, on one copy of the Lehman Report the words would be scrawled, "Save for the Pearl Harbor hearings—if some, or any."[3]

Lehman was greatly aided by McCone's habit of "keeping meticulous memoranda for the record" of actions, meetings, and conversations.[4] Within four days, Lehman had worked up a manuscript of nearly one hundred pages on the events leading up to the missiles' detection. Two weeks later, on November 14, he presented his findings to McCone.

Overall the Lehman Report was accurate and careful, if in some places understated. Although it was not exhaustive—it was only thirty-three pages long—it did reflect the gist of what had happened in the weeks leading up to the discovery of the missile sites.[5] With respect to the operational deficit, Lehman correctly zeroed in on the events of September 10 as being absolutely "crucial to the record."[6]

In 2003, during a telephone interview, Lehman recalled his findings in blunt terms: President Kennedy, he said, had "shot himself in the foot" by attenuating U-2 coverage over Cuba.[7] However, in the report itself Lehman was much more circumspect. He deemed that the U-2 overflights permitted after September 10 were successful inasmuch as they had established new facets of the Soviet build-up. Yet they "did not—and since they were designed to avoid SAM-defended areas, could not—detect the ballistic missile deployments then under way."[8] Lehman astutely observed that responsibility for the cautious overflight policy might appear murkier than it in fact was. Coming away from the September 10 meeting, the CIA had understood in no uncertain terms that any intrusive overflights it proposed would be declined by the NSC's Special Group Augmented for submission to the president; the agency had therefore made no such requests. Thus, the record showed that the president authorized everything the SGA requested (as Bundy would soon claim) and that the SGA had not turned down any written requests or oral appeals from the CIA for intrusive overflights.[9] In other words, a critical limitation imposed on the overflight regime for five weeks had not been captured on paper—a fact that would assume ever-larger significance in the three postmortems that followed.

The Inspector General's Survey

Several days before Lehman completed his report, Jack Earman, the CIA's inspector general (IG) since May, took up virtually the same task, also at McCone's request (McCone's reasons for ordering two internal CIA postmortems remain unclear). Earman finished a draft on November 20. The formal title was "Inspector General's Survey of Handling of Intelligence Information during the Cuban Arms Build-up, August to Mid-October 1962."

This first draft apparently either glossed over the photo gap entirely or treated it in a manner that roused McCone, perhaps by placing too much of the onus on the agency. McCone instructed Earman to take another look at the factors behind the September 10 decision to attenuate U-2 coverage.[10] On November 26 Earman put together a memo describing how he intended to incorporate this request into a revised account: "We have been told by several Agency officers that there was a widespread understanding in CIA that overflights of known SAM sites were forbidden by the Special Group [Augmented]. I believe this understanding stemmed from the desires which Secretary Rusk expressed at the 10 September 1962 meeting in Mr. Bundy's office which was not in fact a duly constituted meeting of the Special Group. However, the records do not reveal that CIA pressed for additional missions or changes in coverage of overflights approved for September 1962."[11] He then went on to recount the history of the September overflights in some detail and gave a preview of his new conclusion—which would not be all that different from Lehman's, although it was not as sharp. The precise wording of his finding, Earman wrote, would be "That extreme caution with regard to U-2 flights . . . affected the planning of Cuban reconnaissance overflights during [September]."[12]

The final version of the IG Survey, completed on November 14, weighed in at seventy-two pages—more than twice the length of Lehman's analysis. Only the USIB postmortem (at ninety pages) would be longer. Earman's report contained extensive information about the inner workings of the intelligence community in the run-up to the crisis, covering the gamut of estimative, analytical, and operational factors. For example, it gave perhaps the most detailed account anywhere of the so-called "publication ban"—strict limitations that had been placed on the dissemination, in intelligence community–coordinated publications, of information about Soviet offensive weapons in Cuba.

With respect to the "photo gap," the IG Survey was much more precise than Lehman's postmortem about what kind of surveillance the COMOR had proposed and when. It included a six-page annex, "Chronology of Cuban Overflights," which added great detail. Perhaps because of McCone's prodding, the IG Survey considered the operational deficit to be one of the most important issues. Counting the annex, it devoted as many pages to the overflight restrictions as it did to any other single topic. Earman put the consequences of the restrictions this way: "Thus, it took nearly a month [from

September 10 to October 14] to get the coverage CIA had sought to get in a single [U-2] mission."[13]

McCone's response to Earman's initial draft had essentially made the final IG Survey consonant with the Lehman Report on the reasons for the photo gap.[14] Neither analysis attempted to shift the entire responsibility for the operational deficit in coverage onto the State Department or the White House. Both were simply candid about the fact that the administration's overweening concern about a possible international incident, together with estimative and analytical errors, had led to a significant degradation of intelligence gathering precisely while the first offensive missiles were being trucked into place.

The USIB Report

On November 14, the day Richard Lehman turned in his analysis, Dr. James T. Killian, the chairman of the President's Foreign Intelligence Advisory Board (PFIAB), asked the CIA to produce an "all-source, all-agency" postmortem.[15] The PFIAB was an elite, ostensibly nonpartisan panel established by President Eisenhower in 1956 and comprised of experienced officials currently outside the government, along with some of the nation's leading scientists. Its purpose was to advise the president directly on all matters concerning US intelligence, from the most technical collection issues to broader counterintelligence matters. The panel's standing as one of the few external overseers of the intelligence community, coupled with its access to the president, meant that the stakes in this postmortem were very high.[16]

McCone transmitted Killian's request to the US Intelligence Board (USIB) the next day. This body, founded in 1958, represented the pinnacle of the intelligence community at the time: its principal members were the CIA, the Defense Intelligence Agency (DIA), the National Security Agency (NSA), and the State Department's Bureau of Intelligence and Research (INR). Thus, the USIB postmortem would represent the coordinated and considered judgment of the intelligence community as a whole, just as most of the community had been engaged in the intelligence operations leading to the missiles' discovery.[17]

McCone then chose Jack Earman to chair the USIB working group that would draft the report.[18] On the surface, this risked making the USIB postmortem simply an elaboration of the internal CIA analysis that Earman was six days away from wrapping up. But the USIB inquest promised to differ in two fundamental respects. The participants would be grading not just their own performance but also, and perhaps more importantly, their comparative performance; and although the findings would, like the Lehman analysis and the IG Survey, be highly classified, they would, unlike those reports, be circulated outside the originating body.

Word of this new study instantly evoked wariness among some of the offices that stood to be scrutinized. Dr. Herbert Scoville, head of the directorate that actually operated the CIA's U-2s, told his staff that he feared that there might be some "buckpassing." He wanted the Office of Special Activities to review carefully all the factors that had led up to the October 14 overflight, taking into account all requirements, COMOR deliberations, Special Group Augmented actions, and the weather.[19] Meanwhile, James Reber, the COMOR chairman, expressed concern about the "validity of people's memories as they unintentionally embroidered the facts."[20]

The USIB working group soon encountered the very same problem that Lehman had already pointed out: the September 10 decision to degrade U-2 overflights was incompletely and imperfectly reflected in the written record. The sketchy accounts were not even in complete agreement about who attended the ad hoc meeting. And the documentation that did exist, moreover, could leave the impression that the CIA had not been very exercised by the limitation imposed by the White House and the State Department. It could easily be made to appear as if the CIA had gotten exactly the coverage it had asked for.[21]

A flawed paper trail might have been less of a problem but for the predispositions one member of the working group, INR director Roger Hilsman, brought to the table. Hilsman viewed the postmortem as a crucial engagement in his ongoing war with the CIA. Like many liberals in the administration, he had come into government service believing that the CIA had gotten so powerful during the 1950s that "it was running the foreign policy of the United States." He had privately set for himself the tasks of "cutting them [the CIA] back in power" and "sav[ing] the [State] Department from the CIA" by reducing the agency's alleged policy-making proclivities and influence.[22]

He was intent on using his position in the working group to scrub the USIB postmortem of any self-congratulatory gestures that the CIA might make at the expense of the State Department and the administration in general. This goal was all the more urgent, of course, because McCone had been the only one of the president's national security advisers who had anticipated the offensive missiles and distinctly warned Kennedy of their possibility. The aftermath of the crisis promised to afford McCone an opportunity to "manipulate [the missile crisis] to his advantage," as Hilsman put it—a forbidding prospect to someone who had strongly opposed McCone's appointment in the first place and who had tried, but failed, to insert himself in the process that led to the September 10 decision.[23]

An illustration of the antagonistic relations between Hilsman and the CIA was an incident that allegedly occurred on October 16, the very day President Kennedy learned of the missiles. Word soon reached the CIA that as Hilsman was preparing to see Dean Rusk that morning, the INR director had remarked he was going to have to report a "tremendous failure on part of U.S. Intelligence." When CIA deputy director Pat Carter promptly called Hilsman and asked him about the reported comment, Hilsman claimed that he didn't recall saying anything of the kind—only that he, along with almost everyone else in the administration, did not expect the Soviet deployment.[24]

In short, from Hilsman's perspective the USIB postmortem afforded McCone an opportunity to "manipulate [the crisis] to [his] advantage," and thereby strengthen the CIA's position within the administration. This was intolerable, given that Hilsman was intent on reining in the CIA's power.[25]

Apparently, there is no easily obtainable record of the deliberations over USIB analysis, which lasted many weeks. The best insight into Hilsman's influence on the process can be gained by considering the postmortem in light of Hilsman's controversial 1967 memoir, *To Move a Nation* (controversial because so-called "kiss and tell" memoirs revealing classified information had not yet become commonplace). Hilsman devoted an entire chapter to the aftermath of the missile crisis, entitling it "The Intelligence Post-Mortem: Who Erred?" He characterized the USIB Report as one of "two attempts by insiders to allege that policy [had] interfered with intelligence." McCone [*sic*] instituted the study, Hilsman disingenuously wrote, "immediately after the crisis to determine if the missiles would have been discovered sooner if the secretary of state had not requested on September 10 that the next [U-2] flight be broken up into four separate flights. For a while there was some uneasiness at the possibility of some real alley fighting developing. But it was not difficult to show, first, that any delay caused by making four flights instead of one was negligible; and, second, that there had never been a turndown of any flight that intelligence had asked to be approved, but that on the contrary both the White House and the State Department had actually pushed for more intelligence all along."[26] Hilsman's loyalty to the administration clearly overrode his loyalty to the facts; his foremost goal from the outset of the process was to insulate the State Department and the White House from criticism. According to Hilsman's deputy, Thomas Hughes, it was feared that an adverse USIB postmortem might lead the PFIAB to submit an even more critical report, or that portions of the USIB analysis damaging to the president might be leaked to the press and perhaps even trigger a congressional investigation.[27]

Of course, Hilsman was just one member of the working group and could not unilaterally impose his agenda. But juxtaposing his memoir with the USIB Report leaves no doubt that his preferred narrative carried the day. "The procedures adopted in September delayed photographic intelligence, but this delay was not critical, because photography obtained prior to about 17 October would not have been sufficient to warrant action of a type which would require support from Western Hemisphere or NATO allies," the report would conclude, in marked contrast to the Lehman Report and IG Survey.[28] Not coincidentally, this position was nearly identical to the administration's public explanation for the delay; and to varying degrees, all the USIB members ultimately had an interest in propagating it to anyone outside the immediate intelligence community.

The USIB postmortem has to be considered a negotiated, if not compromised, document, the product of a bargain between competing factions in the government. It tried hard to give the appearance of presenting evidence in a plain, unvarnished manner. But whenever a problematic fact reared its head, the language was massaged until the presentation was acceptable to all vested interests—bureaucratic as well as those of the administration.[29] And even then, in March 1963 the State Department would belatedly attempt to claim, despite Hilsman's participation at every stage, that the USIB postmortem was not a "coordinated report" but McCone's "personal report."[30]

The PFIAB Report

Despite the intense bargaining over the USIB postmortem, those who commissioned it never viewed it as an end in itself. The nine PFIAB members were nothing if not mindful of their jealously guarded access to the Oval Office, and they always intended to gather additional information and submit their own findings to the president. They recognized that the USIB postmortem was likely to represent a "best foot forward" approach by the intelligence community and its titular head, McCone.[31]

PFIAB members were also inclined to be skeptical because their relations with McCone were uneasy at best. DCIs, it seemed, tended not to like having an independent board looking over their shoulder, "encroaching on their prerogatives." To make matters worse, McCone had long had a prickly relationship with the PFIAB chairman, Dr. James Killian. McCone was of the opinion that "scientists cause trouble" in the federal government because they tended to inject themselves into political matters rather than sticking to what they knew and were supposed to do—which was provide technical advice. The two men had clashed repeatedly when McCone was chairman of the Atomic Energy Commission in the late 1950s and Killian served as President Eisenhower's top science adviser. Their relationship was so poor (at least from Killian's perspective) that after President Kennedy announced McCone's appointment as DCI in September 1961, Killian threatened to resign as PFIAB chairman. He backed down only after a personal appeal from Attorney General Robert Kennedy.[32]

But if McCone truly had a nemesis on the panel, it was Clark M. Clifford, an archetypal Washington lawyer and a skilled, consummate defender of partisan political interests. In the administrative regrouping after the Bay of Pigs invasion, President Kennedy had offered Clifford the DCI position, only to have him decline. Instead, Clifford accepted an appointment to the PFIAB, with the understanding that he would soon replace Killian as chairman.[33] It marked the first time that someone known largely for being a "Washington fixer" had been appointed to the prestigious board.

Clifford, moreover, was operating with the knowledge that he had been Kennedy's first choice for DCI, and he did not regard McCone as a very good second choice, owing to McCone's notorious inflexibility, his standing as a rich Republican businessman who had served Eisenhower and remained close to Nixon, and his reputation as a "deeply ideological anticommunist." To top things off, the fact that the press was hailing McCone for his foresight on the missiles rankled Clifford no end. During the PFIAB postmortem the friction between the two would reach, in Clifford's words, a "crescendo."[34]

Although the record of the PFIAB's deliberations is spotty, Clifford—the member who was almost certainly the most influential in shaping the postmortem—discussed the episode in detail in his 1991 memoir (somewhat like Hilsman vis-à-vis the USIB Report), and several CIA memos declassified in 2003 provide additional insights. "We were faced with a dilemma," Clifford wrote in his book. "We did not wish to criticize the president, who had handled the crisis brilliantly once the Soviet missiles had been positively identified by American intelligence, but we felt the length of time it had taken to discover the missiles was dangerously and inexcusably long. We were particularly disturbed that there had been no overflights of Cuba between August 29 and October 14 despite public charges [most prominently from Senator Kenneth Keating, R-NY] that offensive missiles were being installed." Clearly, Clifford (and possibly the other members of the panel) identified the key operational deficit early on and recognized its political sensitivity. Of course, he was also acutely aware of McCone's prognostication, notwithstanding all the estimates and expert opinion to the contrary, that the Soviets would eventually deploy SSMs in Cuba.[35]

The PFIAB's deliberations began in earnest in early December, when McCone appeared to discuss the ongoing USIB postmortem and answer the panel's questions. He mounted a stout defense of the intelligence community's performance, minimizing the estimative and operational deficits. It was essentially an "all's well that ends well" perspective. Robert Murphy, a former diplomat serving on the panel, asked if "any handicaps had been placed on the collection of intelligence about Cuba." Here, if McCone wanted it, was an opening to criticize policy makers for having put blinders on the CIA. But he loyally desisted from doing so. "No," he answered flatly.[36]

The questioning then became more pointed, according to CIA memos of the meetings. Clifford brought up the issue of McCone's personal estimate about Soviet offensive missiles, first enunciated in August, and asked about the September "honeymoon cables," in which the DCI had repeated the warning. Frank Pace, another panel member, then asked the critical question outright: how much earlier than mid-October might the U-2 have discovered the offensive missiles? McCone, foreshadowing the USIB findings, accurately responded that spotting the missiles was conceivable from about September 20 onward, but then claimed that nothing clinching the case would have been likely until mid-October anyway.[37]

The most that McCone would admit was that some "timidity" and an "attitude of caution" had existed in September. However, he was cavalier about the consequences before the PFIAB. It was a posture diametrically at odds with his alarmist position in late September and early October, not to mention his private belief, after reading two internal postmortems, that the CIA "had been remiss in proposing something less than complete coverage, having been influenced by the existing attitude . . . that complete overflights, if proposed, would not be approved."[38] The PFIAB members found McCone's appearance wholly unpersuasive. His testimony only hardened their inclination to treat the USIB's postmortem with the utmost skepticism.[39]

McCone presented the USIB findings to the PFIAB panel on December 26. Two days later, another meeting was held after the panel had presumably read the report. McCone stressed again that the conclusions were not his own personal views, which differed slightly from the USIB Report about what happened and why. Still, he was more or less in concurrence with its findings. The DCI answered several questions from the panel and, with respect to the photo gap, had every reason to believe that the PFIAB was satisfied with the

USIB's negotiated explanation. Former ambassador Robert Murphy asked McCone whether he had noted any difference "in the philosophy of the State Department in regard to intelligence." Yes, McCone answered, he thought there had been a decided change in State's attitude.[40]

Despite some sharp questions, McCone left the meeting apparently unaware of the depth of the PFIAB's dissatisfaction with both the USIB post-mortem and his explanation. After his departure Clifford declared himself profoundly unimpressed. In his memoir he called the USIB Report a "snow job" and criticized the excessive "delicacy" with which it treated the U-2 over-flights. To a degree, of course, Clifford was right in that the USIB Report was a compromised analysis, having been drafted by the same agencies that had collected and evaluated the intelligence. Still, the findings insulated the Kennedy administration from criticism at least as much as, if not more than, they benefited the intelligence community.[41]

Clifford then posed a hypothetical question: if a similar situation were to be encountered again, would any of them argue that the president had been well served by the intelligence community? There was silence—until Clifford answered his own question. The successful outcome of the missile crisis should not "lull us into a false sense of comfort," he argued. The Republican National Committee had leveled a "preposterous" allegation against President Kennedy, charging that he had deliberately withheld and/ or manipulated information about the missiles for political advantage. The facts proved otherwise, Clifford stated, and they had to be brought out in the PFIAB Report, since the intelligence community was obviously unwilling to face up to its own shortcomings. "The delays had been caused by decisions made *within the intelligence community* [emphasis added] for internal reasons," Clifford declared, citing a "state of mind within the intelligence community . . . which rejected the possibility of offensive missiles in Cuba." He expressed concern that the president "would be hurt by the CIA's efforts to protect itself." In sum, Clifford sought to put the entire blame for the photo gap onto the CIA and its Republican director.[42]

In late December the PFIAB submitted an interim report to the president that contained its most urgent recommendations. When McCone discussed them with the president on January 7, the DCI was more or less in agreement with the PFIAB's partial assessment. He also used the occasion to express his own unvarnished conclusions to Kennedy directly. The intelligence community had done a good job but "could have done better," observed McCone. The principal errors were, in order of importance, the photo gap, the estimative deficit, and, lastly, the failure to analyze correctly some indicators that might, in retrospect, have forced a reconsideration of the September 19 SNIE. But McCone was careful to spread responsibility for the photo gap widely, ascribing it to "timidity throughout the government."[43]

What McCone failed to appreciate was that the PFIAB was still preparing its salvo. The most sensitive section—the panel's findings about the intelligence community's pre-October performance—had not been included in the interim report, for the panel was intent on digging more deeply into the issue. According to Clifford's memoir, this effort involved gaining access to information that went beyond the postmortems and briefings McCone had already made available. When McCone initially balked at supplying these materials, Clifford declared the DCI's obstructionism intolerable. "If McCone was going to set himself up as a censor of what the PFIAB could and could not see," Clifford later wrote, ". . . then [the PFIAB's] functions and rationale would be destroyed." Clifford went so far as to threaten to resign, and when the president heard about the dispute, he urged the DCI to be more forthcoming.[44]

Nonetheless, McCone still did not foresee a problem. He presumed, in all likelihood, that after the panel got all the unhindered access it wanted, it would present a balanced picture of what had happened and why.

On February 4 the PFIAB finished its "comprehensive" final report—comprehensive because it now included the panel's detailed investigation of the intelligence community's performance prior to October 14. Whereas every postmortem had judged that performance to be a triumph overall, albeit by the narrowest of margins, PFIAB considered it a failure "in view of the fact that the Soviet move came dangerously close to success." The panel concluded, moreover, that from August to mid-October the intelligence community was missing a "focused sense of urgency or alarm which might well have stimulated a greater effort."[45]

The president lent McCone the only copy of the report in late February—and the DCI was stunned by the unexpected and blistering criticism. He responded in a memo almost immediately, most of which was devoted to an analysis of the reasons for the surveillance deficit. Somewhat ironically, McCone now adopted the position of at least partly defending the policy that he had so vigorously lobbied against in the fall. The "reluctance and timidity" to direct U-2 flights over Cuba was understandable in context," he told the president in his February 28 memo.[46]

McCone knew that the PFIAB would be meeting with President Kennedy on March 9 to discuss its findings, and on March 7 he telephoned Robert Murphy, the panel member he apparently knew the best. According to

Murphy's account, McCone got quite emotional. If the PFIAB was going to insist on submitting the report as is, McCone said, the top five people in the CIA—including the DCI himself—would have to resign, and perhaps officials from the DIA as well. When Murphy pointed out that it was too late to withdraw the report, McCone stressed his disagreement with its references to a "failure of intelligence." Murphy responded that the criticism was "really mild" but that in his judgment, and he thought in the judgment of the entire panel, there had been in fact a failure and it was PFIAB's duty to so state to the president.[47]

Two days later the PFIAB discussed its findings—a ten-page report—with President Kennedy during a seventy-nine-minute meeting. Clifford's handiwork was manifest: the postmortem read more like a lawyer's brief than a disinterested analysis. It was virtually transparent in its effort to absolve policy makers from any responsibility for the photo gap. The longest paragraph in the report pertained to the September 10 meeting. Owing to the paucity of records, the board members claimed, it was "impossible to determine whether or not there was a restriction" that prevented intrusive overflights of Cuba. They did allow that the CIA was clearly under the "impression" that such an injunction had been imposed. But the panel found fault only with the intelligence community. In what was by now a familiar litany, it noted that the president "granted authorization for all U-2 flights which were recommended to him by . . . the SGA," which "was not made fully aware of the delaying effects on the acquisition of aerial intelligence" that stemmed from the September 10 decision.[48]

National Security Advisor McGeorge Bundy, who was also present, interjected that such a situation would never recur. The Special Group had instituted new procedures to ensure that it would be informed whenever operational delays occurred while previously approved surveillance missions were carried out. The one comment the president made about the photo gap suggested that he knew who was primarily responsible for the curtailment of overflights (having been told the truth by his brother in all likelihood). He was not suggesting, said the president, that this had not been a prudent suggestion by his secretary of state. Aircraft might well have been shot down. But it made him as president more conscious of the fact that there was perhaps a lack of true expertise on the part of policy makers with respect to "certain intelligence operations."[49]

For his part, McCone was unwilling to let the matter drop. One month later he was still bringing up his objections to the PFIAB Report during meetings ostensibly devoted to more pressing issues, urging the president to have it withdrawn or amended. Kennedy, who tended to find such arguments tedious, told him not to persist; he was not going to allow the one copy to circulate, and insofar as he was concerned, the matter was over.[50] McCone's inability to ignore the criticism may well have contributed to the abrupt deterioration of his relationship with President Kennedy, which was never the same after the missile crisis. In any event, McCone had already taken steps to make sure the CIA was never going to get sandbagged in such a way again. He issued a directive ordering agency personnel "to be very aggressive in taking the initiative to obtain permission for any and all types of intelligence operations to obtain required information for national security."[51]

It is impossible to separate the harshness of the PFIAB's findings from the fact that many board members were personally "averse" to John McCone, as Robert Kennedy put it in a 1964 interview. The panel may also have sought to compensate for the USIB's tendency to explain, and implicitly excuse, any shortcomings on the part of the intelligence community. But in its eagerness to tarnish the CIA's performance and cut down McCone's newly won reputation for prescience, the PFIAB erred in the other direction, taking the deficits out of the context in which they had occurred, as if the intelligence community operated in a vacuum, immune from the pressures exerted by policy makers. The document PFIAB produced was a handy tool for rebutting Republican charges about the administration's performance, which certainly served Clifford's primary interest. But it left McCone seething, for he believed the PFIAB was guilty of Monday morning quarterbacking and misstating the facts.[52]

An interesting postscript to the PFIAB postmortem occurred in April 1963, when Clifford was elevated, as planned, to the panel's chairmanship. It is not known whether the *New York Times* knew about the dispute raging internally over the report, but an editorial published in April suggests that it did. Clifford "has a brilliant mind," the *Times* observed, "but, as a long-time trouble-shooter for the Democratic Party, he is inextricably associated with partisan politics. The selection is at best unfortunate. It is bound to give the impression that our intelligence activities will now be monitored—not by a chairman who is an expert in the field—but by one who is essentially a politician."[53]

The Rashômon *Effect*

The government's inability to be consistent or objective in its 1962–63 postmortems is sobering. The four reports were reminiscent of Akira Kurosawa's film masterpiece *Rashômon*, which depicted the same event through the eyes of four different witnesses, who give four quite different versions of what happened. Each postmortem could not be separated from the person(s) who wrote it and the circumstances involved in its production; they could easily be as flawed as the intelligence process they purported to judge, if not more so. With the benefit of hindsight, everyone knew what side to be on.

This aspect of the intense struggle over assessments, if not over history itself, occurred over a period of months and completely behind the scenes. But that would begin to change when Congress—which had been out of session during the entire crisis—finally reconvened in January 1963. Now the struggle over how to characterize the reason for the photo gap would be conducted in different arena.

Stonewalling the House

When the Eighty-Eighth Congress convened on January 3, 1963, its Republican members were livid about the 1962 election. Precedent had all but guaranteed that the Democrats, as the party in power during a midterm election, would lose around five Senate seats and nearly forty in the House. Instead, it was the GOP that lost Senate seats (four), while gaining only two seats in the lower chamber. The election results shored up President Kennedy's political standing, which had been somewhat precarious because of his razor-thin margin of victory in 1960. The Republicans had "lost rather than gained momentum in the incipient race to win back the White House in 1964," as one prominent White House correspondent put it.[1]

Politicians and news commentators unanimously agreed that one issue was responsible for the turnabout in Democratic fortunes. "You remember my prediction a month ago?" House minority leader Charles Halleck reportedly told an aide on October 22, the day the congressional leadership was briefed on the missile deployment. "I said he'll pull the rug out from under the Republicans on the Cuba issue. Well, that's what he's done." A less conspiratorial-sounding explanation came from the president's sometime ally in the Senate, Stuart Symington (D-MO), who wrote Lyndon and Lady Bird Johnson: "Cuba helped."[2] Indeed, the Kennedy administration had all but rewritten the conventional wisdom on its management of US foreign policy. As recently as October 1962, questions about its basic competence in this arena had promised to be a sure-fire issue for Republicans; now it appeared that foreign policy could be one of Kennedy's strongest cards leading into the November 1964 election.

Predictably, Republicans began to attack the administration over Cuba as soon as the new Congress was seated. Losing that issue appeared tantamount to conceding foreign policy as a whole. Encouraged by a few members of the press, they began probing every facet of the missile crisis in an effort to dim the glow of the president's October victory.[3]

During the first half of 1963, Republicans would variously claim that not all the Soviet missiles were being withdrawn from Cuba, that there were secret codicils to the terms of the Soviet withdrawal, and that the administration had been lax in its surveillance of Cuba prior to the discovery of the missiles. A few members would attempt to focus attention on the fact that Castro remained ensconced in power and would call for a belated congressional investigation into the Bay of Pigs.[4] A desperate minority within the GOP would even argue that the administration had timed the missile crisis solely for political advantage.

Most of these criticisms were baseless. Only two were genuinely problematic for the administration—primarily because they were true. The more sensitive of the two, in terms of the Western alliance and the Cold War, was the charge of a secret codicil: Kennedy's private assurance to Khrushchev that he would withdraw the Jupiter missiles from Turkey. Still, in some ways this was not a hard secret to keep. Only eight of the president's advisers had been privy to the pact, and the Soviets had been told that any public reference by Moscow to Kennedy's pledge would instantly render it "null and void."[5]

The allegation about lax photo surveillance—the photo gap—was another matter.[6]

Congress Enters the Fray

The administration's efforts to manage the news about the missile crisis had peaked with the December publication of the Alsop-Bartlett account in the *Saturday Evening Post*. One detail from the adoring article had stood out so vividly that the administration's preferred narrative had become virtually fixed in the public mind. "We're eyeball to eyeball," Rusk was quoted as observing at the climactic moment, "and I think the other fellow just blinked."[7] Against such a backdrop, questions from Capitol Hill were apt to appear political—as potshots from the opposition.

By early January, the White House was guardedly optimistic about getting Cuba off the front pages, and perhaps even turning it into a nonissue. Dogged surveillance of the Soviet withdrawal had demonstrated to the administration's satisfaction that Moscow had removed the offensive missiles.[8] Domestically President Kennedy's prestige was at an all-time high, reflecting a combination of relief that a nuclear war had been avoided and the belief that Moscow had capitulated.[9]

The administration's sanguine attitude was exemplified during a January

5 meeting between the president and John McCone at the Kennedy winter compound in Palm Beach, Florida. The two men started off by discussing the pending report from the PFIAB.[10] McCone gave his impression of the various intelligence deficits, including, and most important, the reason why the discovery of the missiles had been delayed. He said he had concluded that the first offensive missiles had reached Cuba between the second and ninth of September. The reason they were not discovered for more than a month was "timidity throughout the government . . . for fear of a 'U-2 incident.'"[11] McCone did not, however, remind Kennedy specifically of the September 10 meeting in Bundy's office.

In his response the president cast no aspersions, not even at the CIA estimators who had predicted that the Soviets would not place missiles in Cuba. He did ask McCone if he had ever found out who Kenneth Keating's sources were—the senator had always claimed that "ninety-five percent" of his information came from within the government. McCone said he had not been able to verify this claim and believed that Keating's sources were actually Cuban refugees.[12]

Toward the end of the meeting, the two men discussed how to answer questions about the intelligence community's performance, which the new Congress was almost certain to ask about. The president suggested that McCone prepare a briefing for the bipartisan leadership, presumably in the hope that this might staunch any calls for an investigation. McCone offered the opinion that the Senate Foreign Relations Committee was likely to conduct a probe, probably at the instigation of Senator Frank Lausche (D-OH).[13]

During a congressional leadership briefing late the next day, the key issue was whether the Soviets had withdrawn their offensive weapons. McCone reported that aerial reconnaissance showed that Moscow had withdrawn forty-two strategic medium-range missiles, forty-two jet bombers, and four or five thousand associated personnel, leaving behind about 17,000 troops. In keeping with his reputation as a hard-liner, he concluded by stressing that Cuba still represented a subversive beachhead in the region, with the Soviets still firmly ensconced. The leadership asked no significant questions and made no allegations about a deficit in US intelligence.[14]

However, the briefing proved to be the proverbial calm before the storm.[15] The Cuban issue erupted in late January to a degree not seen since the previous fall. There were reports of a new "around-the-clock Soviet military defensive build-up on Cuba" and questions about whether Moscow was withdrawing all its SSMs or might be trying to hide some in caves.[16] In other words, Republicans charged, the crisis was definitely *not* over. The level of "partisan belligerence" was fueled not only by a flurry of unsubstantiated reports but also by lingering confusion over the administration's intelligence gathering the previous fall.[17] There was no dearth of congressmen angling for the kind of fame Kenneth Keating had achieved, and Keating himself was intent on a second act, having suddenly become a "major figure in foreign policy."[18] On January 31 he leveled allegations that the Soviets were not living up to their promise to completely dismantle their missile sites. His supposed prescience the previous fall was a major reason why the renewed controversy gained currency now.

The allegations about hidden missiles were soon proved baseless, and the mostly Republican critics of the administration turned their attention to portraying the remaining Soviet forces as a potent threat anyway. One indirect consequence of their effort, however, was to redirect public attention to the issue of intelligence gathering about Cuba.[19] Representative Gerald Ford (R-MI) told constituents back home that during the missile crisis itself, "the Kennedy administration acted with confidence and in a manner which I certainly applaud. But before that time, especially from the middle of September to the middle of October, the administration had solid evidence which should have, but did not, prompt them to step up surveillance of the island." If it had done so, he added, "we would not have been caught by surprise on October 14th." A Washington correspondent for the *New Yorker* observed later that winter, "It would have been almost impossible to believe in early November of last year that the respect and admiration the President had won by his handling of the previous month's crisis could have almost completely disappeared by February. Yet this seems to be the case—or close to it."[20]

By late January the administration was also facing a slow but steady stream of news stories that tried to make sense of the belated discovery of missiles. As McGeorge Bundy noted, the press had "behaved in a highly cooperative way until the pressure was off and the post-mortems began." Given that the administration was bent on dissembling, these stories were invariably off the mark, except for one consistent strand: the explanations offered to date just didn't add up. The "post-mortem problem is still with us," Bundy advised the president on January 21, referring specifically to a follow-up article by Stewart Alsop in the *Saturday Evening Post* in which he argued that "the American people, not only historians, have a right to know" about White House decision making.[21] And in March *Reader's Digest* published a piece that made the White House "most unhappy."[22] Titled "While America Slept" (an obvious swipe at the president, whose first book was titled *Why England Slept)*, it insisted that there had been an intelligence gap. However, it too was short on details.[23]

The confluence of angry Republicans in Congress (along with some Democrats uncertain about how to respond, given their own hard-line declarations) and lingering questions in the media eventually produced just the sort of congressional investigation the administration had hoped to avoid.[24] The level of scrutiny applied to an event largely perceived as a triumph was somewhat ironic, given that the "perfect failure," the Bay of Pigs invasion, had not instigated much congressional oversight.

Questions in the House

Administration officials checking their work calendars in February 1963 would have seen reminders of the rarely enjoyable task of testifying on Capitol Hill. When they began making their annual appearances before Congress to discuss authorization and appropriations bills for the fiscal year ahead, they often found themselves being grilled by Republicans and even some Democrats about intelligence issues relating to Cuba.[25] Gen. Maxwell Taylor, chairman of the Joint Chiefs of Staff (JCS), observed on February 5 that "Congressional hearings on the Defense Department budget [have] turned into a Congressional investigation on Cuba."[26] His most vivid experience of this came two days later in a closed hearing before the Defense Department subcommittee of the House Appropriations Committee.

Taylor had been the army chief of staff under President Eisenhower. The two had had a frosty relationship, and in 1959 Taylor had retired. Kennedy brought him back into government service first to investigate the Bay of Pigs failure, then as a special military adviser, and now as the JCS chair. Taylor tried to steer his testimony on February 7 and 8 into safe waters, stating, "I, as Chairman of the Joint Chiefs of Staff, am prepared to testify on the budget." But Gerald Ford, Jamie Whitten (D-MS), and especially William Minshall (R-OH) pushed hard on what they viewed as failures in dealing with Cuba, with Minshall suggesting that there had been a photo gap. When Taylor asserted that the Soviet missiles "were discovered virtually at the time when they became visible above ground," Minshall disagreed: "There was quite a time lag there . . . . In World War II, if our G-2 section missed as much as they did on the Cuban build-up, you would be looking for a new G-2." Taylor would have none of it. "No, it depends on time and circumstance," he said.

Minshall replied that "it was not until we had the now famous picture of October 14, that was shown to us and the American public, that you ever believed that they had offensive missiles," even though "everybody" in Washington had known that "increased volume of shipping" into Cuba by the

USSR signified that "something was up." He insisted that US intelligence "could have been improved. I say most respectfully that it could have been improved," and zeroed in on the missed opportunities after early September: "They conducted only six U-2 flights from the period of September 4 or 5 until October 14 and according to the Secretary [of Defense], those U-2 flights did not show anything. The reason they did not show anything was the fact that they did not fly over the right areas . . . . At this time, why didn't they scan the whole island? . . . Here these missile sites went from an empty field, a farm area, to a practically completed missile site before you discovered them." Taylor conceded only that bad weather in late September or early October may have caused some slight delays. In any case, he maintained, "I think we came very near to catching [the missiles] upon arrival." Soon thereafter, Taylor wrote to McGeorge Bundy to suggest that the administration develop "coordinated responses" to questions likely to come up in future hearings—questions like "Why were we so long in detecting the presence of Soviet personnel and equipment?" and "Why were there so few U-2 flights in September and early October?"[27]

During the same time, Secretary of Defense Robert McNamara also found himself answering questions about Cuba rather than military expenditures before committees normally interested only in defense spending. McNamara was a master at reciting information in such copious detail that it was difficult to take issue with his narrative. As one legislator told him later that year, "You are hard to put a glove on."[28]

McNamara appeared before the House Armed Services Committee on January 30, ostensibly to discuss the US military posture and technical procurement issues. Nonetheless, Chairman Carl Vinson (D-GA) asked him to come fully prepared to talk about the deployment of the Soviet missiles. McNamara did so in a disingenuous prepared statement in which he characterized the U-2 surveillance regime as "high altitude reconnaissance missions over Cuba . . . flown on a regular schedule, weather permitting."[29] The September 10 decision to degrade surveillance went entirely unmentioned. McNamara made it appear that the administration had sent the U-2s over Cuba with impunity, scouring the island every time it received a report from refugees about any suspicious activity that could possibly involve missiles. (He would similarly mislead the press a few weeks later, stressing that there had been "six U-2 flights" between September 5 and October 7 and implying that all of them had consisted of substantial flight paths over Cuba.[30])

The committee members were at a decided disadvantage without access to the basic facts, and McNamara was not about to disclose them. An exchange between McNamara and Representative Les Arends (R-IL), the committee's ranking member, demonstrates McNamara's ability to parry every thrust:

> Arends: . . . Then we [the US government] came to the conclusion that something really important was happening in Cuba, although belatedly.
>
> McNamara: I don't believe, personally, that we came to that conclusion belatedly.[31]

When pressed by other members, McNamara vigorously insisted that given Cuba's status as a "denied area," the administration's intelligence collection and evaluation the previous fall were "near perfect" or "remarkable."[32] At the same time, he admitted, without specifying how, that Khrushchev "almost got them in before we had complete evidence of what was going on."[33] The overall impression he gave the committee was that bad weather and the Russians' speed were the main factors behind the apparent suddenness of the missiles' deployment.[34]

This left Representative Frank Osmers (R-NJ), who also sat on the Armed Services Committee's CIA subcommittee, sputtering angrily.[35] Osmers was one of the few congressmen who firmly believed there had been an operational deficit that the administration was intent on covering up.[36] He had said so to McCone and others at a January 17 meeting of the CIA subcommittee. He may have been intrigued by, if unsatisfied with, McCone's statement to the subcommittee that day. In John Warner's summary: "The Director pointed out that during September there was a certain degree of timidity within the Government concerning overflights because of two recent incidents. The first incident was the accidental intrusion of a U-2 mission over the Sakhalin Peninsula and the second was the shoot down of a U-2 over Communist China. However, on the 4th of October, the Director stated he pushed for further overflights regardless of consequences, resulting in the 14th of October flight."[37]

During McNamara's meeting with the full Armed Services Committee on January 30, Osmers (as Warner noted) "delivered a violent attack against the intelligence community, stating in effect that the Cuban situation was the worst intelligence failure since Pearl Harbor." He posited three explanations: "a. criminal conspiracy on the part of the intelligence community to withhold information, b. massive withholding of information by the Executive Branch, or c. gross incompetence on the part of the intelligence community." As Osmers later told Vinson, he believed that the first explanation was wrong, and that the second was "highly unlikely." That left incompetence.[38]

Chairman Vinson challenged Osmers to "recommend a remedy." The following day, Osmers delivered a four-page letter that correctly identified the incongruities in McNamara's testimony and alleged the possibility of a "political 'managing of the facts.'" He suggested that the Armed Services Committee's CIA subcommittee look into the operations of the intelligence community; only a full-blown investigation could prevent "another Cuban near disaster," he argued. "Our inability to confirm the existence of a Soviet offensive ballistic missile complex in Cuba until but a few days before it became operational revealed a colossal gap in our defenses," he wrote Vinson. After all, "many Americans last summer thought it would be logical that offensive missiles were being sent to Cuba," yet the intelligence community had had "no hint." Vinson subsequently wrote to McCone that Osmers had raised "serious questions;" however, McCone told his colleagues at the CIA that "almost every sentence in Mr. Osmers' letter can be refuted."[39]

It is highly unlikely that anything like a full-scale investigation by the subcommittee occurred. The previous year, Vinson had committed the group to meet monthly with CIA leaders in order to monitor the agency more effectively, but especially to ward off efforts by House reformers to create a full intelligence oversight committee. The "monthly" meetings had not come to pass, though the subcommittee did hold nine secret sessions with CIA leaders in 1963. Virtually no information on these hearings has ever been declassified, judging from a summary of one held late in the year; however, they were reasonably substantive and included discussions of recent estimates of conditions in hot spots such as Cuba and South Vietnam as well as CIA descriptions of covert action in Cuba.[40]

On March 21 McCone met with the CIA subcommittee in order to respond to Osmers's criticisms. The details of his response have not been declassified; we do know, however, that McCone planned to rely on his recent report to the PFIAB. Whether he included the report's view that "operational elements" in the intelligence community had considered themselves to be under a "restriction" from flying over the parts of Cuba with SA-2 sites for much of September and October is not known. Whatever the case, the president requested a report from McCone on how he had responded to Osmers.[41] McCone reported that Osmers "seemed reasonably satisfied with my briefing." He added a comment that, decades later, has multiple resonances: "Although Mr. Osmers will never completely understand why there were not very frequent reconnaissance overflights over Cuba beginning in August or September, I believe he has a better appreciation of what the situation actually was." Osmers later expressed satisfaction with what he had learned.[42]

Faced with these sometimes aggressive queries in early 1963, the White House was mainly concerned that all administration witnesses stay on the same page. That was not a worry whenever McNamara or Dean Rusk testified, as both secretaries were strong administration loyalists. McCone was another story.

During his January and February appearances before Congress, McCone tried to stick to the script he had given in late October: there had been little delay in detecting Soviet missile sites in Cuba, and even if U-2 flights *had* gone over western Cuba in September 1962, Soviet progress on the sites was insufficient to result in photographs that the United States could have used to persuade allies of a crisis at hand.[43] But when pressed, or depending on the exact venue, he diverged from the script, as he did during the mid-January appearance before Vinson's subcommittee when he referred in passing to the Kennedy administration's "timidity." A week later he told the House Appropriations Committee's CIA subcommittee that the path of the October 14 overflight was chosen primarily to check the operational readiness of the most advanced SAM sites—*not* because of any suspicions of strategic missile installations.[44] Still, for the most part, he adhered to the administration's general formulation of what had happened and never mentioned the September 10 meeting.

Indeed, McCone's testimony at the House Appropriations' CIA subcommittee was, as a rule, nearly as opaque as McNamara's and Rusk's. After truthfully citing the basis for the October 14 flight path, for example, he reiterated the misleading notion that photos taken earlier than mid-October "would not have been convincing enough to establish the presence" of offensive missiles in the minds of US allies.[45] When testifying before panels that were not strictly engaged in CIA oversight, he blurred the story even more. On February 5 he told the Defense subcommittee of the House Appropriations Committee, "During the month of September we overflew only part of Cuba because we had overflown the western sector on the 29th of August and the 5th of September. The Committee on Overhead Reconnaissance . . . placed in the first priority a survey of the parts of Cuba that had not been seen. We were frustrated during September because of bad weather. As a consequence, we did not get a look at the western part of Cuba until the flight of October 14."[46] Even so, McCone's explanations were sometimes suggestive enough of the truth to set several congressmen to thinking.

On February 6, Herbert Scoville, the CIA's deputy director for research, noted, "A lot of flapping is occurring relative to releases of information on Soviet forces in Cuba . . . all congressional committees are in the act, and exactly what will happen is unclear." That day, McNamara and Lt. Gen.

Carroll, director of the Defense Intelligence Agency, appeared before the same House Appropriations panel. George Mahon welcomed the defense secretary "for the purpose of discussing, really, the fate of the nation." But McNamara and Carroll were about to be grilled on Cuba for days.[47] They began by giving their by-then polished account of the Soviet build-up and subsequent withdrawal of offensive weapons. Mahon directly challenged the account, charging that "people have been saying for at least two years that there was a wide distribution of ballistic missiles in Cuba." McNamara, however, coolly insisted that "at no time were the intelligence reports seriously late, or in error, in reporting on the offensive weapons buildup in Cuba." His statement stunned Mahon, who reminded him, "We were told by representatives of the Defense Department and the State Department along in September and early October that, insofar as they knew, there were no offensive weapons in Cuba, whereas we now know in retrospect the weapons were there at that time."

Jamie Whitten then voiced open skepticism about the adequacy of the photo reconnaissance effort: "You knew all the time that you had the capacity to have the information you now have from the pictures. What restricted you from having that information prior to this build-up of offensive weapons? Why was it that you did not avail yourself of the picture-taking capacity but relied, as you say, on the very tenuous and uncertain types of information that you got under the conditions that you described? Was it because you were not instructed to?" Whitten's instincts in pursuing this line of questioning were sound, but he lacked an understanding of how the U-2 flights and flight paths had (or had not) been authorized over Cuba. This prevented him from effectively countering McNamara's response, which yet again stressed "regular" aerial reconnaissance flights. Whitten could only complain angrily about the administration's withholding of information from Congress, asking McNamara sarcastically, "What percentage of what you know now are you holding out and what percentage are you giving us?"[48]

The defense secretary received a similar tongue-lashing from Glenard Lipscomb (R-CA), who found it "almost inconceivable that we could have nearly perfect intelligence-gathering data and then wake up one day and find out that the Soviet Union had moved in the type of offensive equipment in the magnitude which appears to be just overnight on station, and by the 28th of October, one of the systems was ready to go." But the most challenging cross-examination came from Representatives Ford and Minshall, both of whom were also members of the Appropriations subcommittee on the CIA.[49] Both men had disputed and would continue to dispute Maxwell Taylor's account of events pertaining to Cuba during the Appropriations hearings.

Ford was not only known as one of the most partisan foreign policy critics in the House; he was personally angry at the president for not responding to a letter he had written him two months earlier and for what he viewed as the Kennedys' dishonest public-relations efforts regarding Cuba. One Michigan friend had written Ford, "If he [JFK] could only do as well as he talked," adding, "Every paper you pick up has something about this Cuban situation. Also, Robert Kennedy's high pressure and dictatorial methods." In response, Ford ridiculed "brother Bobbie Kennedy" and his attempts to "rewrite history."[50] For his part, Minshall had been an army intelligence officer in the European theater, rising to the rank of lieutenant colonel. It may have been this experience that enabled him to pick up on a telling fact missed by the other members of the Appropriations Committee: the unexplained thirty-nine-day gap in the photo coverage of the area around San Cristóbal.

Minshall's curiosity had been piqued not only by McCone's testimony but also by a very public event the previous day, February 6, in which the administration had gone to extraordinary lengths to dispel the increasingly wild rumors about hidden missiles in Cuba and to "stem the tide of criticism."[51] McNamara, Carroll, and Carroll's special assistant, John Hughes, held a press conference that aired on national TV. For nearly two hours they laid out all the details of the post-missile-crisis Soviet withdrawal.[52] This represented a release of information that was normally highly classified, including photographs that starkly revealed the precision of US aerial surveillance.

Such a televised event was unprecedented in American television or intelligence history. Its genesis is no mystery, though, at least in retrospect. On February 4 McGeorge Bundy had been warned by a close associate, "Senator Keating's recurrent statements on the Cuban issue are again having the cumulative effect which they gained last fall up until mid-October. Congressional mail is mounting steadily; and the Republicans again see Cuba as the maggot of our Administration."[53] The next day President Kennedy told his ExComm (according to a notetaker) that "if we acted promptly in putting out all our information within the next two or three days, we would be able to stem the tide of congressional opinion, turn it to our advantage, and reduce the problem to manageable proportions." Secretary McNamara enthusiastically agreed, suggesting a presidential press conference or "possibly a television show" to "reveal how extensive our present surveillance efforts have been and are now." But Attorney General Robert Kennedy questioned "the prospect of our helping the Russians by giving the public everything we know about [the] Soviet military presence in Cuba." Perhaps thinking that such a defense by the president's brother of intelligence secrets would prevail, McCone kept his silence. But the president said, no, his efforts and those of the State and Defense departments had been "unsuccessful in convincing many people that we knew exactly what was going on in Cuba. . . . we should go as far as we possibly can in making public intelligence information in an effort to get the situation under control this week." Thus, a "television show" was aired the very next day, with McNamara, not the president, as the star.[54]

A front-page story in the next day's *Washington Post* summarized part of the presentation that suggested a photo gap: "Hughes flashed on a screen U.S. aerial reconnaissance photos taken in August and early September. They showed innocent Cuban countryside. One picture taken Aug. 29 in the San Cristóbal area showed no evidence of military activity. It later became a missile site. Hughes then showed what he called the 'historic photo' in the Cuban crisis. It was taken by a high-altitude reconnaissance plane traveling south to north across the western sector of Cuba early on Oct. 14, 1962. It showed a Soviet medium-range missile unit that apparently had just arrived." Of course, the *Post* reporter had no way of knowing whether the missile had in fact "just" arrived. During a closing question-and-answer session, the Cleveland *Plain Dealer*'s Phil Goulding had noted the apparent lack of photos taken from early September to mid-October and asked McNamara whether this was due solely to bad weather. The defense secretary gave an evasive and misleading answer, claiming he was not showing all the photos taken "simply for a lack of time."[55]

To some degree, the television program achieved its intended result. One newspaper columnist observed, "The president's choice of McNamara was shrewd, sound politics"; the defense secretary was a "strong man" of the Kennedy cabinet.[56] However, it also highlighted precisely the sorts of questions it was meant to deflect.

At the February 7 Appropriations hearing, Minshall pressed McNamara on virtually the same question Goulding had asked, but in more pointed terms. "With all the information you had from various sources," he said, "why were there not more U-2 flights flown?" This time McNamara and Carroll could not simply mislead by omission. However, it seems clear that Minshall assumed that all U-2 overflights were equally thorough, never imagining that the intrusive flight paths routinely flown since February 1962 had been radically altered on September 10. Laboring under this misimpression, he could not understand why there were no pictures of San Cristóbal for almost six weeks. And McNamara, of course, was not interested in clarifying matters; he simply reiterated his assurances about the administration's vigilance. The "U-2 schedule during the period was quite effective and quite satisfactory," he said, and added, in a blatant untruth, "It was directed toward obtaining a complete and frequent coverage of all parts of the island."[57] The only admission Minshall won from McNamara and Carroll—and it was a confusing one—was that in September more emphasis had been put on coverage of central and eastern Cuba than on the western portion of the island.[58]

At one point in the proceedings, McNamara disclosed, perhaps inadvertently, his rationale for giving partial and misleading testimony in response to one particularly pointed question. "I have never withheld from this committee information *which I believed* [emphasis added] the committee needs and requires in connection with its duties and responsibilities," he said."[59] In other words, McNamara apparently took it upon himself to decide what the House Appropriations Committee needed to know. (Among the other topics with which McNamara was familiar but thought the committee did not need to understand was the agreement between Kennedy and Khrushchev about the Jupiter missiles: "I can say without any qualifications whatsoever there was absolutely no deal, as it might be called, between the Soviet Union and the United States regarding the removal of Jupiter weapons from either Italy or Turkey.")[60]

Ultimately, Minshall was unconvinced by McNamara, just as he had been by Taylor. "We were mistaken, surprised, and fooled over the Cuban build-up," he told McNamara. "It is shocking to me to have you sit here and tell us that our estimates on the Cuban missile situation were timely . . . I do not understand why a more intensive program of aerial surveillance was not conducted over Cuba in view of the reports you had when the weather permitted flying. From September 5 until October 14, we have a period of 39 days when we have no pictures of any missile activity in Soviet Cuba."

Minshall was, of course, essentially correct. Still, some Republicans were left thoroughly dazed by the administration's witnesses. In an Associated Press story published in early March, Gerald Ford supposedly explained the delay in discovering the offensive missiles. US intelligence "knew" by mid-September that the Soviets were implanting the missiles, he said; the administration simply did nothing about it until after October 14.[61]

Nothing better illustrates the overall confusion than two stories published by Jules Witcover, a young reporter covering the Defense Department for the Advance News Service. Witcover had to work twice as hard as the many veteran reporters assigned to the Pentagon, all of whom had better sources. He apparently saw the photo gap as an opportunity to make an impression. As of late February, he despaired of ever getting to the bottom of the story. "The mystery of the 'Cuba picture gap' . . . may never be explained publicly," he wrote in an article published in the *Washington Star* on February 27.[62] Yet barely ten days later Witcover came closer than any reporter had so far to uncovering the true extent, nature, and reason for the photo gap.[63] "Fear of another 'U-2 incident' now appears to have been the major impediment to earlier discovery of the Soviet missile buildup in Cuba," he wrote on March 10.[64] Despite its accuracy, however, the story had virtually no impact, most likely because the venue in which it appeared—the then very conservative *Los Angeles Times*—was not considered a newspaper of record on par with the major East Coast dailies.[65]

Some weeks later, when the text of the February 6–7 Appropriations sessions was released, the "situation" would be "very tricky" for the Kennedy administration, as Representative George Mahon had predicted to Undersecretary of State George Ball: the exchange between Minshall and McNamara was treated as the long-sought answer to why the offensive missiles had gone undetected for several weeks—and despite all the obfuscation and misdirection, news analyses somehow came uncomfortably close to getting it right. "U.S. Admits a Gap in Watching Cuba," the March 30 headline in the *New York Times* read, although McNamara had never actually conceded a direct relationship between a gap in photo coverage and a delay in discovering the missiles.[66]

Equally unhelpful testimony about the photo gap was given in what would amount to the only sustained House inquiry into the Soviet build-up, a probe mounted in mid-February by the House Foreign Affairs Subcommittee on Inter-American Affairs. These hearings, chaired by the conservative Southern representative Armistead Selden (D-AL), were prospective rather than retrospective and focused on the threat of subversion in the hemisphere now that a Communist redoubt had been established in Cuba.[67] Inevitably, though, they touched upon the belated discovery of the missiles the previous fall. According to one press report, committee members planned to "pin . . . down" McCone on the issue of the alleged photo gap. However, it did not work out that way.[68] When Representative F. Bradford Morse (R-MA) asked Lieutenant General Carroll the reason for the delay, Carroll responded, "Weather completely."[69] Representative Paul Rogers (D-FL) then proceeded to check weather reports and pointed out that Carroll's claim did not correspond with the facts.[70]

But Rogers's protest fell on deaf ears. House Republicans and conservative Democrats were left fuming, having failed to demonstrate that the Kennedy administration had degraded the single best source of intelligence on Cuba.

The Senate Steps In

A lthough the House was generally more aggressive about trying to poke holes in the administration's account of the Soviet build-up, it was a Senate inquiry that would cause the White House the greatest anxiety.[1] This postmortem was conducted by one of that chamber's most elite bodies: the Senate Preparedness Investigating Subcommittee (SPIS), the investigating arm of the Armed Services Committee. The SPIS had a sterling reputation and was known for its "pitiless but not petty, vigorous but not virulent" inquiries, as one contemporary observer put it.[2] It had first achieved renown as the Truman committee, monitoring defense contracts during World War II. A decade later, during the Eisenhower administration, Senate majority leader Lyndon Johnson (D-TX) used the SPIS to investigate the alleged "missile gap" of the late 1950s. The committee also produced a long series of respected reports about the material needs of the armed forces. Its increased influence and activities during the early decades of the Cold War paralleled broader congressional trends. As historian Joseph Fry has noted, "After the Legislative Reorganization Act of 1946 empowered subcommittee chairs to hire staff, the number of Senate foreign policy-related subcommittees jumped from seven in 1946 to thirty-one in 1966." By the 1960s, the SPIS and other subcommittees rivaled the venerable Committee on Foreign Relations in terms of influence.[3]

Harry Truman's chairmanship of the SPIS had helped vault him into the White House, and Lyndon Johnson had undoubtedly hoped lightning would strike twice. But the chairman in 1963, John Stennis (D-MS), harbored no such ambitions. Stennis had not been seeking the post when Richard Russell designated him chairman in January 1961. Russell, one of Washington's most powerful politicians, viewed Stennis as his natural successor. Running the prestigious subcommittee was to be part of Stennis's maturation. "I think in determining the extent of the subcommittee's activities," Russell wrote Stennis upon his appointment, "you would be well-advised to remember the likelihood of your later becoming chairman of the full committee and to avoid any precedents that might plague you then. . . . The best advice I can offer at the moment is not to spread yourself too thin by undertaking too many subjects initially."[4]

A former judge, Stennis had a self-effacing, exceedingly polite manner that belied a shrewd intellect and at least occasional courage. He had been the first Democrat to demand the censure of Joe McCarthy (R-WI) in 1954. During his first two years as chair, he conducted many meat-and-potato investigations, none designed with headlines in mind. They concerned such issues as housing for military families, construction costs of missile bases, and the cost-effectiveness of the Minuteman and Polaris missiles. Stennis did become involved in one of the hottest issues of 1962, the so-called "muzzling" of the military by Robert McNamara's Pentagon, but this was only because the SPIS, which by then had six professional staff investigators, was the logical body to look into the matter.[5] The probe—the most sensitive one involving the armed forces since Russell's investigation a decade earlier into the firing of Gen. Douglas MacArthur—could easily have turned into another congressional witch hunt. But Stennis kept tight rein on it.[6] In the process, he earned the disdain of his colleague on the committee, Strom Thurmond (D-SC), a dynamic that would come into play in 1963.[7]

Stennis had taken nearly as hard a line as anyone in Congress on the issue of Soviet aid to Cuba. He had advocated a blockade of the island well before the Soviets' nuclear-tipped missiles were discovered, and their removal did nothing to alter his position.[8] As the crisis intensified, Stennis contacted his subcommittee colleagues about incorporating Cuba into an ongoing study of the adequacy of US forces, given their global commitments.[9] Most, including the ranking member, Leverett Saltonstall (R-MA), quickly agreed.[10]

But a wholly separate probe involving Cuba was not on the SPIS agenda when the new Congress began; for one thing, ten other investigations were already under way.[11] Even as Stennis became persuaded, in mid-January, that the SPIS was the best venue for a separate inquiry into the missile crisis, he was decidedly against incorporating a review of the intelligence community's performance, probably on the grounds that anything having to do with the CIA was Russell's turf.[12] His primary concern remained the adequacy of US military preparedness in a fast-changing situation so close to US shores, in keeping with his desire to help shape a "firm policy which will finally rid the Americans of this cancerous growth."[13]

This "order of battle" preoccupation, and the impact of the crisis upon the disposition of US forces worldwide, would remain an SPIS concern throughout. But the focus quickly began to shift because of increasing allegations that the Soviets were reneging on their pledge to remove all the offensive weapons.[14] The adequacy of US intelligence collection, current even more so than past, was soon perceived as the more urgent question. Although the informal Senate Armed Services Committee's subcommittee on the CIA was perhaps a more logical place for such an inquiry, it had no fulltime investigative staff, so the task, with Russell's blessing, fell to Stennis's panel.[15]

On January 25 Stennis attended a closed Foreign Relations hearing that included a briefing by Rusk and McCone on the latest developments in the alleged renewal of Soviet force in Cuba.[16] Later that day, after an SPIS executive session, he formally announced that the subcommittee would make the Cuba investigation its top priority, putting aside for the time being a planned inquiry into the consequences of a nuclear test ban treaty.[17] Stennis said the probe would cover "Cuba's current military strength, the nature of the weapons located in Cuba, and the current and future threat which the Cuban situation poses to the Western Hemisphere from a military standpoint." He expected it to begin in about two weeks and to include testimony from the highest officials at the State Department, the CIA, and the Pentagon.[18] In view of the facts that the SPIS had a reputation for careful, fair, and nonpartisan investigations and that Stennis had Russell's firm backing, the administration could do nothing to stop the inquiry. It promised to cooperate fully.[19]

Kennedy met privately with Russell on February 2, just as the Senate appeared to be getting apoplectic again about Cuba, and the two men spent the better part of an hour discussing the island. The president went over Kenneth Keating's latest public statements in great detail. He would have done so because, in the words of the prominent news reporter Elie Abel, a renewed "hullabaloo has been a-building since Senator Keating, the New York Republican, charged that a military build-up was under way in Cuba, and that it was ten times bigger than last July."[20] Kennedy tried to persuade Russell that the New York senator had not been factual. The Pentagon "had the correct intelligence" on Soviet forces, Kennedy maintained. Although Russell did not disagree, he observed that any media reference to Keating was always followed by the statement "who reported the offensive missiles in Cuba last year before it was known to United States intelligence." Thus, he reminded Kennedy, anything Keating alleged about Cuba "assumed unusual importance."[21] (Keating and Russell would not have known it, but Secretary of State Dean Rusk told Soviet ambassador Anatoly Dobrynin much the same thing a few days later: "It was not so easy for the President to reassure the country over Cuba. The American people remember what Senator Keating had said last

August and what the President had said and they remember . . . [who] turned out to be correct. This situation makes it very difficult for the President.")[22]

Russell told the president he thought the Stennis inquiry would "probably clear the atmosphere," and the president, according to Russell, "expressed the idea that these hearings would be helpful."[23] Nonetheless, anxiety was high in the White House over the only investigation to be genuinely mounted.[24] Not coincidentally, Stennis instantly became a member of the elite group of congressional leaders who were briefed whenever the White House wanted to inform Congress about sensitive Cuban developments.[25]

The White House's growing apprehension about Congress's inquisitiveness did not go unnoticed. The administration "is plainly jittery over the congressional reaction," the conservative commentator Fulton Lewis observed.[26] Hal Hendrix, an influential *Miami News* columnist on Latin American affairs, wrote, "The New Frontier is faced with a double-header probe it maneuvered feverishly to avoid shortly before Congress reconvened last month."[27] The administration's concern was well founded. Two of the president's harshest critics on Cuba—Barry Goldwater (R-AZ) and Strom Thurmond—sat on the SPIS. Goldwater's relish at goading administration defenders on the floor of the Senate that "criticism of the administration's handling of the Cuban problem . . . is completely bipartisan" did not bode well for serene hearings. And Stennis himself, as noted, often took a hard line publicly about the Soviet presence in Cuba.[28] The probe also prolonged the danger that McCone might be tempted to enhance his reputation at the administration's expense.[29]

McCone was in an extremely delicate position, one that had been exacerbated by a tactical decision made by several GOP politicians. They had seized on the idea of making McCone, easily the most prominent Republican in the administration apart from Secretary of the Treasury C. Douglas Dillon, the only "hero" of the affair. To this end, they drew a sharp contrast between McCone and the other top administration officials, all of whom had publicly discounted the likelihood of Soviet missiles in Cuba.[30] This put McCone "on the hottest of hot seats," as the syndicated columnist Marquis Childs noted.[31]

In addition, there was a growing schism in the administration over the nature of the Cuban threat. Although McCone was not necessarily convinced that the Soviets were violating the withdrawal pact, he was far more concerned than any other senior official in the administration about the continued Soviet military presence and the urgency of removing it. The congressional hearings heightened the possibility that these differences would not simply be aired internally. In accordance with the administration's general aim of getting Cuba off the front pages, the president said publicly in February that the

Soviet presence represented "unfinished business" but was not a threat to the hemisphere. Should McCone's views become public, Cuba would certainly stay in the headlines.[32]

Structuring the Inquiry

The SPIS probe began in earnest early in February. By then, the intelligence aspect had become almost as important as any other question to be addressed. As described in a memo by James Kendall, the SPIS general counsel who would oversee the inquiry on a day-to-day basis, the study was to incorporate "an exploration of the intelligence mechanism by which the U.S. government handles the acquisition, analysis, and distribution of intelligence at several levels of operation," while avoiding "the highly sensitive area of the covert operations of the CIA." It would develop a detailed history of the Soviet military build-up; examine essential information, or specific requests for information, that had been generated by the various military services; review the methods that had been used to gather and assess intelligence, along with the roles played by the agencies and services involved; and explore any changes made in intelligence evaluations or assessments from start to finish of the episode, including instances in which information that had initially been discounted was later verified.

Kendall planned to work from the bottom up, calling first the chiefs of army, navy, and air force intelligence, followed by Joseph Carroll, head of the relatively new Defense Intelligence Agency, and then McCone.[33] Once all these sources had been heard from, he intended to gather information from unofficial sources—activists within the Cuban exile community and journalists who had followed the issue closely. The idea was to take testimony from exile leaders such as Manuel Artime, a brigade commander at the Bay of Pigs, and reporters such as Hal Hendrix, who was on the verge of winning a Pulitzer Prize for his 1962 coverage of the military build-up.[34] Ultimately, though, the subcommittee did not take any testimony from unofficial sources. Instead, two staff members spent fourteen days in March interviewing some seventy people in Miami, including several prominent Cuban expatriates, the DOD and CIA personnel who had been in charge of debriefing refugees at the CIA-run processing center at Opa Locka; and Cuban nationals who had pointed to the existence of the Soviet missiles well before US intelligence had confirmed them.

The subcommittee investigators soon found themselves digesting the same hard lesson the intelligence community had learned the previous fall: the information obtained from refugees was easy to believe but hard to confirm. And they eventually realized that the kind of detailed information they were gathering went far beyond the kind of limited inquiry that Stennis had in mind.[35]

From the start, Stennis appeared to be under no illusion that the full story of the crisis had already been told. On February 3, during a rare appearance on TV and radio—he was a guest on a program hosted by Senator Keating—he said that, although he was not accusing anyone of "wrong-doing in keeping information away," he did "not think the people of the United States have been told all the facts." He reiterated this sentiment a few days later on the Senate floor, emphasizing, "We want all of the facts and the entire truth to be known."[36]

After testimony by the military intelligence leaders—the details of which remain obscure but seem to have provided no particular insights into the photo gap—it was McCone's turn.[37] His initial testimony was spread over two days, February 6 and 7. His first appearance, which lasted two and a half hours, was held in unusual secrecy, even for the SPIS: the subcommittee members were not informed of the location until just before the proceedings started at noon.[38] McCone's unclassified, prepared opening statement was fully consonant with the administration's public assurances about the Soviet withdrawal.[39] The ensuing hours with the DCI were devoted largely to this topic and whether Moscow was continuing to deceive the United States. However, some senators asked about the lead-up to the missile crisis. Margaret Chase Smith (R-ME), who had voted against McCone's confirmation as DCI a year earlier, approached him with her customary bluntness, posing a question that—if he had answered it honestly—would have revealed aspects of the photo gap:

> Smith: Mr. McCone, can you explain how Senator Keating was so right and CIA so wrong up to October 15 on the Cuban Situation?
>
> McCone: Well, I can't explain it, no, except that Senator Keating obviously had information, the same information, that we had. . . . The Intelligence Community were obliged to evaluate the information with great care until they could support it with what they term hard intelligence and this was not done for reasons which I have explained, until October 14. I would hasten to say, Senator Smith, that I myself had the same concern that Senator Keating did and expressed it long before he did.

Later Stuart Symington (D-MO) gave McCone a chance to restate his self-serving account:

Symington: I think it is important that the record show that, before anybody, you were suspicious of this and said so in no uncertain terms, and did it again and again and again in August. But the powers-that-be did not agree with your position. You didn't know but you felt sure . . . that they [the Soviets] would not go to this expense of SAM sites . . . unless they were doing it to protect offensive weapons, isn't that correct?

McCone: That is right.

McCone's prescience before the discovery of missiles gave him great credibility with the SPIS members. He did not hesitate to make use of his enhanced stature, telling the subcommittee, "I would be less than frank with you if I did not tell you that I have taken a more alarmed view of the developments in Cuba than others in official positions in Washington ever since the buildup started the first of August." Such a remark could only raise questions about the competence and perhaps the honesty of other key administration figures, including McNamara and the president himself. Yet it passed without challenge or criticism.[40]

As his testimony proceeded, the White House grew increasingly wary. Not only was McCone too candid and self-congratulatory with respect to his own foresight the previous fall, but when pressed about the "subversive threat" in the hemisphere, he gave answers more in line with the views of the administration's conservative critics than those of McNamara and Rusk.[41] In what represented a serious leak of classified information, the syndicated columnists Robert Allen and Paul Scott reported that the gravity with which the DCI viewed the threat posed by Cuba "startled" the senators. The columnist correctly wrote that McCone had "revealed that 1,500 saboteurs and Communist guerrillas were training in Cuba during the past 12 months and are now at work in Latin countries."[42]

Getting the Communists out of Cuba was "imperative," McCone told the subcommittee. A surviving partial transcript shows him driving home the point by describing a recent meeting in Latin America.[43]

McCone: I spent last Monday and Tuesday in Panama with the chiefs of our stations from Mexico south to the Argentine for the purpose of finding out directly from them just what they knew about the Soviet-Castro penetration of their respective countries. Every one of them has a communist apparatus of greater or lesser extent, depending upon the country, and the leadership.
. . . There is no question about the fact that this is the bridgehead of communism into all of Latin America.

Symington: If we don't get them out of Cuba, the chances are excellent that we will lose Central and South America.

McCone: It will erode away rapidly, in my opinion.[44]

McNamara's high-profile televised presentation on Cuba had come on the afternoon of McCone's first day of SPIS testimony. Almost all of the committee members were struck by the differences in the pictures painted by the two men.[45] "I listened with a good deal of cynicism, if that is the right word, to Mr. McNamara, after listening to you," Saltonstall told McCone when the hearings resumed the next day.[46] James Kendall pointed out that "there were some significant divergences, as between your statement and what Mr. McNamara said." Stennis asked, "How could there be such differences in your testimony? Do you have access to the same facts?" Yes, McCone replied, "we have access to the same facts. It is a matter of judgment." Very likely McCone's "tremendously impressive" testimony, as Stennis characterized it, explains why Stennis later told reporters that he did not agree "at all" with McNamara that the military threat from Cuba had been "lessening" in recent months.

In fact, the two presentations led to such different perceptions that McCone prepared a side-by-side comparison for the president, presumably to prove that he wasn't straying from the facts—that it was simply a matter of interpretation. In a cover note, he explained that, while "the basic figures" in the McNamara press conference did "not differ in any major way from those agreed on by the Intelligence Community," the "general impression" left by McNamara and his associates "differed from that which I have expressed to congressional committees in executive session."[47] As one participant observed while taking notes of the daily staff meeting at CIA on February 7, the day after McNamara's press conference, McCone was "something between concerned and angry" because McNamara's analyses of the Soviet presence did not agree with his own.[48]

Struggling to Maintain Unity

With good reason, national security adviser McGeorge Bundy feared that the "first big, internal, high-level personality clash" within the administration was about to occur.[49] And in fact McCone did order an in-house study of intelligence sources and methods that may have been compromised by top administration officials in their attempts to dampen speculation about hidden Soviet missiles—attempts that included but were not limited to what Deputy Director of Central Intelligence Marshall Carter derided as "Mr. McNamara's floor show." McNamara's disclosures, Carter complained, "unquestionably

Senior SPIS members, 1961. *From left,* Stuart Symington (D-MO), John Stennis (D-MS), Leverett Saltonstall (R-MA), and Margaret Chase Smith (R-ME). *Courtesy Margaret Chase Smith Library.*

Director of Central Intelligence John McCone greets Senator Margaret Chase Smith (R-ME) prior to an Armed Services Committee hearing. Between them is Senator Leverett Saltonstall (R-MA). *Courtesy Margaret Chase Smith Library.*

alerted the Soviets to our intelligence capabilities in areas which they might otherwise not have been aware of." McCone, he went on, had not approved the kind of briefing that McNamara gave. McCone had agreed that DIA's General Carroll could give a background briefing to "certain key members of the press," but he had not cleared the "McNamara strip tease" in any way, "either as to content or purpose."[50]

On Capitol Hill McNamara's televised presentation received mixed reviews. Florida Republican William Cramer told House colleagues that it "proved . . . the continuing military buildup in Cuba," but a fellow Republican, Thomas Kuchel of California, found McNamara "quite convincing" in describing Soviet withdrawals.[51]

Since early January, the key question, pursued especially avidly by conservatives, had been, Were the Soviets cheating? In other words, had all the missiles been withdrawn? McNamara's televised briefing decisively changed the parameters and terms of the debate.[52] The emphasis shifted to intelligence gathering and other activities by the Communist bloc in the hemisphere. On February 16 Stennis wrote to McCone that the SPIS was "deeply interested in obtaining such information as is available with respect to subversive, revolutionary and agitational activities from Cuba directed at other Latin American countries," adding, "We need now to obtain detailed information on a country-by country basis."[53]

McNamara's news conference had obviously left open the issue of differing estimates of Cuba's subversive potential. He and others in the administration were soon chafing over McCone's statements to the SPIS on this aspect of the situation.[54] Officials in the State Department monitored McCone's appearances before Congress closely, as if he were an adversary. As soon as a transcript of his testimony was ready, copies were delivered to the State Department and to the White House to be read by an unhappy president.[55]

During a telephone call between INR director Roger Hilsman and Undersecretary of State George Ball in mid-February, both men groused about McCone's performance on Capitol Hill, particularly his February 5 appearance before the House Appropriations Committee. McCone was "going all over town saying that he told everybody again and again and again" about the possibility of offensive missiles in Cuba the previous fall, Hilsman complained, but "he never once mentioned it to us." Hilsman was also unhappy that a Republican congresswoman, Francis Bolton (Ohio), had expressed great satisfaction with McCone's testimony before a House subcommittee. "She said, 'I was just so pleased because several times [McCone] volunteered his viewpoint on developments in Cuba, agreeing with those of us on the Republican side who are dissenting, and it was so refreshing.'"[56]

On February 13 McNamara, DIA director Carroll, and JCS chairman Maxwell Taylor met to discuss the discrepancies between McNamara's testimony and McCone's.[57] At the same time, White House counsel Theodore Sorensen prepared a memorandum for the attorney general on McCone's recent statements, highlighting the divergences from the administration's line and noting that McCone had "a different view" on the subjects the administration preferred to avoid altogether. On February 14 Hank Knoche, one of McCone's special assistants at the CIA, received a call from Bromley Smith, on the NSC staff at the White House, indicating that "the president has directed that it be made a standard procedure from now on that all proposed testimonies by executive branch officials before Congress concerning Cuba be submitted to the White House in advance for clearance" and that "it will also be standard procedure to send a copy of the transcript of an appearance to the White House after the appearance has been made." Knoche should expect a White House memo to that effect soon, Smith said. This change from ad hoc policy to standard procedure would not be implemented easily or fully, facing resistance from some on Capitol Hill and at the CIA.[58]

Just as the administration was struggling to maintain the semblance of unity, its story about the photo gap showed signs of unraveling. Although McNamara's February 6 briefing had helped quell claims about new Soviet missiles, it had inadvertently revived interest in the lack of photo coverage between September 5 and October 15, which had until then been an obscure, side issue. In fact, the phrases "intelligence gap" and "picture gap" now became buzzwords, shorthand that was readily understood. McNamara's explanation—that lack of time precluded showing all the photos—did not satisfy even some friends of the administration.[59]

It was just at this time that McGeorge Bundy committed to paper the supposed "facts" relating to the photo gap for the president's benefit. He wrote JFK on February 14 a memo titled "Overflights of Cuba in September and October." While the national security adviser and the president must have had a frank talk about the topic at some point, Bundy's memo was anything but honest. It made no mention of the key September 10 meeting, nor did it acknowledge that intelligence leaders, especially acting DCI Pat Carter, had made the case for surveillance over western Cuba. Instead, Bundy exploited the fact that Carter had not formally protested the decision to attenuate the U-2 flights: "recommendations presented to the Special Group on behalf of the intelligence community were approved, with modifications in one or two cases [and] were accepted by the intelligence community without appeal to the president. Every request which was presented to you was approved." Since it is highly unlikely that Bundy would have deceived the president about interactions between his foreign policy leaders and the intelligence community heads, it seems probable that the president and national security adviser had agreed that Bundy's memo should lay out the stance the president wished the administration to take as it faced anticipated criticisms.[60]

The Bundy memo may have also been a response toward one of those who took note of the photo gap—Walter Lippmann, one of columnists to whom the White House had selectively leaked the previous fall. Back then, Lippmann had written that the CIA's photo surveillance of Cuba was "elaborate." But now—two days before Bundy wrote the president about photo reconnaissance—Lippmann struck a different note, recognizing that the reasons proffered for the delay did not make sense. The administration "may well have . . . to make a full explanation of what went wrong in September and early October," he wrote in a February 12 column. "I am struck by the fact that there was a blank space from September 5 to October 14." That was the time frame, he reminded readers, "when the administration was telling the country that there were no offensive weapons in Cuba." Therefore, "This is the source of infection which will have to be removed if full confidence is to be restored."[61]

Bundy commiserated later that day by telephone with Undersecretary of State George Ball, whose secretary took revealing (if inelegantly worded) notes: "They discuss the difficulties with admitting the state of their intelligence over the Cuba missile crisis, given that they do not want McCone. This in view of an article by Lippmann."[62] The column prompted the administration to elaborate on its cover story, resulting in an explanation that was more specific but no less disingenuous. Now officials began to stress that they had *increased* the number of U-2 flights, which of course was true only in a narrow, technical sense. Meanwhile, adverse weather continued to be a convenient explanation for any delays in surveillance results from late August through mid-October 1962.[63]

Lippmann's column was soon followed by an editorial in the *New York Times* arguing for closer congressional oversight of the intelligence community because, among other reasons, "there are [still] glaring gaps—for which no responsibility has been publicly assessed—in the intelligence picture presented to the nation for last September and early October."[64] Hanson Baldwin, the first to have raised knowledgeable questions about the issue the previous fall, took it up again. Meanwhile, persistent House Republicans like William

Minshall still dogged the administration at every opportunity, though with little effect. Even Democrats inclined to be loyal to the administration found their interest piqued, though they, too, were far from understanding what had gone on. Lippman "raised an eyebrow over the failure of the government to show pictures during the August–September period, when it was claimed that the pictures revealed nothing," George Mahon told his Defense subcommittee staff. He asked them to "have a look at the photographs [from the San Cristóbal area] prior to about October 14, which revealed nothing significant." That Mahon thought such photos existed illustrates the extent of congressional confusion.[65]

Thus, by the latter half of February, the main issue that had generated the Stennis probe—questions about the completeness of the Soviet withdrawal—had crested, but the controversy over the photo gap had reasserted itself.[66] And although "most people," as the *New Yorker* observed, were inclined to "accept as entirely truthful the official chronology," enough questions had been reopened to put the administration in an uncomfortable position. And there were new questions, too: on March 4 *Newsweek* published an article claiming that the photo gap was not caused by "bad weather" but by a bureaucratic deadlock between the CIA and the air force over who would conduct the U-2 surveillance. (Although this was not the reason for the photo gap, tensions between the two bodies had run high.)[67]

Prompted, no doubt, by this new allegation, CIA legislative counsel John Warner met with Senator Russell on February 28 to see how he wanted to handle the matter. Warner offered to have McCone testify before the full Armed Services Committee to settle questions about the "so-called picture gap" once and for all. Russell demurred. He was extremely protective of the CIA in general and now believed that too much had been said publicly about U-2 surveillance capabilities—particularly during McNamara's televised briefing. Russell told Warner that questions about the adequacy of U-2 operations would be best handled within the ongoing SPIS inquiry. He had already talked to Stennis to that effect.[68]

Later that day Representative Paul Rogers, as noted in the previous chapter, asserted that the photo gap could not have been caused by meteorological conditions. "Just what is the reason?" he asked. Warner therefore approached Stennis and indicated McCone's willingness to appear again before the SPIS. Stennis appreciated the apparent willingness of the CIA to set the matter to rest but did not feel any sense of urgency; he told Warner that he would just as soon have the heads of the other intelligence agencies testify again before a return visit from McCone.[69]

Whatever the order of the testimony, there was never any doubt that the investigation would be taken care of by the SPIS. Senator Russell had made it clear that he wanted all aspects of the Cuban matter handled by the panel.[70] Whether or not the SPIS would arrive at the truth about the photo gap, it was unlikely to blame the CIA; as Warner noted, Stennis "specifically wanted the Director to know that he was not at all in sympathy with reports appearing in the press concerning possible failure by the CIA." Other parties appeared no more likely to come up with a full account. After a brief flurry of activity, the press seemed completely stymied. The Defense Department told reporters that it had no business discussing CIA activities. And the CIA itself remained silent.[71]

Tensions within the Kennedy Administration

Fashioning a Unified Story

With the most sustained and important probe less than halfway through, the administration was jittery.[1] Consequently, it focused on the need to speak in unison about aspects of the Cuban problem, especially the photo gap. In the wake of Lippmann's article, McCone's propensity to speak his mind constituted a great risk. The State Department, the Pentagon, and even the attorney general had complained to McGeorge Bundy about this tendency.[2] At Bundy's apparent instruction, an NSC aide began keeping a chart across February and March of the administration witnesses scheduled to appear before Congress whenever there was the slightest chance the subject would involve Cuba.[3]

On February 18, almost two weeks after the DCI's initial SPIS testimony, Bundy convened a two-hour session after working hours so that the key principals—Rusk, McNamara, Taylor, and McCone—could synchronize their stories.[4] Or, in the words of a State Department notetaker who summarized a telephone conversation between Bundy and George Ball, it was to be "the big meeting they are going to have on Cuban events to forestall the inquiries." At the "big meeting," those present agreed that McCone would take "first responsibility" for any further questions about intelligence collection and evaluation in September and October 1962. They also agreed that "all flights requested of the president were authorized by him" and that "all priorities set by the U.S. Intelligence Board were accepted."[5] To the degree that any operational mistakes, or "discernible weaknesses," would be admitted, the agreed-upon language was intentionally vague. These weaknesses included "a lack of all-out energy in framing and presenting intelligence requirements; that delays in executing approved reconnaissance missions were not reported upward, or monitored downward; and that dissenting recommendations were not carried to the president." In essence, Congress was to judge the CIA's intelligence gathering by the results only—that is, that a denied area was "penetrated accurately and in time."[6]

A week later, however, after receiving comments from McNamara and McCone on his draft memorandum of the session, Bundy had second thoughts. He decided it would be better not to attempt a "resume of agreed guidelines, subject at [*sic*] it might be to misunderstanding."[7] Instead, he gave Rusk, McNamara, and McCone a compendium of the president's public statements, together with the USIB postmortem, which, as detailed in chapter 3, represented a version of events acceptable to all involved.

Prodded in large part by these efforts to develop a coordinated answer, McCone asked Lyman Kirkpatrick, the CIA's executive director, to revisit the photo gap issue and develop a background paper describing what had happened in clear, unambiguous terms to serve as "background information for . . . guidance in testifying before committees of Congress." On February 27, Kirkpatrick produced a candid eleven-page account that put the decisions, for better or worse, in context and dispensed with the USIB finding that the photo gap did not matter. As a courtesy, McCone sent the account to the State and Defense Departments.[8] Not surprisingly, it raised hackles at State, which, of course, bore much of the responsibility for degrading U-2 coverage; it did not consider the analysis a fair or wise rendering. "I wonder whether it would not be practicable and desirable," Undersecretary of State U. Alexis Johnson wrote to McCone on March 6, "for everyone to adopt the same general principle that the President set forth with regard to the [ExComm] discussions . . . that is, there would not be any discussion of the various positions taken by the various individuals or institutions concerned. . . . If we are to maintain within the Government that degree of frankness and freedom to state views out of which sound decisions can be reached, particularly on sensitive intelligence matters, it seems to me that we should seek to preserve the anonymity of our advice and deliberations." Johnson then offered specific advice on how the analysis might be edited to present a "full factual account," but one stripped of "all reference to personalities and institutions as well as debatable subjective judgments."[9] His suggestions so obfuscated the facts that the "explanation" would surely defy outside comprehension. He advocated perpetuating the fictions that the administration had increased rather than attenuated U-2 surveillance and that the photo gap was attributable entirely to poor weather.[10]

McCone responded promptly, telling Johnson it was too late to withdraw Kirkpatrick's memo, which had already been distributed to USIB members preparing to testify on Capitol Hill. However, McCone assured Johnson that no USIB member who had testified to date had "spoken of the position of any individual or Department in connection with the planning or execution of [U-2] flights."[11] And he would caution the USIB members who were yet to testify not to do so.[12] Taken together, McCone's actions strongly suggest that his real impulse behind requesting the Kirkpatrick memo was not to get the facts straight or even, as Johnson feared, to point the finger at the State Department, but to remind everyone what the agreed-on "facts" were so that no one testifying before the SPIS would stumble over them.[13]

Still, Bundy worried that McCone might say something deeply damaging to the president. In late February McCone bluntly informed Bundy that there was a "serious gap" in the administration's Cuba policies, namely, "how we were going to deal with the Soviet presence in Cuba, how we are going to . . . remove the Castro government or control it," and that he had been "repeatedly asked by congressional committees" how these problems would be resolved. The national security adviser had long since concluded that the DCI was selling himself on Capitol Hill as the lone figure in the Kennedy administration who had had the courage and insight to insist in August and September of 1962 that the Soviets were placing strategic missiles into Cuba. While Bundy knew there was some truth to that claim, "The main thing [he told Undersecretary of State George Ball] is that no 'powers that be' got in his [i.e., McCone's] way." Nothing had interfered with McCone's advocacy and influence in the administration during those months so much as "his little honeymoon." So, with corresponding directness, Bundy now told McCone that "policy matters" were "beyond the scope" of the DCI's competence. McCone accepted the admonition, but, as he recorded in a memo on the conversation, "I again reminded him that, irrespective of who says what, we simply did not have a policy on repressive action."[14]

Unable to guarantee uniform testimony on Capitol Hill, Bundy did the next best thing. He arranged for all the committees holding Cuba-related hearings to give the White House transcripts of testimony prior to the transcripts' possible public release. McCone did not object, but he did say he needed to "personally discuss" the matter with Stennis. So that McCone could speak as candidly as possible when testifying before the SPIS, he and Stennis had agreed that only two transcripts of his remarks would be made, that neither would circulate, and that both would be kept at the CIA, subject to SPIS review.[15] This was standard SPIS procedure whenever a CIA official testified before the committee.[16] But McCone could hardly object to Bundy's request. He merely said that if the White House was to receive a copy of any transcript, "it should be for [Bundy's] personal use only."

Finally, the White House took another stab at getting a friendly columnist to write a prophylactic piece. This time the willing administration voice was Joseph Kraft, a young columnist favored by Robert Kennedy. His column appeared in the *Washington Star* on March 1. In it he scored the administration for its laxity and "unusual clumsiness" in handling the domestic politics of the Cuba problem. A prime example of this supposed ham-handedness, he wrote, was McNamara's February briefing, which gave rise to the "theory of the 'photo gap.'" This theory was unsupported, Kraft argued: there had been no operational deficit. Indeed, he wrote, the administration had *increased* U-2 coverage, and the main reason the SSMs were not found earlier was that many scheduled flights were "cancelled because of bad weather."[17]

The SPIS Perspective

The widening fissures within the administration were largely unknown to the SPIS members, though the panel was, of course, acutely aware of McCone's divergent view about the threat posed by Cuba. The small staff was all but overwhelmed by its task. James Kendall was a tireless worker who did the job of two men, but he spent so much time and energy organizing hearings for executive sessions that he was not really functioning as a chief investigator. Nor did he have the background to do so, especially when the group under investigation was the cloaked intelligence community itself.

There were some signs of the administration's nervousness in addition to Bundy's desire to review transcripts. In early February the SPIS had received verbal briefings about the Cuban build-up from the service intelligence agencies.[18] But now that it wanted to take formal testimony from those services, the Pentagon's civilian leadership asked to have Defense Department observers sit in, ostensibly for the "purpose of insuring accuracy."[19] Stennis turned this request down flat, and the administration decided not to appeal his decision. As Pentagon aide Adam Yarmolinsky explained to Bundy, "We think we can live with [Stennis's decision] so long as we get the transcripts directly or under the table."[20] Not everyone at the Pentagon was as sanguine, however. In a routine report to the White House congressional liaison Larry O'Brien, David McGiffert, the legislative liaison at the Pentagon, described the SPIS inquiry as "if not unfriendly, [then] uncooperative, particularly when compared with past relationships." He explained, "No observers from the [Pentagon] are permitted to attend and the subcommittee is clearly trying to so mold its procedure as to maximize the opportunity to bring out any differences of opinion within the intelligence community."[21]

Stennis was not a naïve man, but he was inclined to believe administration officials were acting honorably.[22] On February 27, as the hearings resumed, he stressed publicly that the inquiry was not being undertaken "for the mere purpose of revealing or spotlighting any past errors or deficiencies." The subcommittee, he said, was "concerned largely with the present and the future," although it would insist on "full disclosure" of all available information.[23]

There are limits to what is known about the SPIS's success in obtaining such "disclosure." The Stennis papers do not contain the full transcripts of the hearings or any version of the subcommittee's report other than the one that would be publicly released. Judging from the prepared statements and testimony fragments that are available, one thing is clear: the SPIS members obtained no information unless they specifically asked for it or figured it out for themselves.

The February 27 hearing began with a 2:00 P.M. appearance by Maj. Gen. Robert Breitweiser, the air force assistant chief of staff for intelligence; he was followed the next day by R. Adm. V. L. Lowrance, the director of naval intelligence. Lowrance's testimony concerned the role played by the Office of Naval Intelligence, and since that office had played no role in uncovering the missiles per se, he did not address the photo gap.[24] Breitweiser did address the gap at some length, but only in response to a false allegation that was easily dispelled: *Newsweek*'s charge that the lag in discovering the missiles had been caused by a deadlock between the CIA and the air force over responsibility for the U-2 surveillance. As Stennis told reporters, Breitweiser assured the senators that shifting responsibility to the air force had been "the natural thing to do" and that there had been the "fullest and most complete cooperation" between the two entities.[25] The reporters must have then pressed for an explanation: if a rift between the air force and the CIA wasn't the cause, what was? Stennis said, "I don't think there was a gap when no photos were taken," adding carefully that he did not think there was a "complete" period during which no photos were taken. Surveillance went on as it should have during the transfer, he told them.[26] Clearly, the SPIS was no closer to an answer than it had been at the start of its inquiry.

By now, the committee's procedure was set. Kendall questioned witnesses first, cross-examining them if necessary. He was prepared in advance to cover all the major points a particular witness was supposed to testify about. Once he completed his main questioning, individual senators examined the witnesses, who could bring with them only people actually needed to help them present their testimony. Once the military chiefs began appearing, however, a major obstacle cropped up.

As Kendall wrote to David McGiffert, McNamara's assistant for legislative affairs, on March 2, SPIS members were concerned because the prepared statements of the military witnesses so far—Breitweiser and Lowrance—were not being received in time for close study and consideration, hindering Kendall's ability to conduct a thorough investigation. The statements had apparently been delayed for a "policy review." Kendall advised McGiffert that the SPIS would insist on having prepared statements at least twenty-four hours in advance of testimony. He also wanted precise information on the policy review process, as "we also have information which indicates that these statements are forwarded also to the Department of State and possibly to the White House for review and clearance."[27] If true, Kendall hinted, that would be a serious problem.

On March 6 McGiffert responded that every effort would be made to get prepared statements cleared twenty-four hours in advance of testimony. He also informed Kendall of the DOD's clearance procedures. Statements were referred to "other agencies of the government where there is an appropriate interest," he said, including, "for information," the White House."[28] He did not tell Kendall that *all* written communication between the subcommittee and the Pentagon went through the White House before the Defense Department would respond.[29]

"He's a Real Bastard, That John McCone"

As the administration was wrangling with the subcommittee over these matters, the tensions within the executive branch threatened to explode into the public clash Bundy so feared. The immediate cause was the March 1 release of McCone's February 19 testimony before the House Foreign Affairs Subcommittee on Inter-American Affairs: his estimate of Cuba's subversive potential was now out in the open. The media was quick to pick up the story, with the *New York Times*, for example, running it on page one, column one.[30] McCone was now not just of concern to Bundy, State, and Defense, but was a target of the president's ire as well.[31] The DCI's testimony was fodder for Kennedy's critics, since it came from within the administration and, in particular, from the one official known to have been prescient about the Soviet missile emplacements. If McCone had been right last fall, the argument went, surely his views now should carry more weight than Rusk's or McNamara's.[32]

McCone's standing as a conservative Republican and a Communist hard-liner had been of great utility to the administration at one time—when Kennedy had to replace Allen Dulles after the Bay of Pigs. Then McCone served to protect the president's right flank. But now these same attributes only fueled the Kennedys' worries about McCone's loyalties, particularly after a March 4 column by Marquis Childs in the *Washington Post*. It had an obvious pro-McCone, pro-CIA tilt, depicting the agency as having continually pushed for more surveillance. The piece did not challenge the administration's obfuscation of the photo gap, nor was it the first flattering article about McCone's prescience. Still, it made the president furious, if only because it meant someone was leaking an account that made McCone and the CIA look good at everyone else's expense.[33]

The previous December's story in the *Saturday Evening Post*—the piece carefully orchestrated by the Kennedys—had acknowledged that McCone was "the only major dissenter," the only one who had believed that the Russians intended to put offensive missiles in Cuba.[34] But Childs made a much larger issue of "who was right—and right first." McCone "began saying to top people in government as early as last August, before Senator Kenneth Keating's public missile statements, that he believed the Soviets were about to install offensive capability," Childs wrote, adding that if the "honeymoon cables" were ever released, they "would seem to establish McCone as having been first to be right."[35]

Robert Kennedy, who read the column in the morning's *Washington Post*, was hardly surprised by it, given what he thought he knew about its source. Childs, the chief Washington correspondent for the *St. Louis Post-Dispatch*, was firmly plugged into the Georgetown cocktail-party circuit, as were many CIA officials. The Kennedy brothers discussed the matter during a tape-recorded telephone conversation the day the column appeared. The attorney general reported that Childs had told Ed Guthman (RFK's press secretary) that "they're really pouring that stuff out of CIA against the administration . . . on behalf of John McCone . . . they're trying to make themselves look good." "Yeah," the president responded. "He's a real *bastard*, that John McCone. . . . Of course, everybody [within the administration] is onto him now. . . . Everybody's saying he's a horse's ass." "Well, he was useful at one time," the attorney general replied. "Yeah, but boy, it's really evaporated," the president said, referring specifically to recent headlines about McCone's contradictions of Secretary McNamara.

The president's anger against the DCI had been building for weeks, as he had heard stories about McCone promoting his image on Capitol Hill. And now, on top of the Childs column, he had heard from national security adviser Bundy that McCone's relations with the President's Foreign Intelligence Advisory Board were so explosive (as recounted in chapter 3) that the DCI had seriously suggested to Bundy that the board should be abolished. Bundy also knew, and reported to the president, that the DCI had threatened to resign over the PFIAB's critical report about the intelligence establishment's handling of the photo gap and other issues. About McCone's abolishment suggestion, Bundy noted, "I rather carefully told him I did not think the president would agree to the recommendation (which is a very mild statement compared to what the president said to me. . . .) It is too bad to have to be careful in this kind of thing with a colleague." Of McCone's threat to resign (made to a PFIAB member), Bundy thought it "most extraordinary" news.[36]

The Childs column particularly rankled the president, though. Even before talking to RFK, Kennedy had immediately judged (correctly) that it was thoroughly based on McCone's leaks. It is easy to imagine his all the greater anger when he read a paragraph that concluded: "The unanswered question, as McCone has testified to before several committees, is why the Kremlin, knowing that high-level aerial reconnaissance was bound to pick up the missile sites, should have gone ahead. Was it because Khrushchev believed the United States would not respond, or not respond in time?" Other readers might have barely noticed that analysis, but probably not JFK. Earlier in his presidency he had been livid and enduringly unforgiving toward the famous poet Robert Frost for merely reporting, after meeting Khrushchev, that the Soviet leader thought the United States was "too liberal to fight." Now McCone was apparently implying, by way of Childs, that Khrushchev had seriously thought Kennedy might not have responded to Soviet missiles in Cuba!

In his recorded conversation with Robert Kennedy, the president also singled out for particular scorn another aspect of McCone's February testimony before the House Foreign Affairs Committee, which was widely cited in newspaper headlines in March. In 1962 alone, McCone had testified, 1,500 students from Latin America had received guerrilla training in Cuba. "That's the trouble. [McCone's] stupid himself," Kennedy told his brother. "They've got fifteen hundred *students*. How many of them are being trained as terrorists and guerrillas . . . is another question."[37]

The president then suggested that RFK inform McCone that the Kennedys were aware of the information pouring out of CIA at the administration's expense: "So maybe he would then decide it wasn't so *wise*." The attorney general, who was having McCone over for dinner in two days, promised to make that message clear. (McCone would subsequently tell him that he had been Marquis Childs's source, but only because Childs came to him already armed by several senators with information about the honeymoon cables.)

That afternoon the president requested McCone's presence at the White House at 4:30 so that he could underline the seriousness of the situation. Before the meeting Bundy tried to explain to Kennedy part of the reason for McCone's seeming indifference to the White House's desire for loyalty. "McCone is getting told by the Stuart Symingtons of the world that we're out to get him . . . and he believes all that kind of crap, unfortunately," Bundy said. He also drew up a list of talking points for the president. They amounted to reading McCone the riot act, saying, in essence, that if McCone persisted in his candor, the White House would place the entire burden for the operational deficit on the CIA:

1. President authorized every overflight requested.
2. Acting DCI accepted for CIA responsibility for arranging necessary overflights
3. . . .
4. There was no report of concern because of weather delay to either the DCI or the White House.
5. . . .
6. The President may want to emphasize that Mr. McCone should be extremely careful in criticism of Sec/State request for a rescheduling of September flights into four shorter ones. There was no reclama of this [September 10 decision]—and no report to anyone that it was leading to delay.[38]

Judging from McCone's memo on the conversation, however, the meeting was not nearly as contentious as it might have been. "The president stated he felt that an attempt was being made to drive a division within the administration, most particularly between CIA on the one hand and State and Defense on the other," McCone recounted. "He hoped we could avoid any statements on the Hill, publicly or to the press, which would exacerbate the situation." During the meeting McCone summarized Kirkpatrick's late-February analysis—namely, that the CIA "had operated under an inhibiting policy" and "had recommended only most limited overflights in September, as they felt that recommendations for a more aggressive program would undoubtedly have been refused to them."[39] He read the president excerpts from the honeymoon cables in which he had urged greater vigilance and went over the findings of the exculpatory USIB postmortem, which had concluded that photo coverage prior to mid-October would not have yielded the kind of evidence necessary for allied action anyway.

By reciting this chronology, McCone was, in effect, signaling a retreat from the position he had put before the president in January while discussing the forthcoming PFIAB postmortem; then he had emphasized that "timidity throughout the government" had foreclosed earlier detection of the offensive weapons in Cuba. It was only a partial retreat: McCone was unwilling to have the onus for September's "extreme caution" put on the CIA: "I did point out that it was necessary for everyone to recognize and to understand that extreme caution was used through September in considering U-2 operations over Cuba." The president remarked that there was "bound to be something of an internal problem, but felt that we should minimize it and should not get into an interdepartmental row." McCone readily agreed: "I assured him this would not happen." Apparently Kennedy felt he got his point across without having to use Bundy's talking points.[40]

Bundy himself would do a turnabout in short order and advise the president to handle McCone with kid gloves. The national security adviser had arrived at the conclusion (as he dictated into a tape recorder one evening) that "John McCone is not so much crooked as he is sensitive and not very brave until he makes up his mind to it."[41] After talking to RFK and McCone, he explained to JFK that it was "very important to deal gently" with McCone, who was actually "in a relatively cooperative mood at the moment." McCone was hearing from some on Capitol Hill that the administration "was out to get him." He "is just fantastically sensitive and he *believes* that there are wolves in every woods," Bundy observed. "And I'm not sure that the way to straighten *that* out isn't for you to say something nice about him at a press conference soon."[42]

On March 6 Kennedy did so. "I am satisfied with Mr. McCone, with the Intelligence Community and the Defense Department, and the job they did in those days particularly taken in totality," he said in response to a question about Cuba. He also made his most direct comments to date about the "photo gap."

> I think in hindsight, I suppose we could have always, perhaps, picked up these missile bases a few days earlier, but not very many days earlier, because the missiles didn't come in, at least in hindsight it now appears, until some time around the middle of September. The installations began at a later date. They were very fast, and I think the photography on the same areas, if we had known that missiles were going in, 10 days before might not have picked up anything. The week before might have picked up something. Even the pictures taken October 14th were only obvious to the most sophisticated expert. And it was not until the pictures taken really the 16th and 17th that you had pictures that would be generally acceptable. So this was a very clandestine and fast operation.[43]

In other words, he told the press, Republican Congress members were wrong in charging that there had been an intelligence gap between the CIA and the Defense Department in the surveillance operations of Cuba. "When you think that the job was done, the missiles were discovered, the missiles were removed, the bombers were discovered, the bombers were removed, I don't think that anybody should feel that anything but a good job was done."[44]

The administration's anxiety peaked during that first week or so of March. There was not a scintilla of doubt now that what McCone termed the administration's timidity would be a campaign issue in 1964 if the truth should come to light. Republicans, still seeking to whittle down the perception of a sweeping foreign policy triumph, were harping on the issue of ongoing aerial surveillance of Cuba and whether any offensive missiles were still on Cuban soil.[45] Now that the formerly villainous U-2 had been transformed, practically overnight, into a heroic tool, it was awkward for the administration ever to admit that the CIA, in Helms's words, had been "enjoined to stay well away from what we called the business [western] end of the island."[46] President Kennedy faced the uncomfortable prospect of explaining why his administration had degraded the only intelligence-gathering tool that was obviously indispensable until it was almost too late.[47]

Kennedy was right, of course, about how close the cover story was to unraveling. Two days after the SPIS released some of McCone's more pessimistic testimony, Senator Keating jumped into the fray again. Sensing the administration's internal fissure, he sought to align himself with the intelligence community and McCone. Previously, he had been as critical of the CIA as he had been of anyone else; his conversations with McCone about Cuba had been rather testy, and he had refused to disclose his sources to McCone in early February.[48] Suddenly he was "lavish in his praise of McCone," as one reporter put it.[49] If the White House was suffering a "crisis of credibility" over Cuba, Keating claimed, it was not because there had been an "intelligence gap." Rather, it was because a top administration official, the secretary of defense, was glossing over the facts. The proof of his argument, as he put it, lay in the decidedly different estimates given by McCone and McNamara about the threat Cuba posed. Keating topped off his new round of allegations by concluding that there were "disturbing indications that an attempt is being made to use the intelligence community for a scape-goat and whipping boy for the crisis of confidence in the government's handling of the Cuban situation."[50]

In the House Gerald Ford echoed some of these charges. "The whole situation has a very peculiar odor," he said.[51] But Ford wasn't as willing to absolve the CIA or Defense Department. "It all adds up to irresponsibility," he proclaimed. Ford, like others, was still thrashing around for an explanation that made sense. To him, the one that best fit the known facts was that "U.S.

intelligence knew as early as mid-September that the Soviets were setting up missiles in Cuba, but the administration did nothing about it until after October 14." Such a farfetched theory only muddied the waters, and it tended to make the president's critics as a group appear dyspeptic and incapable of being satisfied. As Representative Morris Udall (D-AZ) said, "I sometimes get the impression Senator Goldwater thinks our enemy is not Khrushchev, or Mao Tze-tung or Castro, but John F. Kennedy."[52]

Still, it was not surprising that the intelligence community had so far stuck to the administration's cover story, or close enough to it. The two parties had a common interest: if the true story came out, the CIA stood to be criticized for yielding too easily the previous summer and early autumn to the administration's overcautious policy. The longer the controversy continued unabated, the more likely it became that the facts would eventually spill out. As Hanson Baldwin observed in a March 11 *New York Times* story headlined "Again the Cuba Problem," despite the administration's efforts "to dampen public discussion, there was no end to the dispute in sight." Baldwin prominently noted the "contradiction" between McCone's and McNamara's testimony. He then returned to the issue of the still-unexplained gap in intelligence gathering—the issue that, months before, he had been the first to raise. Although he was unsure about the details, he wrote now, he was certain "beyond doubt" that "Washington . . . did not use all its intelligence resources in and around Cuba prior to the sudden crisis last fall."[53]

In the meantime, the White House was heartened by a statement from George Mahon, the chairman of the House Defense Appropriations subcommittee and the CIA subcommittee and one of the more inquisitive Democrats on the Hill. Although interested himself in getting to the bottom of the photo gap, Mahon may have been enraged by Ford's or other Republicans' allegations.[54] On March 7 he spoke on the House floor about the "outrageous and intolerable" damage the discussion in Congress was doing to the intelligence community.

"There is an intelligence gap. The gap is in the intelligence of those who are daily revealing the secrets of the intelligence operations of the United States government," Mahon asserted. "There has been a great excess of talk about the procedures of our intelligence apparatus. Critics have made public statements on matters which should never be discussed in public." Here the Texan showed himself trusting of the White House and CIA and dubious about the more critically minded members of Appropriations. Just three days earlier Mahon had informed CIA leaders that some of his colleagues on the committee were concerned that fears of another U-2 incident had caused a "stand down" of U-2 flights over Cuba the previous fall. In other words, that there had been a photographic intelligence gap. According to John Warner, though, Mahon himself "did not appear concerned."

Mahon's address on the House floor predictably struck an enthusiastic chord in President Kennedy, who called that day to congratulate him. "I get god-damned sick every day of reading about some intelligence officer up there saying what we know and don't know," Kennedy said, indicating concern about the "three hearings going on over there" at Congress.[55] Of course, his interest in protecting legitimate secrets was inextricable from his desire to protect his administration's image. And it was not "some intelligence officer" or legislator who had released the most detailed intelligence publicly; it was Robert McNamara.[56]

Success for Whom?

By mid-March the SPIS was almost through taking the final round of testimony from the services' intelligence chiefs. It heard from Maj. Gen. Alva Fitch, the army's assistant chief of staff for intelligence (and a survivor of the Bataan "death march"), on March 6 and from DIA director Gen. Joseph Carroll on March 11.[57] Given that army intelligence had not played an instrumental role in detecting the offensive weapons, it is doubtful that Fitch gave the subcommittee any useful information regarding the photo gap.

The Defense Intelligence Agency was very much the junior agency appearing before the subcommittee, having been constituted only in October 1961; but because Carroll was taking the lion's share of the credit for piecing together the intelligence that supposedly prompted the October 14 overflight, his testimony was second only to McCone's in importance. Three drafts are extant in the White House national security files, suggesting that his prepared statement was closely coordinated with Bundy's office and had to meet with Bundy's approval. In keeping with his earlier testimony before the House, Carroll presented the discovery of the Soviet missiles as a seamless example of intelligence collection and evaluation. His prepared statement contains no hint of the existence of a photo gap or of any analytical, estimative, or operational deficits. The only whiff of caution was his observation in passing that "up to this time [early September], high-altitude reconnaissance missions over Cuba were flown on a regular schedule, weather permitting."[58]

Following Carroll's evasive testimony, McCone again appeared before the subcommittee, meeting on March 12 in Stennis's hideaway office.[59] Only a short fragment of McCone's transcript is available, so it is impossible to know the precise language he used in the hope of settling the photo gap issue once and for all. But records from a telephone conversation between McCone and Undersecretary of State U. Alexis Johnson on March 12, shortly before McCone's testimony, provide some insight.

McCone called Johnson because he wanted to dispense with sending on-the-record memos back and forth with State about its objections to the USIB postmortem. Johnson reiterated the arguments raised in his March 6 memo: first, the USIB study implied Rusk had been seeking to delay coverage on September 10, "whereas everyone had promptly agreed to [Rusk's] suggestion and did not then nor later ever point out that any delay was involved." He also pointed out that it had been unfair to imply that there had been a "strong suspicion" that SSMs were in western Cuba, a charge with which McCone, his previous statements notwithstanding, readily agreed.[60]

Just as McCone had promised the president on March 4 that he would not make an issue of the near-crippling caution of the previous fall, he now told Johnson that his testimony would not highlight the September 10 meeting or the adverse "climate" in Washington with respect to U-2 overflights. He specifically mentioned Bundy's "famous phone call" to the CIA that led directly to the September 10 meeting and the degradation of U-2 coverage. In a memo to Rusk about the phone conversation, Johnson said he thought McCone was "laying too much emphasis" on the "climate question." "I did not know of any request for [U-2] coverage that had been turned down," Johnson wrote, repeating Bundy's refrain. McCone did admit that it was fair for Rusk "to take the position that no one at the September 10 meeting warned him that his insistence on four flights (two peripheral, two in-and-out) might cause a delay."[61]

Whatever their remaining differences with respect to the facts and context of the previous fall's decisions, McCone's promise not to raise what Rusk or other officials had done or said on September 10 mollified Johnson. Ultimately McCone's loyalty to the administration exceeded his partisan instincts, although ambition, too, may have played a part: like several others, McCone fancied himself a possible successor to Rusk, who was widely thought to be a one-term secretary of state.[62]

The March 12 SPIS hearing lasted more than three hours. Judging from the three summaries of McCone's testimony available from CIA files and the few pages of transcript in the White House files, McCone kept his promises to President Kennedy and Alex Johnson. At the outset, Stennis asked McCone to "cover the picture gap." McCone immediately referred to the USIB study (which he disingenuously called an "independent investigation"), reading aloud its conclusions, which thoroughly papered over the photo gap.[63]

Then, aided by the NPIC's head, Arthur Lundahl, he walked the subcommittee through the chronology of surveillance: "... utilizing photographs and charts, the Director gave details on the U-2 flights over Cuba of 29 August; 5, 26 and 29 September; and 5 and 7 October. For each of these flights the Subcommittee was shown graphically the exact information discovered during each flight, i.e., SAM sites, cruise missiles sites, etc. It was pointed out that the planned flight for September 10 was broken down into four individual flights in view of the potential hazard from the SA-2 systems, first photographed on the 29 August mission. The delays in accomplishing these flights due to weather was also discussed." This misleading summary was apparently the closest he came to describing the September 10 decision to degrade photo coverage.

Whether any of the SPIS senators or staff understood the implications is unclear; judging from the brief snippet of testimony that is available, it appears they did not. Senator Margaret Chase Smith heaped praise on McCone, prompting the following exchange:

> Smith: During this period, it seems to me, we have been led to believe that weather was the reason why we did not see all of this. Weather had very little to do with it. If we had not had the bad weather we would [still] not have known about those bases.
>
> McCone: We would not have known any earlier.
>
> Smith: Any earlier.
>
> McCone: In the location. Now, it may have been caught in convoy or at a dock or something such as that. I would not want to say that we absolutely would not have found it.[64]

Leaving Senator Smith and her colleagues with this misimpression was consistent with the USIB finding (and State Department position) that the missiles had been found as early as possible.[65]

The SPIS members seem to have been easily distracted during this hearing. Some were interested in exploring the already-known September 1962 failure to estimate Soviet actions in Cuba. Others were concerned about the Soviet order of battle and the threat Cuba posed as a staging area for Communism in the hemisphere. This left little time for exploring photo gap questions. Strom Thurmond, one of the most outspoken critics of the administration's handling of the Cuban crisis (Richard Russell once told JFK that Thurmond was a "fanatic"), was absent throughout, although he left written questions to be answered for the record.[66] The effect of his absence, if any, is impossible to gauge. Stennis had had a heart-to-heart talk with Thurmond in late February.

"We all go off at tangents some time," Stennis said, adding that Thurmond was capable of being "one of the best members" of the subcommittee, but that depended on whether he was cooperative or adversarial toward the chairman and other members and on his willingness to stand behind the report being prepared. "If I come out on one note and you on another," Stennis advised, "the press will have a field day, but the [subcommittee] and the country will suffer."[67] Even had Thurmond been present, then, Stennis's admonitions in February might have neutralized him as someone who might have pushed to get to the bottom of things.

By the time the session ended, at 5:15, the senators—must notably Barry Goldwater—were universal in their praise of McCone personally and the CIA in general, tossing around such words as "magnificent" and "outstanding." They spent a considerable amount of time discussing, off the record, whether the subcommittee should issue a public statement in advance of its report, giving its unanimous opinion that the CIA had done "an excellent job."[68] Finally, they decided to release, as soon as practicable, an interim report covering the first, intelligence, phase of the inquiry—thus putting to rest all outstanding public questions about the intelligence effort.[69] To McCone, the SPIS seemed completely won over.

On March 13 McCone told the president and then the NSC of his success with the SPIS the previous day. For Kennedy, he reviewed his testimony and the subcommittee's reactions in detail, culminating in the SPIS's decision to issue an interim report that would vindicate CIA and extinguish all criticism "of the so-called photographic gap." The committee members "were positive and without reservation," McCone said.

But the president asked, in effect, whether the CIA's vindication might lead to criticism of the administration or of other departments. McCone hastened to assure him that he "did not believe this would be the case." He emphasized that he had been "very careful" and that "no one could possibly draw a false conclusion from anything" he had said. (McCone would eventually be backed up by Bundy, who would assure the president two weeks later that the DCI had put in "a remarkably effective and loyal performance before the Stennis Committee.")[70]

McCone gave a briefer account at the NSC meeting, which was attended by every high official with any equity or involvement in the photo gap issue—the president and his brother, Bundy, Sorensen, Rusk, and McNamara—along with several lower-ranking officials in the State and Defense Departments. The SPIS "will make a favorable report," he said. "All members appear to be satisfied with the performance of the Intelligence Community and their public report will cite no intelligence gap to be criticized." He concluded with another forecast: the investigation of past actions in Cuba "was about finished on the Hill."[71]

His triumphant report probably annoyed the president on at least one score, though. Only two weeks after McCone had been reminded by Bundy that "policy" was beyond his "competence," he told the NSC that, having been "pressed" by the Stennis subcommittee to give his personal policy views, he had advocated "taking positive steps to prevent any other country from falling to communism," adding, "As regards Cuba . . . we must get the Soviets out and, after that, the Castro government can be broken up by a military coup favorable" to US interests. Few believed that such a coup would happen without US backing; in essence, McCone had advocated a significant covert operation before an audience of legislators, many of whom doubted the president had the guts to see such an action through successfully.[72]

A few days later, at the regular weekly USIB meeting, McCone briefed the members of that body as well. INR director Roger Hilsman, who had fought so tenaciously to make the USIB postmortem inoffensive to the State Department, could not help but be impressed. He called McCone's office to ask for an opportunity to read the complete transcript of the hearing. Hilsman wanted "his people" to be able to put forward the same line of argument.[73]

End of the Trail

The "Interim" Report

By April 4, two weeks after McCone's final testimony and after receiving additional answers promised for the record by all the witnesses, James Kendall finished a first draft of the SPIS report.[1] Stennis wanted a step-by-step chronological account of how the build-up had occurred and what efforts had been made to detect it. The draft also included a section compiled by Charles Donnelly, a former colonel working at the Library of Congress. This concerned the extent and nature of subversive activities promoted by Cuba in the hemisphere.[2]

On April 5, 9, and 24 the subcommittee held executive meetings, with no transcripts being made.[3] It is clear from other documentation that, as a result of the meetings, some changes in language were incorporated into the draft. Still, the substance and thrust of the report remained more or less intact.[4]

On April 10, very much after the fact, Stennis learned about the vetting of the prepared statements of the service intelligence chiefs by higher-ups. He was stunned and immediately contacted McNamara. "I was greatly dismayed to learn that the intelligence chiefs . . . were compelled to submit their formal prepared statements to your office for review and screening," he wrote. "Quite frankly, I cannot understand why these officers should not be permitted to come before us in closed sessions and give the facts as they know them without prior review. I feel so strongly about this matter that I am seriously considering making a statement . . . on the floor of the Senate."[5]

During the April 24 meeting, at which the SPIS members reviewed the "final" language of the interim report, one of the first things to come up concerned two paragraphs about the vetting. Strom Thurmond had argued vigorously that the report should mention the screening of the statements. Upon reflection, however, Stennis decided that the paragraphs in question "would tend to weaken rather than strengthen the interim report." He wrote Thurmond, "It might suggest to those not familiar with the details of the inquiry that we did not get the real facts. I think you will agree that such an impression would be both unfortunate and unjustified in view of the fact that all of the witnesses were subjected to extensive questioning under oath."[6] Stennis added that he was in complete agreement about getting unvarnished testimony before the subcommittee in executive session and intended to pursue the matter with McNamara. Thurmond reluctantly agreed to drop the paragraphs, and Stennis informed McNamara of the change, though warning that SPIS reports "will make mention of this practice should it recur . . . under similar circumstances." Rather belatedly McNamara assured Stennis that the Pentagon had not subjected the statements to review by State Department officials.[7] He said nothing about reviews by the White House.

Coming into the April 24 SPIS meeting, at least one Republican senator, Margaret Chase Smith, had sufficient reservations to make a unanimous report unlikely. Smith was a unique legislator in many ways, not the least of which was that only one other woman, Maurine Neuberger (D-OR), served in the Senate (as a very junior member) in 1963. Smith had been in the House for almost a decade before her election to the Senate in 1948. "Mrs. Smith, slight, attractive and gray-haired, is a lieutenant colonel in the Women's Air Force Reserve. She frequently has given high-ranking generals appearing before the Armed Services Committee a hard time," one reporter wrote in 1963.[8]

Smith was skeptical about the administration's actions concerning Cuba. In February she told her constituents, "Americans held their heads high the morning of October 23, 1962, after the President made his speech the night before announcing that we would fight if Khrushchev did not remove the Russian missiles in Cuba." But now there was a national "feeling of resentment of the possibility of having been misled with reports that were too rosy and too sugar-coated." Her characterization of the SPIS investigation must have made John Stennis squirm: "This action of investigation drowns out the heated denials of the Kennedy administration—for the American public recognizes that the Cuban situation has gotten so bad that a member of President Kennedy's own Democratic Party has ordered a congressional investigation of the matter."[9]

Smith's normally smooth relations with Richard Russell and Leverett Saltonstall had become difficult over the preceding year. She had assumed that she would become the ranking Republican on the Armed Services Committee after the death of Styles Bridges (R-NH) in November 1961 and also take his place on the exclusive subcommittee on the CIA. But for this to happen, Saltonstall—the newly senior Republican on both Armed Services and

Appropriations—would have had to voluntarily give up his "ranking" status on one of them. Drew Pearson adroitly captured the situation: "Saltonstall, a very proper Bostonian . . . has been strangely silent about rising and graciously asking Mrs. Smith to take the top Republican position on the Armed Services Committee. One reason is discreet opposition from the Pentagon about letting the independent lady from Maine get more power over the military."[10]

In the end, Salstonstall did not do the "gracious" thing. Furthermore, Russell named Milton Young (R-ND) to replace Bridges on the Appropriations CIA subcommittee and decided not to replace Bridges at all on the Armed Services CIA subcommittee.[11] Whatever explanation Saltonstall and Russell may have offered for blocking Smith's rise is undocumented in her surviving papers, but one of her top aides later told a CIA official that she had wondered if "Mr. McCone had had any part in this, since Senator Smith had voted against Mr. McCone's confirmation as DCI."[12] (Tellingly, Smith would soon place into the *Congressional Record* a political novella written by her Senate aide Bill Lewis, with whom she shared a home. In it, the DCI, clearly patterned on McCone, speaks to the president about "that woman" on the Armed Services Committee: "They won't be able to ignore her seniority and keep her off the Subcommittee on the CIA forever.") Still, there is no evidence that the CIA influenced Russell's decision, and McCone had earned Smith's grudging admiration in his first two years as DCI.[13]

Smith's reservations in April 1963 at the SPIS hearings included the fact that because on-site inspections had not been permitted, there was no iron-clad assurance that Cuba no longer posed a military threat. She also felt that the testimony of Cubans in Florida, who had been interviewed by two SPIS staff members, had not been taken into proper account.

For weeks during the investigation, Stennis, Saltonstall, and others had lobbied Smith to relent in some of her criticisms. Smith's papers show that Saltonstall sought to visit her privately in her office in late March; they probably did meet eventually. On April 10, when the SPIS members were reacting to an early draft of the report, Stuart French, Saltonstall's top aide on the SPIS staff, left word that he "would like an appointment to sit down and talk with the senator about it and find out what she liked and what she did not like." On April 17 Smith made a notation on her office calendar: "I saw him—Cuba."[14]

Later that day, Smith appeared for the taping of a weekly television interview program hosted by Kenneth Keating. (Like many other legislators, Keating taped programs for broadcast in his home state.) He wasted little time introducing her before moving to his topic of interest:

Keating: You've been holding Executive Sessions on the subject of Cuba. When do you expect there will be a report?

Smith: Senator Keating, the report is in the making now. We've been working on it for the past ten days or two weeks. It could very well be ready—the interim report, not the final report—by May first.

Keating: Do you expect there will be any division in your committee?

Smith: There is quite apt to be.[15]

A week later, she made some notes of what to say to her Preparedness colleagues: "I cannot join in the commendation of the intelligence community. The most that I could ascribe to would be written recognition of the good job that the photo reconnaissance pilots and interpreters did in obtaining the aerial evidence and making determinations from it." She added, among other points, that she had "never received satisfactory answers" to her questions about "information we had on Russians being brought in by ships to Cuba."[16]

The next day, Smith summoned Stuart French back to her office. "He'll be over in 15 minutes, as you suggested," a staffer responded. Smith wrote out her message for that meeting thus: "Rewrite report Tighten up." On Tuesday, April 30, her receptionist recorded, "Senator Stennis came in the office to see the Senator." Smith described the point of Stennis's visit: "Report—wants it unanimous—done again." Stennis telephoned twice on May 2, and Smith saw him twice in her office that day. Her notations about the two sessions were identical: "Cuban report."[17]

The report was apparently massaged until Smith was satisfied. On Friday, May 3, the CIA legislative liaison John Warner recorded in his work diary, "Mr. Kendall called later in the evening and advised that the Report had been finished. Arrangements were made for a courier to pick up the report and bring it to the Agency on Saturday morning."[18]

Even as CIA reviewed the "finished" draft in order to prevent any disclosures of classified information, SPIS members continued to offer critiques and suggestions. One of the first to comment was Barry Goldwater, who had an interest in dissenting from any findings that praised the administration's handling of the missile crisis. Reflecting the subcommittee's unstinting commendation after McCone's second appearance, the draft found that "there has been no instance in the history of this or any other nation when intelligence was able to do that which was done at this time." Goldwater objected to so sweeping a statement. Unwittingly demonstrating how successfully the administration's witnesses had prevented the SPIS from uncovering the troubling facts, he then noted, "There is no question that the information was gathered but some place between the CIA and the Executive Branch it was very badly evaluated, if not completely ignored, and if we are going to praise, we are going to have to explain this strange inability of this country to act on well-gathered intelligence, so I would steer carefully clear of any sweeping praise." Ironically, given McCone's role in getting the administration off the hook, he was the one official Goldwater regarded as blameless and "worthy of our recognition."[19]

The final draft was issued to the subcommittee members on May 8. By this time, if not before, the section on Cuba's subversive potential had been jettisoned; the panel intended to include it in a subsequent report. Stennis was anxious to get the report out, so instead of scheduling a final meeting to review it, he polled each senator personally to gain his or her assent. Another reason for speed was to prevent leaks, or even word that the report's release was imminent. "I have had repeated inquiries and have given assurances to the press that all will be treated equally in the public release of the report," Stennis told Stuart Symington.[20] The document was sure to be highly sensitive. There was talk that the White House was making an "astonishing demand" on the SPIS. "It wants to examine [SPIS's findings] before they are published," the syndicated columnists Robert Allen and Paul Scott wrote. One constituent sent Stennis a copy of the column and said, "I know you will expose the naked truth, no matter whom it may embarrass."[21]

With the final language agreed upon, the SPIS planned to make a classified version of the interim report available to the full Armed Services Committee and possibly the Appropriations Committee. But it also wanted a declassified version printed for release to the public, which would require screening by the Defense Department and the CIA. Of course, the line between reviewing for classified information and vetting for political acceptability could be easily blurred. In his cover letter to McNamara and McCone, Stennis underlined that he expected no comments on any aspect of the report "except those matters as to which the national security might be affected adversely by public release of the information."[22] Although details are lacking, there is no question that parts of the report were rewritten after an expeditious review by the CIA and Pentagon.[23]

As publication of the report approached, Drew Pearson reported in his daily column in the *Washington Post* (reprinted in hundreds of newspapers nationwide) that "CIA chief John McCone has been growling about President Kennedy's policy in Cuba, has said it permitted Khrushchev to take over." Nonetheless, it was soon apparent that the administration's efforts to quell criticism and turn attention away from Cuba were finally bearing fruit.[24]

When Nixon criticized JFK for having "goofed" the Bay of Pigs invasion, the president shot back that his Republican predecessors had been in a position to prevent Fidel Castro from having come to power in the first place. (In February Kennedy had entertained an idea—"Why we should not permit and even encourage a congressional investigation of the handling of Cuba before 1961?"—but was dissuaded by McGeorge Bundy.)[25] When Nelson Rockefeller—a possible 1964 GOP nominee—suggested that there had been "secret communications" between Kennedy and Khrushchev and an element of appeasement in the administration's policy, a number of newspaper columnists roundly criticized him for making undocumented charges (although, of course, they happened to be true).[26] Meanwhile, highly critical articles in the media, such as a column by Allen and Scott alleging the existence of another intelligence gap owing to the degradation of low-level reconnaissance flights, had little impact. As one reporter noted, by late April even Keating was sounding "moderate, even sometimes gentle."[27]

By the first week in May, the SPIS was ready to resume its probe into the latest nuclear test ban treaty proposals and put Cuba behind it. On May 8, soon after another SPIS session, Stennis sent a letter to each subcommittee member accompanying what he hoped would be a final draft—Kendall's second major draft—of what came to be called the "Interim Report on the Cuban Military Buildup." "I am most hopeful that you will find nothing objectionable in the enclosed draft and that it will be possible to release it without a further Subcommittee meeting," he wrote, adding that he would be in touch by telephone or in person later that day to secure approval. In Smith's case, he phoned. Her note on the call reads, "Unless hearing by 9 a.m., release for noon 5-9-63." In other words, unless someone insisted by 9:00 the following morning on discussing further changes, the report would be released.

Apparently no one objected, and Stennis took to the Senate floor on Thursday, May 9, at noon. "Mr. President, the Preparedness Investigating Subcommittee of the Committee on Armed Services has filed a report with the full committee on the first phases of the hearings it has been conducting with reference to the military buildup in Cuba and with particular reference to our intelligence activities and operations in connection with Cuba during the year 1962 and to date," he announced. He noted "some difference of opinion among the members of the subcommittee as to what should be in the report," but said that "as a result of an exchange of thought and suggestions," the report had been "agreed to by all the members." This was technically true in that all the members had signed the report.

Stennis began his presentation by reminding the senators that "last October, we escaped being confronted with operational strategic missiles on our very doorstep by a very narrow margin." Then he walked them through the subcommittee's conclusions: "a reasonably competent job was done by the intelligence community in acquiring and collecting intelligence information and data." There was, however, faulty "evaluation of the data," heightened by the intelligence community's tendency to discount reports from Cuban refugees and exiles, coupled with a "philosophic conviction on the parts of intelligence officials that it would be contrary to Soviet policy to introduce strategic missiles into Cuba." Therefore, "it was not until photographic evidence was obtained on October 14, 1962, that the intelligence community concluded that strategic missiles had, in fact, been introduced into Cuba."

Stennis then summarized a judgment that indicates the extent to which the SPIS had failed to grasp events: "The subcommittee found no evidence that there was a photography gap between September 5 and October 15." After treating that topic briefly, he went on at length about the inability of US intelligence to know how many Soviet military personnel were in Cuba before, during, and—most important to him—after the missile crisis.[28]

The subcommittee's succinct eighteen-page report closely paralleled Stennis's speech. The SPIS, it said, had "uncovered no evidence" of a photo gap. Inclement weather had made detection of missile sites difficult. (This was accurate, but the SPIS obviously had not learned of, or been told of, the CIA's own account of its weather reports, which showed some days with "good" weather over western Cuba that featured no overflights.)[29] A "reasonably competent job" had been done in acquisition of raw intelligence, but "several substantial errors were made by the intelligence agencies" in terms of "evaluation." There had been "a disinclination on the part of the intelligence community to accept and believe the ominous portent of the information which had been gathered." Neither Stennis nor the report itself made any judgments about the White House's management of intelligence efforts.

Other senators soon took to the floor to voice their disagreements. Stennis allowed Henry "Scoop" Jackson (D-WA), a junior SPIS member, to respond first. Jackson focused on McCone's warnings during August 1962. He was probably aware that an early draft of the report had expressed "confidence in and respect for Mr. John A. McCone," calling him "an able and outstanding administrator and public servant"—a passage that had been cut. As Stennis had begun his opening remarks, Jackson telephoned John Warner, asking that McCone's March 12 testimony, in which he acknowledged his early "intuitive" suspicions about missile deployment, be declassified. Unsurprisingly, the DCI did not object.[30]

McCone, Jackson said, was "the only one in the intelligence community who had come to this conclusion early in August," and he proceeded to read aloud part of "the censored testimony":

> Jackson: You were one of the first to suspect, based on judgment on your part, that the Soviets might put in missiles, MRBMs or IRBMs, in Cuba.
>
> McCone: That is correct. . . . I emphasize that there was no hard intelligence to support my position. Intuitive[ly], I could reach no other conclusion, I couldn't understand why these surface-to-surface missile sites were there. . . . They must be there, in my opinion, to shield the island against observation from aerial reconnaissance.

Without explicitly criticizing the interim report, Jackson said, "I wish the record to show that Mr. McCone foresaw what was later to be developed." Stennis responded, "We can come back to this point later," but he had no real interest in doing so. He knew that some SPIS members were wary of handing out too much praise for the CIA's handling of an incident that had so closely courted disaster.[31]

Barry Goldwater was one of them. On the Senate floor he allowed that McCone was "competent in judgment" and "did a good job" but said "there was an error in judgment somewhere. We cannot point the finger, nor can we select the spot." For all his animosity toward the White House and the State Department, Goldwater seems to have understood no better than the rest of the subcommittee that the errors in judgment had stemmed from those quarters. Stuart Symington also failed to take those offices to task; instead, in his floor speech he concentrated, somewhat incoherently, on "the Air Force and the other departments which have to do with our intelligence." Even though McCone had "wisely told his own organization about his apprehensions . . . that information was not passed on to the intelligence apparatus. Therefore, there can be no criticism of the president or the intelligence apparatus for not having acted on such information." Reporter Peter Clapper wondered if Symington's remarks indicated that "senators might be trying to tell the CIA chief to shape up or ship out." After all, "What good is it to leave uncanny intuitions at the top, untapped?"[32]

Still, on the Senate floor criticisms of the SPIS for not being able to "point the finger" were barely voiced that day. It was left to Jack Miller, a Republican from Iowa with just two years' service in the Senate, to tell Stennis, "I, for one, was hopeful that the committee would be able to fix responsibility in the so-called Cuba build-up and indicate to us whether this was due to a slip-up in our intelligence systems or a slip at the policy- or decision-making level." Stennis, who had been enjoying the dialogue with his colleagues up to that point, simply said that the interim report would "speak for itself on that point."[33]

It was almost four hours before Margaret Chase Smith spoke. By that time, neither Stennis nor the other SPIS members were in attendance.[34] Kenneth Keating, however, was. "Compromise is inevitable in a unanimous report on such a serious matter as the Cuban military build-up," Smith said. But she had "individual observations" to offer about the "treachery of the most reckless sort yet to be experienced in the nuclear age," which had occurred "virtually in our own backyard," and about the government's response. The United States' acceptance of "bland assurances" by the Soviets that the build-up was solely intended to bolster Castro's defensive capabilities had been foolish.

Moreover, the SPIS report ought to have included "the lessons to be learned and remembered from the crisis." One was that "governments, as with people," need to resist being trapped by preconceived notions. The debates between the White House and Keating were really over whether "those in official positions" were giving sufficient credence before mid-October to information that, while lacking "conclusive proof, nevertheless suggested a high probability that strategic weapons were introduced by the Soviet Union."

Smith also scorned the administration's "maligning" of the character of Cuban exiles while ignoring their warnings. "Those who were interviewed upon their arrival in the United States by representatives of our intelligence agencies" had given innumerable indications that a strategic Soviet move was unfolding in Cuba, including stories about "trailers transporting large cylindrical objects draped with canvas." Administration officials "obviously . . . were not able to pass judgment on the offensive or defensive nature of these objects, but they knew they were missiles—and big ones, at that," she emphasized. Since U-2 flights "could detect none of this clandestine activity," the intelligence community persisted in adhering to the view that the build-up was defensive.

Smith made no mention of McCone's late-summer suspicions that the Soviets were placing strategic weapons in Cuba, and by implication, she gave him no credit; in fact, she did not even mention his name. Still, she drew on the same logic he had used. The confirmed presence of surface-to-air missiles should have made it obvious that "these sites were surely not meant for repelling any possible future invasion attempts," she argued. The SA-2 was "relatively ineffective against low-flying aircraft, which would normally provide close ground support to an invading force." The SAMs must have been "for the purpose of denying to us further aerial reconnaissance by U-2s, in order to hide something of real significance—strategic missiles, perhaps?" None-theless, Smith failed to perceive that there had been a significant gap in the photo coverage of western Cuba, much less solve the mystery of why that had happened.[35]

Based on contemporaneous correspondence, it appears that Stennis, the subcommittee's other members, and its staffers genuinely believed the lan-guage of the report concerning the photo gap. One of the clearest indications of this is James Kendall's response to a detailed paper about the performance of the intelligence community, which he received unsolicited in the mail about a year after the report was published. The paper's author, Allen Forbes—prob-ably a college or graduate student—recognized that the published versions of events did not make sense. Either there had been an "extremely slip-shod sur-veillance operation"—a scenario he was not inclined to believe—or, as Gerald Ford had argued and as Forbes thought more likely, the administration was not telling the truth about when it had first gained hard evidence of the mis-sile sites and had only acted after Keating forced its hand. But Kendall wrote, "I do not agree that there was a 'photographic gap' . . . I have seen a great deal of documentary evidence on this which is far more extensive than the interim report indicates."[36] More recently, Kendall reaffirmed the SPIS's 1963 finding in a 2003 interview.

The lower body of Congress seldom took notice of studies issued by the upper body, but the interim report became the subject of extended comment in the House of Representatives. Here, too, the remarks were inextricable from the politics of the issue. Representative Samuel Stratton, a conservative Democrat from upstate New York who intended to run for Keating's Senate seat in 1964, had been hoping the SPIS report would "slap" Keating down.[37]

In a May 16 speech on the House floor, Stratton, former naval intelligence officer, said he was "baffled, mystified, and disappointed" by the report. "All charges [against the CIA] have been factually disproved" according to the subcommittee, he said, "but somehow the defendant has still not been acquit-ted. Instead he remains under suspicion, if he is not indeed actually found guilty at least on some counts." Surely the questions that had prompted the inquiry deserved specific answers. Instead, "Here is a jury verdict with some-thing for everybody, a strange amalgam of both fact and fancy which comes out clearly and positively exactly nowhere."

The allegation of a photo gap—an allegation that had "made big head-lines," Stratton reminded his colleagues—was one of the grave charges that had been "specifically and conclusively disproved," according to the SPIS report. At the same time, the report criticized the intelligence community for dismissing indications of a military build-up. As Stratton pointed out, this criticism made no sense if, as the report stated, the intelligence community had done everything within its power to investigate reports of missile sightings. Stratton also sent a copy of his remarks to McCone, scribbling a cover note: "Your 'friends' seem to me to be throwing you in!"[38]

A second critique in the House came from a group that included many of the Republicans who had been riding herd on the administration since January. The House Republican Policy Special Subcommittee on Cuba and Subversion in the Western Hemisphere prepared a commentary on the report, including a section titled "Unanswered Questions."[39] Chief among them was how the missiles had escaped detection for so long. In its zealousness, however, the GOP task force revived and focused on the incorrect charge that the administration had consciously deceived the public—thereby completely missing the point, just as Gerald Ford had.

The media treated the report with relative lack of interest. All the major outlets took note of it—and *U.S. News & World Report* printed a long excerpt—but with little commentary. One exception was a critical article by the syndicated columnist Max Freedman, which ran in the *Washington Star* on May 16.[40] Freedman discussed the report in light of a lecture on the missile crisis given by Ted Sorensen, the president's special counsel, at Columbia University on May 9. Sorensen had contrasted the freedom individual congressmen had to spread rumors and make unsubstantiated allegations with the president's sober responsibilities.[41] Freedman suggested that the criticisms in the SPIS report were of the same ilk as Keating's charges the previous fall. "It is very easy for the [sub]committee to be wise after the event," he wrote. The column did not genuinely deal with the report itself, however; as one aide wrote to Stennis, it was an attempt to "discredit the report by belaboring a straw-man."[42]

At the White House the president requested a copy of the Stennis report for his weekend reading on May 17.[43] He did so for good reason: his congressional liaison office reported that letters from citizens to legislators gave "every evidence that the public is convinced there is no definite U.S. policy relative to Cuba."[44] But his aides were comfortable letting a senator (Hubert Humphrey) respond to the Republican National Committee chairman William Miller's assertion that "if we believe Senator Stennis and his bipartisan group, we can only conclude that President Kennedy, presidential assistant McGeorge Bundy, Defense Secretary McNamara and Under Secretary of State George Ball were deceiving the American people." Humphrey retorted, "Simple, mischievous nonsense."[45]

Indeed, for the president and his closest associates, the release of the Stennis report was mostly anticlimactic. The only issue that raised hackles was the subcommittee's judgment that 17,500 Soviet personnel remained in Cuba. The president wrote McCone, "I find some difficulty in reconciling the statement of the Stennis committee with the statements that I have made. I was informed that there had been a withdrawal of some 4,000 personnel from Cuba." Kennedy worried (according to an aide) that "there is something funny going on about this business in Cuba. . . . CIA is contradicting what they have already given him."[46] But McCone explained that order-of-battle estimates were highly technical and that deployed military units were assumed to be in place unless there was absolute proof to the contrary. The CIA still believed there had been a 20 to 30 percent reduction in the estimate of 17,500 troops; it was just that there had never been a foolproof head count.[47]

In the main, the administration officials had achieved their goal. Their success was succinctly reflected in Strom Thurmond's acknowledgment, on the floor of the Senate on June 4, of an essential fact: "The administration has not given the subcommittee any evidence of a photography gap." Better still, from the administration's point of view, would have been Nebraska Republican senator Carl Curtiss's remarks to colleagues some weeks later: "It has sometimes been said that committee hearings and committee reports are fine, but that once they are made, they are put on the shelf and forgotten, unless some researcher or historian digs them out. I come back again to the investigation made by the Subcommittee on Preparedness."[48]

The SPIS did penetrate one of the administration's main secrets: the quid pro quo involving the Jupiter missiles in Turkey. In mid-February, some weeks after the administration announced it had made an agreement with Ankara to remove the Jupiters, Stennis telephoned Kendall with urgent instructions.[49] He wanted Kendall to obtain all the evidence that he could about the history and reasons for the removal, especially about whether there had been any differences of opinion at the Defense Department about the decision.

What prompted Stennis to speculate about a connection between the Jupiters' withdrawal and the Cuban crisis in October is not known. Possibly Margaret Chase Smith had some influence on his thoughts. She had told her constituents on February 10, "Americans still wonder if a deal wasn't actually made during the crisis—with an agreement that the American missiles would be removed from Turkey after the crisis blew over."[50] Over the ensuing weeks Kendall obtained sufficient corroboration from the SPIS's excellent Pentagon sources to convince himself that the two events were directly connected; he reported as much to Stennis.[51] This dramatic finding, however, did not make it into the interim report. Perhaps Kendall believed it could not be included without compromising his sources. Or perhaps Stennis judged that the matter was outside the subcommittee's mandate.

Ironically, the person in the administration most upset with the Stennis report was McCone. Stuart French spoke to him about the matter in late May, then told Saltonstall in a memo that the director felt "betrayed" by the subcommittee because the "substance and tone" of the interim report were in marked contrast to the "praise which was so lavishly heaped upon him by each and every committee member . . . on March 12."[52]

Although French was unaware that McCone had dissembled in order to protect the administration, he correctly reported to Saltonstall that McCone was not yet "off the hook" with the White House. French mistakenly thought McCone was in trouble for the "frankness" of his testimony before the SPIS. But he concluded—again correctly, although not for the right reasons—that prolonging the debate over the intelligence community's performance would only "jeopardize [McCone's] position with the administration even further" and that McCone would "much prefer to let the matter rest."[53]

And so it would. The SPIS never issued another Cuba report; the "interim" report proved to be its final word. The Kennedy White House had succeeded in obscuring the facts about the photo gap from wide public knowledge, preserving its reputation for having masterfully handled almost every aspect of the Cuban Missile Crisis, both before and during the event.[54]

The Costs of Managed History

John McCone's reputation on Capitol Hill in 1963 was still far better than that of Allen Dulles after the Bay of Pigs. During one of the SPIS Cuba hearings in March, with McCone present, Margaret Chase Smith told her colleagues matter-of-factly, "I think Mr. McCone has been more direct and frank than his predecessor." Voicing a sentiment held by some other Republicans as well, she expressed concern about making "difficult his position in the administration."[1]

A few weeks after that hearing, one of Gerald Ford's constituents urged him to be tougher regarding Cuba. Legislators should initiate a total blockade and, if necessary, employ military force to achieve "a complete withdrawal of Russian troops," she wrote. After all, she insisted, "Congress has the power to exercise authority over and above the president." But speaking to a group of Republican women in Michigan weeks later, just before the release of the SPIS interim report, Ford spoke of the limits of congressional powers in the face of a resistant White House: "The president *is* keeping the Congress and the public in the dark; he *is* managing the news; he *is* preventing the lawfully elected representatives of the people from making informed judgments of the past conduct of our government and therefore the future hazards we face."[2]

Although McCone had many admirers on Capitol Hill, he as much as anyone had enabled the Kennedy White House's successful resistance. And in any case, Ford and his aggressive constituent were relatively lonely voices: most Americans, including those in Congress, thought the president was handling Cuba fairly well. Far fewer were interested in whether the administration had shared all relevant information with legislators.

Nonetheless, the failure by Congress and the news media to learn the truth about the run-up to the missile crisis had real and varied consequences. Most obviously, it enhanced, or at least left intact, the administration's preferred narrative of the crisis. The same could be said, of course, about the quid pro quo with Moscow and the role Operation MONGOOSE played in fomenting Cuban acceptance of Soviet designs. One can speculate about the various effects these events, had they been revealed during the Kennedy presidency, might have had on US domestic politics and on later administrations. Some scholars have made the case, for example, that the false depiction of what occurred before and after the crisis created an impossible standard for all subsequent presidents during the Cold War.[3] Even Bundy, in hindsight, seemed to admit tacitly that the enhanced image that was projected did not necessarily serve the Kennedy administration or its successors well over the long term. "In particular," Bundy wrote in his 1988 history/memoir, "I think we could have done more than we did to discourage the conclusion that this was a case of wonderfully coordinated and error-free 'crisis management.'"[4] At the time, though, the temptation to repair the image of a president who had just fumbled his way through the Bay of Pigs was obviously too great.

Scholarship about the missile crisis, of course, was demonstrably affected by the failure to get the story straight at the time. The record of how the photo gap was treated in the vast literature on the crisis, and how the real story came out in dribs and drabs over forty years, is addressed in a historiography that follows in the appendix. The seeming inability even over time to incorporate the operational failure of intelligence into histories of the missile crisis and biographies of President Kennedy suggests that the myth created by the administration became so firmly embedded in the popular and scholarly psyche that perhaps nothing will ever shake it. As John F. Kennedy said himself, during a 1962 commencement address at Yale, perhaps the greatest enemy of truth "is very often not the lie—deliberate, contrived, and dishonest—but the myth—persistent, persuasive, and unrealistic."[5]

If what is known now had been known during the crisis or soon thereafter, it is difficult to believe that the episode would have the exalted status it enjoys in the annals of American Cold War history. A pusillanimous effort at the Bay of Pigs was followed by the vast, misguided covert Operation MONGOOSE, which helped make the Cubans receptive to becoming an outpost of Soviet power. The Kennedy administration then miscalculated the effects on Moscow of its 1961 declaration that the United States enjoyed decisive nuclear superiority.[6] After the Soviet build-up in the Caribbean began, there was a near-catastrophic failure of US intelligence, owing as much to Washington's self-deception as to Moscow's deception of the United States. Finally, the crisis was settled on terms that, had they been widely understood at the time, would have markedly influenced perceptions of who had and who had not "blinked."

The dominant narrative of the missile crisis depicts John F. Kennedy in his "finest hour," a "courageous young American President, always cool under fire, [who] successfully resisted the aggressive designs of the Soviet Union and its puppet regime in Cuba to win a decisive victory over Communism."[7] Notwithstanding all that has been learned, even the less charitable interpretations remain highly favorable. As one scholar recently pointed out, the most recent, slightly modified iteration of the "finest hour" thesis is that the United States was "fortunate" that Kennedy was the president "charged with managing the crisis."[8]

Perhaps the most instructive lesson of the photo gap, however, and the struggle to control history in general, concerns the hoary clash between the executive and legislative branches of the US government. Months after its release, the Stennis report was used mainly to chide the Kennedy administration about the unrelieved threat posted by Castro's Cuba. If evaluated for its usefulness in understanding how and why the US government had almost been handed a fait accompli by Khrushchev, however, the report was nearly useless.

This points, in turn, to a larger problem pertaining to congressional attempts to confront the intelligence community. Even today's standing Senate and House intelligence committees (created in 1976 and 1977, respectively) face formidable obstacles when they choose to investigate the intelligence community or an intelligence-related event if the incumbent administration is inclined to obscure basic facts. House Republicans, with their more aggressive and partisan posture in 1963, came much closer to unraveling the truth about the lead-up to the Cuban Missile Crisis than did the prestigious, relatively deliberate inquiry headed by Stennis in the Senate. But what made the obstacles then, and makes the obstacles now, nearly insuperable is the fact that Congress itself is riven by politics: at the end of the day, it is very hard to be effective as a primary truth-seeking body while acting in an oversight capacity.

As for the intelligence establishment's functioning within the executive branch and specifically its relations with the White House, it has commonly been argued that notwithstanding the delay, the system basically worked. "Fortunately, the decision to look harder was made in time, but it would have been made sooner if we had listened more attentively to McCone" is the formulation McGeorge Bundy gave in his book.[9] This "system worked" view has been endorsed by every participant in the crisis who has written a memoir, as well as by most scholars.[10] And it may well be that given the intangibles of human behavior, the most one can ever expect is a kind of dogged performance by an intelligence service that somehow manages, in the end, to prevent a strategic surprise.

Yet some students of the missile crisis have undoubtedly gone too far, making the counterfactual argument that the CIA's misestimates were the most significant shortcoming in the episode and that the photo gap, in essence, did not even matter. "Discovery [of the missiles] a week or two earlier in October . . . would not have changed the situation faced by the president and his advisers," Raymond Garthoff, one of the most esteemed scholars of the crisis, has written.[11] Given that the missiles were found none too soon, a more significant question is: what would have happened if the missiles had been found even slightly later?

What actually happened, of course, matters more than what might have been. Yet by that measure, too, the photo gap was more significant than the consistently wrong intelligence estimates.

The last aspect of the photo gap that merits comment is the effect the secret had on the all-important relationship between the nation's chief intelligence officer and the president—actually, both Kennedys. McCone's prescience and his loyalty—even when that loyalty prompted him to go along, in congressional testimony and elsewhere, with the administration's carefully crafted fiction—did not win him admission to the innermost circle of presidential advisers. It had the opposite effect. McCone became mightily resented, not only for having been right—which he was not inclined to let anyone forget—but also for being privy to an embarrassing truth.[12] The Kennedys now distrusted their DCI more than ever.

The photo gap speaks to issues of moment today, not the least of which is the difficulty of being the nation's chief intelligence officer and the qualities that make for an effective one. Telling the president and his top advisers something they would prefer not to believe, or advocating taking a risk they would prefer to avoid, is not a job for the faint of heart. The story of the photo gap is a reminder that the success or failure of the US intelligence establishment unavoidably depends on the human factor: the character and capacities of the men and women in critical positions and the nature of relationships among those at the very top.

In January 1969, during his farewell address as director of the State Department's Bureau of Intelligence and Research, Thomas Hughes remarked on pressures applied by policy makers: "Over the long run, the prospect for preserving intelligence and policy in their most constructive orthodox roles will depend on the real-life resistance which intelligence officers apply to these pressures, as well as to the self-imposed restraints which impede the policymakers from originally exerting them."[13] Hughes's observation came after eight years of firsthand exposure to the often troubled relationship between the intelligence community and the Kennedy and Johnson administrations, years that included McCone's entire tenure as DCI.

The run-up to the missile crisis may not represent the model behavior Hughes had in mind, but decades later the government seems as far as ever from following his prescription. Judging from such episodes as policy makers' failure to act against al-Qa'ida in the 1990s and their misappropriation of flawed estimates about Iraq in 2002, it seems clear that at critical junctures US policymakers still sometimes seek, receive, and absorb the intelligence they prefer rather than the intelligence they need. The creation in 2004 of the position of director of national intelligence—a job with an august title but limited powers—did not solve this problem, nor is it likely to do so.

A Historiography of the Photo Gap, 1963–2011

Speculation about an "intelligence" or "photo" gap began to mount as soon as the acute phase of the crisis peaked in October. Chapter 1 addressed media coverage of this issue for the remaining months of 1962. This historiography traces the presentation and interpretation of key facts in the public and classified literature, and the varying interpretations given the collection deficit, beginning in 1963 and thereafter. As will be seen, the deficit remained a matter of great confusion in the public literature for decades and even, to some degree, in the classified literature.

The first partly accurate explanation appeared as early as March 1963 in a story by Jules Witcover, the Pentagon beat reporter for the Newhouse Newspapers' Washington bureau. The account as published in the *Washington Star* missed some important details. Still, Witcover managed to convey the genuine reason for the intelligence deficit.[1] The major omission in the story was that it made no mention of the pivotal meeting in McGeorge Bundy's office on September 10, 1962, that resulted in attenuation of U-2 surveillance.

Despite its accuracy, Witcover's account had little impact.[2] Other reporters and columnists continued to put forward the administration's proffered explanation or simply muddled the issue, which served the same end. More importantly, two months later the Senate Preparedness Investigating Subcommittee, chaired by John Stennis, released its report, which flatly declared that allegations about a photo gap were "unfounded."[3] This influential finding became the dominant one. As a consequence, it would not be understood for at least a decade that the run-up to the missile crisis was, in fact, a near failure of the first magnitude.[4] The Kennedy administration's initial obfuscation of the issue remained so successful that scholarly consensus on this point never achieved unanimity.

The First Publications: 1960s

The first book published about the missile crisis appeared in August 1963, written by Henry M. Pachter, a German émigré and professor of history. He had sent dispatches to European papers the previous October, writing stories about the crisis from the perspective of the United Nations Security Council. He relied upon public documents, interviews with diplomatic sources "who prefer[red] to remain anonymous," and government information officers. According to Pachter, McCone "ordered weekly surveillance" of Cuba after the SA-2s were discovered, and U-2 sorties were planned for September 5, 17, 26, and 29 and October 7. But U-2 incidents over Soviet and Chinese airspace thwarted McCone's plans, and all U-2 flights were canceled on September 4. At the end of September U-2 surveillance resumed, Pachter wrote, "since the risk of an incident now seemed of lesser consequence than the risk of ignoring what was going on." The missiles were not discovered until October 14 because unfavorable weather conditions forced a delay.[5]

In an intriguing footnote, Pachter wrote that administration sources "have vaguely hinted that . . . reconnaissance flights during September were limited to 'sideways approaches' outside territorial waters or may not have involved U-2 planes. Another story says that the pilots did not find the places indicated by underground informants, or that the flights had been directed to the wrong end of the island."[6] Yet Pachter also wrote, without seeming to worry about the contradictions, that the Stennis report bore out both "Senator Keating's contention that information was available but evaluation inadequate" and the administration's argument that "no 'hard evidence' was available until October 14."[7] Ultimately, Pachter's explanation was very muddled, although he had some elements of the story right. Nor was he very concerned about deconstructing the issue since the clear emphasis of his book was on great-power coexistence in the nuclear age.

A 1964 article in *World Politics* by Klaus Knorr, a political science professor at Princeton University, purported to examine the performance of the intelligence community prior to the missiles' discovery and precisely why the US government was "surprised" by the deployment.[8] Knorr's analysis was based on a close reading of the Stennis report, but he concentrated almost exclusively on the estimative deficit, that is, the failure to predict the deployment either before or in the midst of the Soviet build-up. In the same *World Politics* issue an article by Arnold Horelick, a RAND Corporation analyst, also adhered to the line of reasoning presented in the Stennis report. Horelick subscribed to the view that the deployment had been carried out with a "rapidity that the US intelligence community found 'remarkable.'"[9]

By contrast, in the government's internal, classified literature (as distinct from the classified documentary record) it was established by no later than 1964 that an operational error had occurred. A brief article in the CIA's in-house periodical, *Studies in Intelligence,* published in the fall of 1964, clearly had the photo gap in mind, although it was short on details. The authors, Harlow Munson and W. P. Southard, pointed out,

> There may be lessons [from the missile crisis] for the policy-maker too. One
> of these was apparently learned very rapidly and expressed in the decision
> of late September [*sic*] to restore the pattern of *thorough* [emphasis in the
> original] aerial reconnaissance over Cuba. The lesson was that a nation might
> be embarrassed by the utilization of a given intelligence asset but might be
> destroyed by the failure to use it.
>
> The other lesson relates to the adversary's reading of U.S. behavior . . .
> including the failure to make a maximum reconnaissance effort between 5
> September and 14 October, which could have been read by Moscow as indi-
> cating tacit agreement. The policy-maker may be able to use more help than
> he normally gets in judging how the signals he is sending—or things that he
> is doing which may be taken as signals—will be read.[10]

Still, Dr. Sherman Kent's article in the very same issue of *Studies in Intelligence* revealed either confusion or a lack of understanding about the collection deficit. In his essay, "A Crucial Estimate Relived," Kent wrote, "Not only did [aerial photography in September] fail to spot the ominous indicators of missile emplacement, but over and over again it made fools of ground observers by proving their reports inaccurate or wrong." But there were no overflights of western or central Cuba in September, and U-2 surveillance could not have played a role in disproving reports from human sources that were coming in, as Kenneth Absher, an analyst working under Kent, would point out decades later.[11]

Probably the most influential of the early analyses was written in 1965 by Roberta Wohlstetter for *Foreign Affairs.* Her 1962 book about the December 1941 attack, *Pearl Harbor: Warning and Decision,* had become an instant political science classic for its analysis of how the Japanese had managed to pull off a strategic surprise.[12] Her *Foreign Affairs* article, however, mostly revealed how even a shrewd analyst like Wohlstetter could be misled by inaccurate accounts in the press and too much reliance on testimony before Congress. While enumerating all the intelligence collection efforts, Wohlstetter asserted that U-2 surveillance had actually been stepped up. "High-level photographic reconnaissance by U-2s over the island of Cuba was taking place at the rate of one flight every two weeks until the month of September, *when it increased to once a week* [emphasis added]." Wohlstetter then attributed the "irregularity" of the actual dates to bad weather.[13]

The article did specifically address the photo gap, which Wohlstetter defined as the "lag of 39 days between September 5 and October 14, during which no flights covered the San Cristóbal area." She credited some "inquiring Congressmen," specifically, William Minshall, for eliciting this information during his cross-examination of administration witnesses. Still, she found Secretary of Defense Robert McNamara more credible than his semi-informed critics. Wohlstetter dismissed Minshall's contention that the weather could not explain the gap because it was not as adverse as claimed by the administration. "No one pointed out at [the hearing] that weather forecasts, not actual weather, determined the schedule of U-2 flights," she wrote.[14]

Wohlstetter came close, nonetheless, to penetrating the administration's obfuscations before accepting its point of view that, prior to October 14, the "data was ambiguous and incomplete." At one point she observed that "the layman can only wonder why it was not possible to cover more than one section of the island on a single U-2 sortie, or why it was not possible to make several simultaneous sorties when good weather prevailed." Without citing Jules Witcover's March 1963 article, she speculated that "perhaps the flight schedule was sensitive to the political atmosphere." Ultimately, Wohlstetter concluded there had not been a collection deficit or a failure to obtain a true "signal" amid all the noise. Rather, "the rapidity of the Russians' installation was in effect a logistical surprise comparable to the technological surprise at the time of Pearl Harbor."[15] She seemed overly inclined to reach a conclusion that meshed with her earlier analysis of Japan's successful attack.

Arthur M. Schlesinger Jr., in his 1965 biography of President Kennedy, drew heavily from Wohlstetter's analysis. There was no attenuation of overflights— quite the opposite. In mid-September, President Kennedy took "the precaution of doubling the frequency of the U-2 overflights of Cuba." Meanwhile, Khrushchev "could hope that the hurricane season might interfere with the U-2 overflights." The real reason the deployment came as a surprise was that "Soviet engineering had enormously reduced the time required for the erection of nuclear missile sites," wrote Schlesinger, echoing Wohlstetter's key finding.[16]

That same year, 1965, saw publication of a Kennedy biography by Theodore Sorensen, who had been the president's special counsel. A member of ExComm, unlike Schlesinger, Sorensen was privy to the innermost secrets of the missile crisis. He did not reiterate the fiction that more overflights had been ordered or cite Wohlstetter's notion of a logistical surprise. Rather, Sorensen cautiously took refuge in the formulation that the president "throughout this period . . . authorized all flights requested of him." He then sidestepped the attenuation in the surveillance regime by treating every over-flight as equal and noted in a carefully parsed footnote: "Missions were flown on September 5, 11, 26, and 29, and October 5 and 7. Bad weather held up flights between September 5 and 26 and made the September 11 photography unusable. Two U-2 incidents elsewhere in the world also led to a high-level re-examination of that airplane's use and some delay in flights.[17]

Journalist Elie Abel's 1966 book, *The Missile Crisis*, was the first volume devoted solely to the episode since Pachter's. Although the text was not foot-noted or well sourced, in a subsequent, paperback edition Abel described how he wrote the book:

> I resolved after [JFK's 1963] death to piece together, within the limits of
> official secrecy as it is variously understood in Washington, Moscow and
> Havana, the fullest possible account of [the] crisis. For months, I searched
> out documents and the recollections of some three dozen men who played a
> part, large or small, in the crisis deliberations. Some drew on their memo
> ry alone. I am particularly grateful to Dean Acheson, George Ball, Douglas
> Dillon, Lord Harlech and Robert McNamara. Their recollections, freely
> given, were sharp and clear. Paul Nitze helped mightily in another way. He
> was a compulsive note-taker.[18]

Following these interviews, Abel sought out Senator Robert F. Kennedy (D-NY). During an initial interview in June 1965, Abel "had more questions than [Kennedy] had answers." Kennedy mentioned that he had dictated a lot of notes about the crisis, and Abel pleaded with him to refresh his memory before their next session. A few days later the notes were located, and for several hours the senator "read aloud while [Abel] filled [his] notebook with the kind of material no one but Bob Kennedy could have supplied."[19] This procedure allowed RFK, of course, to edit his notes as he read them.

Abel's exclusive access to indispensable material meant that *The Missile Crisis* revealed several facets that had gone unreported. Most importantly, he was the first to pinpoint the meeting on September 10 in McGeorge Bundy's office and, indeed, the very existence of the COMOR, which had been a closely guarded secret. Yet because Abel had no recourse to the docu-mentary record and relied solely on interviews with ExComm members, he did not accurately describe the decision to attenuate coverage—though he came close.

With the discovery of the first SAM installation on August 29 "the schedule [of overflights] was stepped up," Abel wrote. A few paragraphs later, he noted that while Cuba was overflown six times beginning September 5, "all but the September 5 flight . . . had limited their photographic sweeps to that portion of Cuba lying east of Havana." He attributed this attenuation not to the White House and State Department, but to the COMOR: "This was the result of a policy decision by the COMOR meeting in McGeorge Bundy's office at the White House on September 10." Abel accurately recounted some of the context for the September 10 decision—namely, the downing of a U-2 over China—but neglected to mention the near-simultaneous U-2 intrusion into Soviet airspace: "No one round the table in Bundy's office wanted to see another pilot lost or a fresh outcry raised round the world that might force the abandonment of future U-2 flights, thus denying to the United States its most reliable source of information. COMOR quickly agreed that the U-2 flights must continue, but decided to alter the flight pattern. Dean Rusk, the secretary of state, suggested that instead of covering the whole island in a single flight (up one side of a line through the middle of the island, then back down the other), the flights should be shorter and more frequent, 'dipping into' Cuban air space."[20] Thus, by 1966, as evinced by Abel's book, the story of the administration's "near-crippling caution" was essentially out, but with one significant qualification. The onus for the decision had been shifted to the intelligence community rather than attributed to the White House and State Department, where it belonged.[21]

The next year saw another journalistic treatment of the missile crisis by Edward Weintal, a contributing editor at *Newsweek,* and Charles Bartlett, the nationally syndicated columnist who had coauthored the controversial *Saturday Evening Post* article in December 1963. Although Weintal and Bartlett did not enumerate their sources, their book, like Abel's, was based on extensive interviews with key officials. They wrote about the concern within the administration after the U-2 incidents in early September but made no reference to the key September 10 meeting, already disclosed by Abel; nor did the authors discuss the decision to attenuate overflights. The fact that four overflights between August 19 and October 14 had found nothing was attributed to a "combination of bad weather, bureaucratic wrangling, and caution."[22] In this respect, their account was a step back from the version Abel offered.

The year 1967 also saw publication of a book/memoir by a senior administration official: Roger Hilsman, INR director at the State Department during the missile crisis.[23] *To Move a Nation* featured a chapter devoted to the aftermath of the missile crisis, and it dealt extensively with all the intelligence deficits (estimative, analytical, and collection). Hilsman flatly asserted that there was "no evidence of any attempt by the policy-makers to suppress information or to hamper intelligence-gathering activities. No request from the intelligence community to fly a U-2 over Cuba was ever refused."[24]

It was disingenuous to claim, of course, that the September 10 decision had not markedly interfered with the collection of hard intelligence. Simultaneously, Hilsman admitted that there had been *some* kind of delay in discovering the missile sites, presumably because he knew better than to adopt Wohlstetter's claim of a logistical miracle. Nonetheless, Hilsman asserted the belated discovery was a nonissue because it was reasonable to believe that the U-2 flight on October 14 "found the missiles at just about the earliest possible date."[25] This was a return to the formulation first offered by Robert Kennedy, that is, that the operational deficit had been meaningless.

The former INR director also engaged in some legerdemain. He wrote that the Special Group Augmented had lifted the ban on flying over known SAM positions in western Cuba on October 4, when in fact this decision was not reached until October 9. By moving up the date, Hilsman made it appear as if the administration had acted with alacrity after receiving new human intelligence reports alleging the presence of large missiles. In fact, even after these reports percolated to the top, the State Department had argued *against* resuming U-2 flights over known SAM sites, and discovery of the SSMs had been postponed by at least an additional five days.[26]

Ultimately, Hilsman found that the discovery of the missiles had to be "marked down as a victory of a very high order" for US intelligence, though "it had also been—in one sense at least—a little lazy."[27] His account was influential, as on the surface it seemed a thorough vetting of the issue by someone with firsthand exposure to the facts.[28]

In 1968 Arthur Krock published his autobiography. The *New York Times* columnist whose views had prompted so much concern within the administration wrote nothing about the intelligence deficits. Instead, he presented a story concerning Philippe Thiraud de Vosjoly, a high intelligence official in France's embassy in Washington, who supposedly provided McCone with his eyewitness confirmation that Soviet offensive missiles were being implanted in Cuba. There was a correlation, presumably, between de Vosjoly's information and the chronology of how the former CIA director had pressed his case. Krock asserted that de Vosjoly's claim, if established as factual, "would make certain sequences even more inexplicable," including the long delay before the Kennedy administration was moved to act.[29]

Robert Kennedy's posthumous memoir of the missile crisis was published the following year. Edited by Theodore Sorensen, it was taken from the journal Kennedy kept during the crisis, portions of which had been read to Elie Abel in June 1965. *Thirteen Days* shed no light on the photo gap, even though Kennedy had been present in Bundy's office on September 10 when the decision was made to restrict surveillance. The book did allow, "We had been deceived by Khrushchev, but we had also fooled ourselves."[30] Kennedy and Sorensen were short on specifics, however, apart from mentioning that the White House too willingly accepted the intelligence community's incorrect estimates. *Thirteen Days* ended by reiterating the findings of the USIB post-mortem, which, of course, had been negotiated until its findings were not critical of the administration: ". . . the same post-mortem study also stated that there was no action the United States could have taken before the time we actually did act, on the grounds that even the films available on October 16 would not have been substantial enough to convince the governments and peoples of the world of the presence of offensive missiles in Cuba. Certainly, unsubstantiated refugee reports would not have been sufficient."[31]

This recounting was virtually indistinguishable from the Kennedy administration's initial cover story about the photo gap. In contrast, *Thirteen Days* provided the first hint, from an impeccable source, about the quid pro quo: the connection between the Soviet withdrawal and the administration's secret assurance about the Jupiter missiles in Turkey.

Ronald Steel's review of *Thirteen Days* in the *New York Review of Books* led to an interesting exchange between Steel and Roger Hilsman. In the review, Steel had talked about the "failure of intelligence" and why the administration was so surprised by the deployment. Though erroneous in detail, he conveyed essence of the issue correctly: ". . . why were photographs not made earlier? When McCone returned from his honeymoon in early October, he discovered that the eastern part of Cuba had not been photographed for more than a month. He immediately ordered the entire island photographed, and the U-2s returned from the flight of October 14 with the proof we now know."[32] In response, Hilsman accused Steel of misquotation, inaccuracy, and suggestive rhetoric that had no basis in fact—since the missiles had been found "at just about the earliest possible date." The INR director appeared to have a better command of the facts, but Steel was not off the mark when he responded by noting, "I am really not sure what is the purpose of his letter, unless it be to preserve from further tarnish the reputation of the administration he served."[33]

1970s

Hugh Thomas's magisterial history of Cuba, published in 1971, contained a good account of the crisis as a whole. Because he relied on the tendentious accounts of Hilsman, Schlesinger, and Sorensen, however, he missed the administration's self-imposed restriction on U-2 overflights. Indeed, his book was a good indicator of the confusion then rampant. He noted that the "U-2s could cover all Cuba in one flight"—which was true enough but was precisely what had not happened. Thomas then indicated that "bad weather" was not the sole cause of delays in the schedule of overflights and that "some caution" was shown, though he did not go into details.[34]

That same year, Harvard scholar Graham Allison published what would become a political science staple about the crisis, *Essence of Decision.* Its "frames of reference" analysis ostensibly allowed for more profound ways of understanding the event. Although the history upon which Allison erected his explanatory models turned out to be wrong, the book is still regarded as a minor classic.[35]

Allison's formulation of the collection deficit was a more sophisticated version of Abel's account and consonant with Hilsman's. Allison acknowledged there was a gap, but according to him, it was the intelligence community that "feared" an incident, not the White House and State Department; the COMOR was responsible for attenuating the overflights. He took note of some inconsistencies in the testimonies given before Congress in 1963 by Robert McNamara and General Carroll, but they were not sufficient to persuade him that there had been a deliberate obfuscation of the record. Allison also devoted far more attention to the supposed ten-day delay that occurred from October 4 to October 14 (in contrast to the impediment caused by the September 10 decision), erroneously terming it the result of a bureaucratic struggle between the CIA and the air force over who would pilot the U-2s (which, of course, fit with his thesis about the primacy of bureaucracies). Allison also made much of the "notorious" intelligence estimate and, in comparison, minimized the degradation of U-2 surveillance. In sum, he created the impression that the latter was not a point of great political sensitivity, nor should it have been.[36]

In 1972 Gen. Maxwell Taylor, chairman of the Joint Chiefs of Staff during the missile crisis, published *Swords and Plowshares.* His memoir was the first book to be candid about the significance of the photo gap; he did not perpetrate the fiction that the missiles had been discovered at the earliest possible opportunity. However, Taylor placed the onus for the collection deficit on the intelligence community, if only because it failed to impress on the White House that the attenuated regime was dysfunctional. Taylor wrote, "September turned out to be the critical month for our intelligence collection efforts. We now know that in this month very important activities were taking place in Cuba which could have been photographed had we had a U-2 at the right place at the right time, but our limited flights were woefully unproductive for a variety of reasons. . . . when allowed to fly, they were hampered by bad weather and by operational restrictions. My impression is that the president was never made fully aware of these limitations on our primary source of information, mainly because the intelligence community did not bring the situation forcibly to his attention."[37]

That same year, Stanford University professor Stephen D. Krasner published an influential article in *Foreign Policy* that took issue with Graham Allison's claims for the supremacy of bureaucratic politics and his analysis of the missile crisis. One of the main points he challenged was Allison's emphasis on the supposed ten-day delay in October. Krasner correctly pointed to the far more debilitating decision (insofar as U-2 surveillance went) taken on September 10—although he erred in attributing it to the COMOR rather than portraying it as an edict imposed on that body by Bundy and Rusk.[38]

In 1974 Abram Chayes, the legal adviser in the Department of State from 1961 to 1964, published a book that looked at the crisis from the perspective of international law. Relying on Abel, Hilsman, and Allison, Chayes reiterated the assertion that the COMOR "decided to alter the [U-2's] reconnaissance flight pattern to avoid going directly over the western end of the island." He did not perpetuate Hilsman's legerdemain, however, about when the decision to fly over western Cuba was made. Chayes correctly put it as having occurred on October 9 rather than the October 4 date claimed by Hilsman.[39]

That same year, 1974, another Stanford University professor, Alexander L. George, published an account that was the first to recognize that the photo gap was an error at least equal in magnitude to the estimative failure. George's understanding of the issue was probably facilitated by his contacts with knowledgeable officials in Washington, particularly within the intelligence community, since he had no special access to documents. And while short on details, he captured the essence of the problem like no one had in the twelve years since the missile crisis.

George began by noting the initial obfuscation that had occurred: "An interesting and important aspect of this case concerns the fact that some of the latent risks of relying so heavily upon U-2 flights did materialize and led to a near-failure of intelligence. This part of the story was obscured in early disclosures and in testimony before congressional committees that held hearings in 1963 on various aspects of the missile crisis. In several early efforts to explain the sluggishness with which intelligence appraisers responded to available clues of the missile deployment, the peculiar role which over-reliance on the U-2 had played was not recognized or given weight."[40]

He then zeroed in on the policy decision taken on September 10. Contrary to Hilsman and Abel, however, George did not assert that the COMOR was responsible for the decision. Rather, "high-level officials in the administration . . . preferred to impose constraints on the flight paths taken by the U-2s." While he characterized this decision as reasonable, given the estimates and views of America's best Kremlin watchers, that context did not deter George from concluding that the episode "must be classified as a near-failure of American intelligence." This was a striking conclusion, at odds with virtually the entire literature. Further illustrating George's grasp of the issue, in a bibliography he included what amounted to a brief historiography of the photo gap, taking note of what all the major works on the missile crisis had said—or not said—about the collection deficit. He took issue, in particular, with Graham Allison for failing to deal clearly with the issue and adjusting the facts to fit his artificial models. "Allison gives misplaced emphasis in his explanation to the 'routines and procedures of . . . the U.S. intelligence community' and to the role of 'overlapping bargaining games' among the suborganizations engaged in the intelligence effort. . . . Allison tends to impose . . . theories on the data, which distorts the explanation for the sluggishness and near failure of the US intelligence effort."[41] Professor George returned to the subject in a 1991 essay on the missile crisis that was part of an edited volume but did not expand on his pathbreaking analysis.[42]

Although George's explication was the best analysis yet, it did not register in books or articles that appeared subsequently. In *The Making of a Missile Crisis: October 1962*, published in 1976, Herbert S. Dinerstein focused on public statements, diplomatic maneuvering, and superpower strategizing.[43] The next year, 1977, *American Heritage* magazine published Don Moser's thorough account of the U-2 and its role in detecting the Soviet missiles. Moser attributed the decision to curtail overflights to the COMOR, however, and his article gave no hint of the internal strains and suspicions over the issue. The intelligence-gathering system had worked flawlessly, in other words.[44]

In 1978 Arthur M. Schlesinger Jr. took another cut at the missile crisis, this time in a biography of Robert F. Kennedy. There were no references to the photo gap, although, if anything, the chapters dealing with Cuba were far more detailed than those in *A Thousand Days*. In large part, this was because Schlesinger felt compelled to absolve the Kennedys of any responsibility for the CIA-sponsored efforts to assassinate Fidel Castro during 1961–63. The run-up to the missile crisis was treated in a cursory manner, except that Schlesinger claimed, citing RFK, that McCone "never communicated his presentiments" about the emplacement of offensive missiles to the president.[45] The biography was also notable in that it explicitly acknowledged the quid pro quo, although Schlesinger attempted to take the edge off by calling it a "personal, but not official, pledge."[46]

A 1979 article in *Army* magazine by Justin Gleichauf, a CIA officer who debriefed Cuban refugees arriving in Florida, told the story of the Caribbean Admission Center, which had been established in early 1962 at a former Marine air base in Opa-Locka. Gleichauf, who reiterated his account in a 2001 *Studies in Intelligence* article, described taking down the first reliable report about SSMs on Sunday, September 16. However, he incorrectly linked this report to the October 14 overflight and attributed the delay of nearly a month to "bad weather and heavy clouds."[47]

Meanwhile, David Detzer's 1979 book, *The Brink*, observed, "Later, after the crisis, some critics of the Kennedy administration demanded to know why Washington had been surprised by the missiles, why it had taken so long to discover them. In fact, however, in some ways it is remarkable the American government found out so soon."[48] Detzer did describe the meeting held on September 10, although he made it seem as if it were a routine COMOR gathering rather than special meeting demanded by Bundy. Rusk's suggestions for avoiding an incident were described, but again, the final decision was depicted as "COMOR's decision" rather than one imposed by policy makers. Moreover, Detzer claimed, the decision to avoid the western and central regions of Cuba was "neither foolish nor timorous."[49]

1980s

The first article in the 1980s to raise the matter of an intelligence failure was Joseph C. Arnold's "Omens and Oracles." Arnold noted that prior to September 1962, U-2 overflights had occurred every two weeks. However, it was not clear that he appreciated the degree to which they had been attenuated, because he ascribed the surprise emplacement of MRBMs to "significant changes [that] could occur in a matter of hours."[50]

In 1982 another memoir by an ExComm participant appeared. Although the State Department had been the prime instigator of the decision to attenuate coverage, in *The Past Has Another Pattern*, George Ball, undersecretary of state during the crisis, did nothing to clarify the issue. Rather, he harked back to a formulation that had been all but discredited by Alexander George's penetrating analysis. Ball wrote, "Until [September], we had been sending biweekly flights of U-2 spy planes to overfly Cuba, but, once the SAMs were discovered, the schedule was *stepped up* [emphasis added]."[51] In the same paragraph, however, he acknowledged that no overflights occurred over western Cuba out fear of a U-2 incident. The book served to muddle the issue again, as evinced by John Prados's *The Soviet Estimate,* published in the same year. "The secretary of state could not be charged with obstructing collection since both Rusk and the White House had been pressing for better information all along," wrote Prados. Meanwhile, a thoughtful article in the *Wilson Quarterly* by Robert A. Pollard somewhat more accurately noted that "cloud cover and fear of the new SAMs had inhibited reconnaissance by the U-2s in early October." But there was no further explanation than that for the belated discovery of the Soviet missiles.[52]

The twentieth anniversary of the missile crisis marked publication of an article that contained a striking admission. In a two-page essay published in *Time* magazine, six of President Kennedy's top ExComm advisers expressed, with the benefit of hindsight, their perspectives on the crisis two decades later. The second of their eight points (the first one being "the crisis could . . . have been avoided") was a direct rebuff of Roger Hilsman's account. Dean Rusk, Robert McNamara, George Ball, Roswell Gilpatric, Theodore Sorensen, and McGeorge Bundy wrote, "Reliable intelligence permitting an effective choice of response was obtained only just in time. *It was primarily a mistake by policymakers, not by professionals* [emphasis added], that made such intelligence unavailable sooner." This disclosure was completely overlooked by the media, which focused on the other secret that had always garnered more attention, that is, the quid pro quo. The ExComm veterans maintained that there was no deal involving the missiles in Turkey; rather, it was a "private assurance."[53]

In 1984 a historian working for the intelligence arm of the Strategic Air Command (SAC) produced a classified study of SAC's role during the missile crisis. Sanders Laubenthal's account was most notable for straightening out any lingering controversy about the transfer of the overflight responsibility from the CIA to the air force in early October, which Allison had exaggerated as a reason for the belated discovery of the missiles. She also showed that SAC analysts had begun to believe that offensive missiles were being implanted, but that their concerns had been discounted during the estimative process culminating in the September 19 SNIE.[54]

Career diplomat U. Alexis Johnson published his memoir in 1984. Johnson, who had functioned as Rusk's alter ego during the Kennedy and Johnson administrations, was more familiar with the collection deficit than his former colleague George Ball. Johnson had represented the State Department at the

October 4 meeting where McCone vigorously protested the degradation of the overflight regime. Johnson was also very familiar with the intense jockeying that had occurred over the USIB postmortem when responsibility for the photo gap was a major bone of contention. Naturally, he was inclined to present the State Department in the best light: "Some have charged that the missiles should have been discovered earlier. . . . These assertions are wrong. As soon as the intelligence community got wind that something new having to do with missiles was going on in Cuba (by analyzing reports that by themselves were vague and inconsistent), additional U-2 flights were programmed. Unfortunately, weather conditions over the target area were cloudy for long periods, delaying flights already scheduled. . . . We had to be cautious about approving U-2 overflights, given the potential presented by these anti-aircraft sites for shooting them down."[55]

Johnson also wrote, "I can state categorically that there were no requests from anyone rejected by the State Department or otherwise, that could have led to earlier discovery of the missiles." This was a misleading construction, of course, as the COMOR had been led to believe, in no uncertain terms, that any requests to overfly the Cuban regions where SAMs were deployed would not be approved. Johnson did portray accurately the October 4 meeting and his own role in delaying coverage of western Cuba for another five days.[56] But ten years after Alexander George's breakthrough analysis, it was still being argued that the missiles could not have been discovered earlier.

Erroneous accounts could also be found in more specialized books about intelligence. Walter Laqueur's 1985 book, *A World of Secrets*, attempted to analyze how the "chain of evidence" had been acquired; without access to primary documents, the result was a muddled account.[57] John Ranelagh's history of the CIA, published in 1986, was the first comprehensive account of the agency in more than a decade, based on interviews and the secondary literature. Ranelagh sidestepped the photo gap issue entirely and attributed the delay to "bad weather."[58]

John McCone never wrote a memoir and never was the subject of a full-length biography. In 1988, however, Peter S. Usowski wrote an article about McCone that paid particular attention to his role during the missile crisis. With most of the primary documentation still unavailable, Usowski had to rely on the secondary literature and congressional documents; nonetheless, he managed to piece together an accurate account of the degradation in U-2 surveillance (which he attributed only to Rusk), and McCone's role in having the self-imposed restrictions lifted in October.[59]

In 1988 McGeorge Bundy's history/memoir was published. It was notable for being the most candid exposition yet of the quid pro quo, though he tried to maintain the pretense that it was something less than an official promise (he termed it a "unilateral private assurance"). But while this former secret was addressed more candidly, Bundy declined to explore the other issue that had preoccupied the White House, notwithstanding the admission he had made in 1982 along with five other ExComm veterans. Bundy's formulation in his memoir was that the system worked, and discussion of the photo gap was relegated to a footnote: "The photographs of October 14 were taken in good time, but they had been delayed first by our own caution in overflying Cuba, then by an unworthy bureaucratic squabble between the CIA and the Air Force over control of the mission, and finally by weather. If our primary interest here were in the intelligence process, these matters would deserve further attention." Bundy endorsed Hilsman's 1967 analysis as "being a good participant's account and assessment."[60]

John Newhouse, a longtime staff writer on the *New Yorker,* wrote the last book of the decade. There was no belated discovery, according to *War and Peace in the Nuclear Age.* "Cuba was putting surveillance to its stiffest test," he wrote. All the intrusive hardware—aircraft and satellites—relentlessly patrolled the skies over Cuba."[61]

1990s

The waning of the Cold War meant the gradual release of previously unseen archival documents. Because the missile crisis was the superpowers' iconic confrontation, that event was among the first to benefit from the new openness and collaborative efforts involving American and Russian scholars and former officials.[62] Although occasionally an important aspect was brought out in the open during these conferences—such as when Dobrynin successfully insisted that the quid pro quo was part of the official settlement—there were also drawbacks in carrying out historical inquiries in such a forum. It was difficult to examine key issues in anything like a systematic matter. Thus, *On the Brink,* an edited volume by James Blight and David Welch, presented highlights from a conference attended by key American and Soviet actors, yet it did not address the photo gap at all.[63]

Meanwhile, the publication of individual memoirs continued. In 1990 Dean Rusk weighed in with his account, which turned out to be less revealing than what George Ball and U. Alexis Johnson had had to say. Insofar as Rusk was concerned, "Reconnaissance overflights and on-the-ground espionage within Cuba yielded little new information" about rumored offensive missiles until the U-2 flight on October 14.[64]

That same year, Dino Brugioni, a former senior CIA officer at the National Photographic Interpretation Center (NPIC), came out with the "inside story" from the perspective of someone several levels deep in the intelligence-evaluation process.[65] Here, for the first time, was a narrative that gave depth and detail to the analysis put forward by Alexander George in 1974. Brugioni's book was a compelling account of how close to failure the CIA had come, if failure was defined as not detecting the presence of the offensive missiles before they were deemed operational. He revealed the messy, nontextbook process by which the missiles had really been detected—and it was a far cry from the coolly methodical depiction that was the dominant narrative. Colorful anecdotes and pungent quotes were sprinkled throughout Brugioni's account.

Eyeball to Eyeball had to rely on fading memories rather than the archival record and therefore contained some small but mostly inconsequential errors.[66] Still, Brugioni got the essence and import of the story down accurately, and the book was a valuable corrective to a literature rife with misleading accounts by much more prominent figures. "It wasn't the weather," he concluded at one point, "but rather the dereliction, bumbling, and intransigence of Rusk and Bundy that kept the U-2s from flying over Cuba and learning about the missiles far earlier than October 14."[67]

Despite Brugioni's book, the collection deficit was still not integrated into subsequent histories or memoirs. In 1991 Michael Beschloss published *The Crisis Years,* a history of the Cold War during the early 1960s. There was no conscious degradation of U-2 surveillance, no near failure of the intelligence community, according to Beschloss. Rather, cloud cover impeded discovery of the missiles.[68] Clark Clifford published his memoir in 1991 also. Unlike the accounts produced by other administration officials, he was frank that the "length of time it had taken to discover the missiles was dangerously and inexcusably long." But he attributed sole responsibility for the collection deficit to McCone and his supposed mismanagement of the CIA rather than acknowledging that the agency had bent to the will of policy makers.[69]

In 1992 the CIA released a compendium of primary documents to mark the thirtieth anniversary of the crisis, edited by agency historian Mary S. McAuliffe. The volume contained two of the four postmortems, along with documents pertaining to the September 10 meeting in Bundy's office, telling diagrams of the U-2 flight paths, and details about U-2 surveillance of Cuba before, during, and after the crisis.[70] The documents confirmed the contemporaneous significance of the collection deficit inside the intelligence community and the fact that the photo gap was not a merely construct of either the media or Congress. Administration infighting over U-2 overflights had been real, and they had been curtailed in September.[71]

Resistance to changing fixed perceptions about the crisis was illustrated by another document compilation published in 1992, this one by the privately funded National Security Archive. The edited volume was the first to integrate information about Operation MONGOOSE into a history of the crisis. But the photo gap received short shrift; for example, September 10 was not given any significance in the volume's extensive chronology.[72] Similarly, a book edited by James Nathan considered U-2 surveillance an important issue only insofar as the downing of a plane on October 27 over Cuba threatened a negotiated settlement.[73] Lastly, Robert S. Thompson's history, *The Missiles of October*, ignored the internal debate over U-2 flights almost entirely.[74]

One book published in 1992 did provide some new insight into the attenuation of overflights. *The Spy Who Saved the World*, the story of Col. Oleg Penkovsky, by Jerrold C. Schecter, a former *Time* journalist, and Peter S. Deriabin, a Soviet defector, was one of the few books to feature a direct interview about the missile crisis with John McCone. Although the book did not make much of the collection deficit, it quoted the former CIA director as asserting in 1988 that before he boarded an ocean liner for his honeymoon in southern France, "I left orders to overfly Cuba every day and the ship had hardly left the dock when my order was canceled by Rusk and McNamara [*sic*], especially Rusk who feared a US plane with a civilian pilot would be shot down and create a hell of a mess."[75] McCone also told Schecter and Deriabin that once he returned to Washington, he found that there had been "no" overflights in his absence. "Everybody seemed to be rather relaxed about that. I was furious, so we immediately started a program of overflights. . . . After ten days or more of bureaucratic infighting aided by cloud cover over Cuba the question was resolved by the facts of the first flight on October 14."[76] While both statements are subject to amendment by the documentary record, they conveyed McCone's general recollection about the pre-October 14 period more than twenty-five years later.

In 1993 Mary McAuliffe, who had edited the CIA document set released the previous year, published an article that highlighted what she believed was the most extraordinary revelation to come from the documents and the agency's corresponding October 1992 symposium. Washington "came perilously close to not discovering the missile in time," McAuliffe wrote. A "complex web of attitudes and events . . . almost blinded the United States in 1962 to what was happening only ninety miles from its shores."[77] McAuliffe corrected one of the errors most frequently made by pointing out that it was

Dean Rusk who pressed for a curtailment of U-2 overflights on September 10, not the COMOR. However, McAuliffe assigned most of the credit for the October 14 overflight to DCI McCone, which prompted Samuel Halpern, the former executive officer in the CIA's Operation MONGOOSE task force, to respond with an article clarifying the record. He revealed, for the first time, the maneuver that resulted in the DIA getting the lion's share of the credit for prodding the COMOR into sending a U-2 over the San Cristóbal trapezoid.[78]

In 1993 James Blight and two colleagues published another edited compilation of oral reminiscences, this time with the participation of Cuban officials, including Fidel Castro. Again, only the October 27 shoot-down of a U-2 merited extensive discussion. Castro confirmed, however, that there had been a very strict order not to fire on the U-2s, meaning that the Kennedy administration's earlier caution had been unwarranted, though the White House had no reasonable way of knowing that.[79]

The missile crisis composed one-third of a 1994 book about the Cold War coauthored by scholars Richard Ned Lebow and Janice Gross Stein.[80] Although relevant chapters exploited all of the new sources that had come to light, like the majority of the literature about the crisis, it focused on the events after the discovery of the missiles. The photo gap was not an issue. That same year, an article in *International Affairs* listed the new interpretations that had come about because of the wealth of new books, documents, and oral histories. Number 12 (out of 16) was a new interpretation of why discovery of the missiles was belated, the new understanding being defined by Brugioni's book. The delay, however, was still not deemed critical—certainly nothing approaching the importance that Alexander George, Dino Brugioni, or Mary McAuliffe had already attached to the issue. Reflecting the still-extant confusion over exactly what had happened, authors Len Scott and Steve Smith wrote, "There were no direct overflights between 5 September and 14 October." That was not quite correct in that two of the four flights (on September 26 and 29) had violated Cuban airspace, albeit briefly.[81]

Also in 1994 an American general, William Y. Smith, and a Soviet general, Anatoli I. Gribkov, collaborated on a book, *Operation ANADYR*, which looked at the crisis from their respective vantage points. Smith, who had served on Gen. Maxwell Taylor's staff in 1962, was familiar with both the intelligence-gathering and covert operations directed against Cuba. He did not mention the September 10 decision to degrade coverage and claimed that a "business-as-usual" surveillance schedule prevailed after discovery of the first SAMs. Nonetheless, the primary difficulty in conducting overflights of

Cuba was not the hurricane season, Smith wrote, but "the obsession in the White House and State Department about the political costs America would supposedly have to pay if a US reconnaissance plane were shot down." Meanwhile, Gribkov, who had overseen planning in 1962 for what the Soviets code-named Operation ANADYR, marveled over the fact that the missiles' presence had "stayed a secret for a full month" after they first reached Cuba. The book also provided the first clue as to why Khrushchev thought the deployment could be kept secret despite the U-2's known capabilities. The Soviet premier wrongly believed the missiles could be camouflaged, and no one in authority had dared contradict him.[82]

In 1996 and 1997 the Department of State released two volumes in its *Foreign Relations of the United States* (*FRUS*) series that documented the Kennedy administration's entire policy toward Cuba from 1961 to 1963. Scores of State Department and CIA documents, all vital to understanding the photo gap, were included in the volumes. For the first time, there was archival evidence that reflected the administration's deep concern in 1963 over congressional inquiries, most notably Stennis's investigation.[83]

Sandwiched in between the *FRUS* volumes, in 1996 Roger Hilsman published a slim volume entitled *The Cuban Missile Crisis*. It was essentially a revised and updated version of relevant portions from *To Move a Nation*. It's instructive to compare the 1967 account with the 1996 treatment. Previously classified information about the September 10 decision was now public, leaving him little choice but to amend his earlier account. In 1996 Hilsman wrote as follows (his emendations are italicized): "It has also been suggested that policy somehow inhibited the intelligence agencies. But there is no evidence of any attempt by the policy makers to suppress information or to hamper intelligence-gathering activities, *except for Dean Rusk's suggestion that the U-2 make peripheral flights around Cuba and only for special reasons actually 'dip into' Cuban airspace. But his motive was mainly to avoid a diplomatic brouhaha that might prevent any further U-2 flights, as happened after Gary Powers was shot down.* No request from the intelligence community to fly a *U-2* over Cuba was ever refused."[84]

Notwithstanding this incorporation of Rusk's "suggestion," Hilsman argued his position as strenuously as he had in 1967. As before, he claimed that the decision to overfly western Cuba was taken on October 4, when in actuality it was October 9. He again asserted that the October 14 overflight found the missiles at just about the earliest possible date. Indeed, he even claimed that but for the administration's watchfulness, the missiles might not have been discovered until much later: "If one wishes to consider a nightmare scenario, suppose a U-2 had flown over the sites on September 15, and construction at that time had not been far enough along to recognize anything significant. The United States might have been lulled into starting once more at the other end of the island and not gotten around to the fateful trapezoid until very late in October or even early November!"[85]

Another book published in between the FRUS volumes was Mark White's history of the missile crisis. Although his narrative included an extensive description of how Senator Kenneth Keating's charges influenced administration policy, White made no reference to the decision to attenuate coverage amid Keating's allegation.[86]

In 1997 the first book based on privileged access to Soviet archives was published: "One Hell of a Gamble," by historians Aleksandr Fursenko and Tim Naftali. The authors' account indicated just how slowly an accurate rendering of the photo gap was seeping into histories of the crisis. Although they described the September 10 meeting in some detail, the narrative erroneously stated that on October 9, "the Kennedy administration geared up for the first direct overflight of Cuba in six weeks."[87] As the illustrations in the 1992 CIA compilation revealed, a direct overflight had occurred as recently as September 29; the problem was that the incursions over Cuban airspace were far too limited.[88] Overall the authors did not give the issue the prominence it deserved in the first narrative to feature Soviet as well as American archival sources.

That same year, Harvard professors Ernest May and Philip Zelikow produced their first volume of annotated transcripts from the ExComm meetings, which had been secretly tape-recorded by President Kennedy.[89] Although the John F. Kennedy Library had originally estimated that it would take one hundred hours of listening to produce a reasonably accurate transcript of a one-hour recording, May and Zelikow claimed to have pulled off this feat in a much shorter amount of time.[90] But their transcripts, which had been prepared initially by court reporters, turned out to be riddled with errors that went uncorrected by the editors.[91] One of the major revelations from the tape recordings—the extent to which the administration mounted a public relations offensive to obfuscate the belated discovery of the missiles—went largely unnoticed.

In 1998 the CIA released a second volume pertinent to the missile crisis. This book was a declassified history of the U-2 program, originally written by Gregory Pedlow and Donald Welzenbach for internal use. Citing many still-classified primary documents, the book described the story of the surveillance regime over Cuba in 1962 in considerable detail and with few excisions. The significance of the September 10 meeting in Bundy's office was accurately conveyed and put into context. "Although these changes [to the overflight regime] greatly reduced the danger to the U-2, they slowed the gathering of information on the Soviet buildup by reducing each mission's coverage," Pedlow and Welzenbach wrote.[92] The authors paid particular attention to the issue of whether the CIA or the air force would assume responsibility for the October 14 overflight but showed that it had no bearing on the delay.

In 1999 the journal *Intelligence and National Security* published a special issue devoted to the missile crisis; edited by James Blight and David Welch, it was later issued as a book.[93] Several of the seven articles touched upon the photo gap. The topic received the most extensive treatment in an essay on US intelligence written by Raymond Garthoff, a CIA analyst during the 1962 crisis who had subsequently become one of the episode's leading scholars. After analyzing the estimative, analytic, and collection deficits in turn, he deemed the photo gap relatively inconsequential, basically arguing that the CIA's misestimates were the most significant shortcoming: "At best, however, the missile sites would only have been discovered a few weeks earlier; indeed, coverage in September in most cases would have shown nothing yet identifiable as missile site construction. Discovery a week or two earlier in October (when weather caused delay) would not have changed the situation faced by the president and his advisers."[94]

A more significant counterfactual question would have been: what might have happened if the missiles had been found even slightly later? In *Thirteen Days*, Robert F. Kennedy wrote, "The important fact . . . is that the missile were uncovered and the information was made available to the government . . . before the missiles became operative and in time for the United States to act."[95] That recognition was the basis for Alexander George's judgment that the belated discovery represented a "near failure" of US intelligence of great magnitude. Two other essays in the issue, by scholars James Wirtz and Beth Fisher, were essentially in agreement with Garthoff on the inconsequentiality of the photo gap.[96]

The analysis offered up by the special issue's editors was even more surprising. In their introductory essay, Blight and Welch wrote that the only real question was "whether Rusk and Bundy prevented earlier detection." They promptly dismissed the issue as a "red herring" for the most part, "less interesting to students of intelligence than to followers of sordid Camelot subplots."[97] And Blight and Welch's minds were unchanged at the end: "As we explain in our introductory essay, we believe the two most commonly asked 'why' questions about American intelligence in the Cuban missile crisis— (1) Why did DCI McCone, but not his analysts, anticipate a Soviet deployment?; and (2) Why did American intelligence discover the missiles only in mid-October?—are both relatively unimportant and fairly easy to answer when understood—as most historians of the crisis have understood them—as questions of historical detail. McCone got lucky (an insight devoid of practical implications for intelligence); the weather in Cuba was bad (ditto). We do not propose to consider them further here."[98]

A year later *Intelligence and National Security* published an article that took the opposite position. In "The 1962 Cuban Intelligence Estimate: A Methodological Perspective," author Gil Merom leveled the harshest criticism of the US intelligence community's performance to appear since Alexander George's 1974 article. "The intelligence product was deficient due to operational, as much as analytical, reasons (i.e., the collection effort was inadequate and thus also partially responsible for the wrong assessment of Soviet intentions, capabilities, and time tables)," Merom wrote. And, he continued, "we should reject claims such as that of Raymond Garthoff that 'the real shortcoming in the intelligence estimative process was not owing to flows in intelligence collection, or analysis.'" While making a strong case for the photo gap's significance, Merom simultaneously contributed to confusion about the issue. He wrote about the doubling of U-2 overflights in September, which was true in only a technical sense, and assigned responsibility for alteration of the surveillance regime to the COMOR.[99]

In 1999 Graham Allison, in collaboration with Philip Zelikow, published a revised *Essence of Decision* to reflect the new sources that had become available since the end of the Cold War, including the ExComm transcripts (which Zelikow was in the process of rendering). The new version dispensed with an account that had been virtually identical to Hilsman's version. Instead, *Essence of Decision* now provided a brief narrative of how U-2 aerial surveillance had been degraded. It stopped well short of depicting the photo gap as a "near failure" of US intelligence, however, possibly because that finding would have been at odds with the book's tenor of expert crisis management—a perspective unchanged from the first edition. At the same time, the authors did not go so far as to subscribe to Garthoff's finding that the photo gap was of no consequence. "Discovery of the missiles two weeks earlier or two weeks later could have made a significant difference in the outcome of the crisis," wrote Allison and Zelikow, although they did not speculate as to how.[100]

2000s

Professor Lawrence Freedman, author of *Kennedy's Wars*, wrote matter-of-factly about the attenuation of U-2 overflights in 2000. He attributed the decision to Rusk's State Department, without getting into the details of the

September 10 decision, and refrained from characterizing it as a near failure that might have changed the contours of the crisis.[101]

In 2001 Ernest May and Philip Zelikow released an extensively revised volume of ExComm transcripts.[102] While a marked improvement over the initial volume—this time the transcripts were prepared exclusively by historians—their revised work nonetheless fell short of being an "authoritative reference work." The transcripts still contained many errors, some of which modified the meaning or intent of what was captured on the tape recordings. One still had to listen to the tapes to grasp how seriously the administration regarded the controversy over the photo gap.

Jeffrey T. Richelson, author of numerous works on the intelligence community, published *The Wizards of Langley* in 2001, the first history of the CIA's Directorate of Science and Technology. Although Richelson did not highlight the decision taken on September 10 to attenuate U-2 coverage, he did convey that the photo gap existed because of "reluctant senior Kennedy administration officials . . . who feared a shootdown and an international incident."[103] Robert Weisbrot's 2001 study of the crisis, *Maximum Danger,* presented a good account of the domestic political considerations weighing on President Kennedy prior to missiles' discovery but made no effort to integrate the September 10 decision into that discussion.[104]

In 2003 the first memoir by a senior CIA officer was published. Richard Helms was a reluctant memoirist—so much so that his book appeared posthumously. His account was almost cryptic and concise when compared with Brugioni's; nonetheless, he was clear that an inhibiting limitation had been imposed on the agency.

> . . . each U-2 mission over Cuba had to be authorized by the president. We tried to keep to a monthly schedule for these flights, but cloud cover and occasional equipment problems meant that some flights had to stand down. When this happened, President Kennedy insisted that we wait for the next scheduled mission. We were also enjoined to stay well away from what we called the business end of the island—the western area where the SA-2 surface-to-air missiles were most heavily concentrated.
>
> . . . . To my considerable satisfaction, it was a report from a spy that triggered permission for the U-2 to undertake its history-making mission.[105]

That same year, Sheldon M. Stern, from 1977 to 1999 the historian in residence at the John F. Kennedy Presidential Library, published a narrative history of the ExComm deliberations based on the tape recordings, the last of which had become available in 1997. The ExComm discussions were critical to establishing the degree of concern that existed over the gap and the public relations offensive that began on October 22, the same day the missiles' deployment was revealed to the American public.[106] This information could be derived only from a close listening of the tape recordings.

In a prize-winning biography of Nikita Khrushchev published in 2003, historian William Taubman did not address the reason that enabled the Soviet deployment to go undetected for four weeks. He did cite, however, several Soviet sources confirming that the deception worked surprisingly well—up to a point. "The surprise is not that Soviet rockets were discovered before they were ready but that it took so long for Khrushchev's scheme to unravel," he perceptively wrote.[107]

In 2004 journalist Eric Alterman published *When Presidents Lie,* a book tracing the history of presidential deception in foreign policy. One of the episodes was the Cuban missile crisis. Alterman zeroed in on the quid pro quo that settled the crisis, but addressed other aspects of the crisis that had been misrepresented as well (such as Stevenson's alleged softness). But he missed the story of the collection deficit and the subsequent effort to obfuscate the record. That same year, Max Frankel, who covered the missile crisis for the *New York Times* in 1962, came out with a memoir/history. In the vast literature no one had conveyed what happened more succinctly and accurately than Frankel. As he put it, "American intelligence . . . went blind for five crucial weeks."[108]

Cynthia Grabo's *Anticipating Surprise,* originally written as a training manual for her colleagues in the intelligence community, was declassified and published in 2004. Grabo was the first scholar to point out that it really didn't matter what the intelligence community "thought" about the probability of offensive missiles in Cuba; rather, it was imperative to collect the data that permitted a firm judgment.[109] Her book also pointed to a deficit in the intelligence literature about the crisis. There were innumerable articles about the estimative failure, such as the issue of "mirror imaging," but no scholar had fully explored the relationship between the belief that the Soviets would not implant offensive missiles and the operational decision to attenuate U-2 coverage.

Beginning in 2000, the CIA began making available a database of declassified intelligence documents at the National Archives in College Park, Maryland. The CIA Records Search Tool (CREST) is searchable by title, data, terms, names, and dates. Incremental additions to the database over the years have added critical documents about the U-2 surveillance of Cuba, the September 10 meeting at the White House, the decision-making process leading up to the October 14 overflight, and the struggle over the postmortems. In 2005 Max Holland, following up the work of Alexander George and Dino

Brugioni, published a fully documented account of the photo gap, based on CREST records, and in 2007 wrote a follow-up article on the politics of the intelligence postmortems.[110]

In 2006 another full treatment of the missile crisis appeared, written by Norman Polmar and John D. Gresham. The authors zeroed in on the September 10 meeting in the White House and accurately portrayed the reason for the delay in discovering the offensive missiles. When John F. Kennedy approved the October 14 overflight, wrote Polmar and Gresham, he did not realize that "he had just saved his presidency." The authors continued:

> A delay of the U-2 flights of just another week would have allowed the SS-4 missiles to become operational. As it was, the same men who had denied McCone and the CIA permission to overfly Cuba during the most critical phase of the Soviet build-up would spend the next four decades proclaiming an "intelligence failure" by the CIA. Those self-serving opinions failed to place the blame where it rightfully belonged: on McGeorge Bundy, Dean Rusk, and John F. Kennedy. While an intelligence failure occurred in the late summer of 1962, it was *not* a failure of the intelligence community. The men and women of the CIA, NSA, NPIC, and other agencies had done everything asked of them and more. In the final analysis, the failure was one of intelligence collection policy and of officials more concerned about not risking doing something wrong, rather than doing what was necessary to be sure and secure."[111]

Also in 2006 Robert Johnson published the first history of the role of Congress during the Cold War. Although he identified the Senate Preparedness Investigating Subcommittee as one of the key congressional bodies during the superpower conflict, Johnson's book neglected to cover Stennis's investigation into the missile crisis.[112] Nor was the collection deficit addressed in the Office of the Secretary of Defense's official history of the missile crisis, published in 2006.[113]

Tim Weiner's *Legacy of Ashes* in 2007 aimed to be the first complete history of the CIA since John Ranelagh's 1986 work but with the added advantage of having mined the documents declassified in the CREST database at the National Archives. In line with the book's emphasis on the CIA's inadequacies, *Legacy of Ashes* devoted several pages to the photo gap. Weiner's account contained many inaccuracies (e.g., "There had been no spy flights over Cuba for nearly five weeks;" the photo gap was closed "at McCone's insistence."). In addition, Weiner uncritically accepted the postmortem conducted by the PFIAB, which was overly inclined to absolve the White House of any responsibility for the collection deficit.[114]

Two Canadian-based scholars, Don Munton and David A. Welch, published a concise missile crisis history in 2007. In contrast to the *Intelligence and National Security* special issue that Welch had coedited, in this account he produced a more accurate rendering of the issue and its significance. The book noted that the Kennedy administration became "skittish" on September 10 about authorizing too many flights over Cuba and that "these timid flights proved highly unsatisfactory." However, the account glossed over the intense wrangling that occurred in early October and was so concise as to be misleading—namely, "Kennedy decided it was time to have a look and rescinded the prohibition on direct overflights."[115]

The most recent history of the missile crisis to be published, journalist Michael Dobbs's *One Minute to Midnight,* picked up the narrative as of the day President Kennedy learned about results of the October 14 U-2 overflight and thus did not address the photo gap. A short afterword did not include the collection deficit as one of the political problems plaguing Kennedy in the aftermath of the crisis.[116]

Jonathan Renshon's 2009 article on the estimative failure, "Mirroring Risk," touched upon the diminution in U-2 overflights.[117] But like his predecessors, Renshon did not explore the relationship between the collection deficit and the prediction that the Soviets would not implant offensive missiles. In this same year Kenneth M. Absher, who began his thirty-one-year CIA career as a Latin America analyst in the Office of National Estimates (ONE) in October 1962, published a detailed chronology and analysis of the intelligence failures and successes during the missile crisis. He focused on the deficits in estimates and collection, terming the latter a case of "self-induced blindness." Absher also delved into the PFIAB report and pointed out its basic unfairness, without getting into the politics behind the postmortem.

Although there was nothing especially novel about Absher's approach to these issues, his firsthand involvement meant he could provide several insights that had eluded other writers. Perhaps his most striking recollection was that most analysts in the intelligence community were simply unaware of the strictures that had been placed on U-2 surveillance. Absher recalled that "among the ONE staff, there was the assumption, even mind-set, that the lack of reconnaissance intelligence meant that the U-2 had flown but not found any missile sites."[118]

Acknowledgments

For providing various kinds of support in the researching and writing of this book, we would like to thank Susan Altenburger, Mike Ballard, Barton J. Bernstein, Don Bohning, William Burr, David Coleman, Mary Lenn Dixon, Nicholas Dujmovic, Kathleen Friesen, the late Alexander George, Cynthia M. Grabo, Joseph Hernandez-Kolski, Thomas L. Hughes, Loch K. Johnson, Aaron King, Mark Kramer, the late Richard Lehman, Brian Latell, Thom Lemmons, Douglas MacEachin, Richard McCulley, Erin Mahan, Dan Mallinson, Augustine Marinelli, Heather Moore, Ken and Marlene Nyman, Jeffrey T. Richelson, Rob Spice, Sheldon M. Stern, Angie Stockwell, Alison Tartt, the late John E. Taylor, Bruce D. Thiel, Maria Toyoda, Sheryl Vogt, Albert D. Wheelon, and Fred Woodward.

We also wish to single out several editors for their encouragement and cooperation: Richard R. Valcourt, editor-in-chief of the *International Journal of Intelligence and CounterIntelligence*, and Barbara Pace and Andres Vaart, editors, respectively, of *Studies in Intelligence*.

The authors are also deeply indebted to Amy Meeker for her skill in fashioning the material into a cohesive book.

Notes

Chapter 1

1. Despite its best efforts, the CIA had discovered only thirty-three of the forty-two medium-range ballistic missiles (MRBMs) in Cuba. Indeed, the Soviet order of battle in Cuba was more complex and much larger than the weaponry designated by Washington as "offensive." The size of Soviet forces was underestimated by half, and the tactical nuclear weapons present went largely undetected. The best discussion of the issue is by Coleman in "The Missiles of November, December, January, February."

2. US Senate, Select Committee to Study Government Operations with Respect to Intelligence Activities, *Alleged Assassination Plots Involving Foreign Leaders*, 134–69. In early August, just as the Soviet build-up in Cuba was becoming manifest, high-ranking administration officials talked repeatedly at SGA meetings about liquidating Castro; indeed, the remarks were so blunt that reminders had to be issued about the "inadmissibility and stupidity" of saying such things at meetings where detailed notes were being taken. See ibid., 154–69; "Editorial Note," *FRUS, 1961–1963*, vol. 10, 923–24; "Memorandum for Deputy Director (Plans)," August 14, 1962, *FRUS, 1961–1963*, vol. 10, Document 290, Microfiche Supplement; "Telephone Call [to Rusk] from Mr. McCone," August 21, 1962, Records of the State Department, Office of the Secretary of State, Transcripts of Telephone Calls, box 46, NARA.

3. On the disclosure of MONGOOSE and the assassination plots, see Associated Press, "High U.S. Officials Reportedly Discussed Assassination of Castro in 1962 Meeting," *LAT*, May 24, 1975; Kitts, *Presidential Commissions*; and Johnson, *Season of Inquiry*. For a more recent treatment of US covert efforts to overthrow Castro from 1959 to 1965, see Bohning, *The Castro Obsession*.

4. Operation MONGOOSE did not envision direct US intervention until and unless an internal revolt erupted. It has been suggested, nonetheless, that the Kennedy administration was contemplating an overt military attack on Castro's regime by the fall of 1962. McGeorge Bundy and Secretary of Defense Robert McNamara discounted that notion during a 1987 conference in Cambridge, Massachusetts, on the missile crisis. "Covert action [was] a psychological salve for inaction," observed Bundy. McNamara asserted that the administration had no intention of invading Cuba, though of course there were contingency plans. Hershberg, "Before 'The Missiles of October': Did Kennedy Plan a Military Strike Against Cuba?" in Nathan, ed., *Cuban Missile Crisis Revisited*, 237–80; and Blight and Welch, *On the Brink*, 249.

Notwithstanding the threat of US subversion, if Fidel Castro and his top advisers had engaged in a cold-blooded analysis of Khrushchev's proposal to implant missiles on Cuban soil, they would have realized that defense of their revolution was not the Soviet premier's primary aim. Rather, Moscow was seeking to redress an acute imbalance in nuclear weaponry, and the Castro regime's interests were subordinate to this purpose. If otherwise, the Soviets would have openly installed the offensive missiles and/or built up Cuba's conventional defenses only. The surreptitious nature of the deployment, which Moscow insisted upon, was perhaps the clearest indicator that Soviet interests were being served first and foremost—and the fact that once the crisis began in earnest, there was little coordination and no consultation between Havana and Moscow. Seen in this context, Operation MONGOOSE had the effect of blinding the Cuban regime to what was strategically obvious about the Soviet plan. Philip Brenner, "Thirteen Months: Cuba's Perspective on the Missile Crisis," in Nathan, ed., *Cuban Missile Crisis Revisited*, 187–217; Blight and Brenner, *Sad and Luminous Days*, 15–18.

5. Secretary of State Dean Rusk, Secretary of the Treasury C. Douglas Dillon, Secretary of Defense Robert McNamara, Attorney General Robert Kennedy, Undersecretary of State George Ball, Deputy Defense Secretary Roswell Gilpatric, ambassador-at-large Llewellyn Thompson, Theodore Sorensen, special counsel to the president, and McGeorge Bundy, the president's special assistant for national security affairs, knew about the private assurance at the time it was given. Rumors about the deal subsequently became rampant by February 1963. In his memoir/history Bundy discussed at some length the reasons for the deception, as seen from the point of view of one of the few officials in the know. Naturally, his account tends to be self-serving and minimizes the nature and extent of the cover-up. Besides keeping the assurance secret, the effort involved the conscious omission of information, the propagation of untruths (the so-called Trollope Ploy cover story), and outright untruths. President Kennedy deceived Dwight Eisenhower, for example, probably because he was miffed that the former president had recently criticized his foreign policy stewardship as "weak," thereby violating the convention that former presidents did not publicly criticize their successors. Kennedy also kept CIA director John McCone out of the loop, despite his instrumental role in helping to detect the missiles before they were operational, and left Vice President Lyndon Johnson in the dark about the true contours of the settlement terms. Some historians have suggested that LBJ's false understanding of the missile crisis contributed later to errors with respect to South Vietnam, in that Johnson, often in the same room where ExComm had met, tried to live up to a perceived Cold War victory that had been falsified. See Henry J. Taylor, "Did U.S. Doublecross DeGaulle and Talk Turkey with Kremlin?" *LAT*, February 8, 1963; Nathan, "The Missile Crisis"; Bundy, *Danger and Survival*, 432–35; Barton J. Bernstein, "The Missiles of October Revisited: Beyond Kennedy's Cool and Khrushchev's Motives," *San Jose Mercury News*, October 26, 1997; Stern, *Averting the 'Final Failure,'* 421–25; Alterman, *When Presidents Lie*, 158–59; Holland, "What Did LBJ Know?"; and Dobbs, *One Minute to Midnight*, 5. The exclusion of McCone from the inner circle of Kennedy advisers stemmed, in part, from his continuing and close relationship with former President Eisenhower, whom he regularly briefed as a courtesy. Since Kennedy intended to withhold from the former president the true parameters of the settlement, telling McCone the truth was impossible. Holland, "The 'Photo Gap,'" 29–30; and Stern, *Averting the 'Final Failure,'* 388.

6. In January 1989 former Soviet ambassador Anatoly Dobrynin insisted at a Moscow conference that the deal he had worked out personally with Robert Kennedy included the Jupiters in Turkey, an assertion borne out when Dobrynin's October 28, 1962, cable to Moscow was later published. Dobrynin's cable read, "In parting, R. Kennedy once again requested that strict secrecy be maintained about the agreement with Turkey. 'Especially so that the correspondents don't find out. At our place for the time being even [Pierre] Salinger does not know about it.' . . . I responded that in the Embassy no one besides me knows about the conversation with him yesterday." Dobrynin to Khrushchev, "Telegram from Soviet Ambassador to the USA Dobrynin to USSR Ministry of Foreign Affairs," October 28, 1962, CWIHP *Bulletin*, no. 5 (Spring 1995), 76. See also Barton J. Bernstein, "Reconsidering the Missile Crisis: Dealing with the Problems of the American Jupiters in Turkey," in Nathan, ed., *Cuban Missile Crisis Revisited*, 55–129; Lebow and Stein, *We All Lost the Cold War*, 524–26; Dobrynin, *In Confidence*, 86–89; and Hershberg,

"Anatomy of a Controversy," 75–80. The definitive treatment of the US missiles in Turkey is Nash, *The Other Missiles of October.*

7. Pfeiffer, *Official History of the Bay of Pigs Operation,* 1:78.

8. Richard Lehman, interview by Max Holland, June 3, 2003. On the Soviets' efforts at secrecy, subterfuge, and strategic disinformation, see Gribkov and Smith, *Operation ANADYR,* 33–44; and Hansen, "Soviet Deception." The best account of Cuba's complementary efforts is Amuchastegui, "Cuban Intelligence and the October Crisis," 100–102.

According to Thomas Hughes, INR deputy director during the missile crisis, after US ambassador-at-large Chester Bowles met with Soviet ambassador Anatoli Dobrynin on October 13, Moscow "surely recognized that we were conducting massive aerial surveillance." If so, there was not much time for the Soviets to absorb and act on this information; the U-2 flight that detected the missiles occurred the next day. Hughes, *Perilous Encounters,* 112; "Memorandum from the Ambassador at Large (Bowles) to President Kennedy, 13 October 1962," *FRUS, 1961–1963,* vol. 11, 26–29.

9. Bundy, *Danger and Survival,* 459. Republicans coined the term "photo gap" after the infamous (and non-existent) "missile gap," which Democrats had exploited to such good effect in 1960. It was also referred to as the "intelligence" or "picture" gap. On the Democrats' exploitation of the non-existent missile gap, see Preble, *John F. Kennedy and the Missile Gap.*

10. Bundy, *Danger and Survival,* 459.

11. Roger Hilsman Oral History, August 14, 1970, JFKL, 15; Hughes, *Perilous Encounters,* 89.

12. In one widely publicized incident, McCone, a Caltech trustee, accused some Caltech scientists in 1956 of being taken in by Soviet propaganda when they came out in support of a nuclear test ban. McCone's relationship with Dr. James T. Killian, a former president of MIT, typified the former AEC chairman's prickly relationships with the scientific community. Killian was both President Eisenhower's first science adviser and, simultaneously, chairman of the President's Foreign Intelligence Advisory Board (PFIAB) and also the President's Science Advisory Committee. McCone, however, was of the general opinion that "scientists cause trouble" in the federal government because they tended to inject themselves into political matters rather than sticking to what they knew and were supposed to do, which was provide the best technical advice. Killian, naturally, took exception to McCone's attitude. After President Kennedy had announced McCone's appointment as the new DCI in September 1961, the *Washington Post* reported that Killian "was so out of sorts over the appointment that he threatened to resign as [PFIAB's] chairman." Although Killian promptly denied the story, it was accurate. "McCone had made a lot of enemies. [Killian] said he was going to put out a report against John McCone," Robert Kennedy recalled in 1964. "I had to call him and had a long conversation with him. . . . We finally got it straightened out." See Chalmers Roberts, "McCone Selection Criticized by Some," *WP,* October 23, 1961; and Guthman and Shulman, eds., *Robert Kennedy in His Own Words,* 253–54.

13. Kistiakowsky, *Scientist at the White House,* 257.

14. John McCone Oral History, August 19, 1970, LBJL, 7; Henry W. Wilson to Lawrence O'Brien, January 25, 1962, Congressional Liaison Files: Wilson, box 1, JFKL; Cable to McCone from John Warner and [name deleted], undated (from late January 1962), CREST; and Hughes, *Perilous Encounters,* 70.

15. Hughes, *Perilous Encounters,* 88–89.

16. *Current Biography,* 1959, 274. See also Campbell, "John A. McCone"; and Lincoln White, Diary Notes, October 31 and November 21, 1961, CREST.

17. Congressional oversight of the CIA, while remaining quite informal and limited, had increased toward the end of Allen Dulles's near decade as director. In his early years as DCI he would make perhaps eight to ten appearances on Capitol Hill to explain the CIA's activities and

budgets, usually facing few probing questions. By 1958, it was more like two dozen appearances, with far more questions and even complaints. John McCone could not know it, but 1962 would set a record (with thirty-two appearances by him or other agency leaders before Congress). Barrett, *The CIA and Congress*, 321; John Warner to McCone, "Report on CIA Relations with Congress—1962," December 3, 1962, CREST.

18. The policy of two overflights of Cuba per month, each of which traversed the island from west to east and back, was reaffirmed in mid-July. Memorandum for the Record, "Reconnaissance of Cuba," October 21, 1962, CREST.

19. The Special Group was a committee of the National Security Council that reviewed and coordinated covert actions carried out by the CIA. The committee was chaired by McGeorge Bundy, the president's special assistant for national security affairs, and its other members at the time of the missile crisis were Deputy Undersecretary of State U. Alexis Johnson, Deputy Secretary of Defense Roswell Gilpatric, Director of Central Intelligence John McCone, and Gen. Maxwell D. Taylor, chairman of the Joint Chiefs of Staff. The Special Group Augmented had the same membership as the Special Group, save that it included Attorney General Robert F. Kennedy and dealt solely with Operation MONGOOSE, a major covert action program aimed at overthrowing the Castro regime in Cuba.

20. Brugioni, *Eyeball to Eyeball*, 96.

21. Walter Elder, "John A. McCone: The Sixth Director of Central Intelligence," 1987, CIA Miscellaneous Files, box 1, JFKARC.

22. Ball, *The Past Has Another Pattern*, 288.

23. During a February 1965 interview with Robert Kennedy, Arthur J. Schlesinger Jr. asked, "How much validity is there to [McCone's] feeling that he forecast the possibility of missiles in Cuba?" "None," answered the former attorney general. Guthman and Shulman, eds., *Robert Kennedy in His Own Words*, 15.

24. Davis, "Sherman Kent's Final Thoughts," 9. At the time, the USIB (in existence since 1958) represented the pinnacle of the intelligence community and functioned as the DCI's principal machinery of coordinating all the elements belonging to the intelligence community. USIB counted among its principal members the CIA, the Defense Intelligence Agency (DIA), the National Security Agency (NSA), and the State Department's Bureau of Intelligence and Research (INR).

25. Thomas L. Hughes, interview by Max Holland, July 2, 2005.

26. Brugioni, *Eyeball to Eyeball*, 104.

27. Pedlow and Welzenbach, *The CIA and the* U-2 *Program*, 201.

28. Brugioni, *Eyeball to Eyeball*, 105. It has been said that McCone was "right but for the wrong reasons." The Soviet plan did call for the SA-2s to be ready before offensive missiles were operational, but for the sole purpose of defending them against an air attack. Khrushchev falsely believed, apparently, that the missiles could be camouflaged. Gribkov and Smith, *Operation ANADYR*, 16, 28, 39–40, 51–52.

29. Memorandum for DCI from Richard Lehman, "CIA Handling of the Soviet Build-up in Cuba, 1 July–16 October 1962" (hereafter Lehman Report), November 14, 1962, CREST, 12.

30. "Memorandum from the Central Intelligence Agency Operations Officer for Operation Mongoose (Harvey) and the Acting Chairman of the Board of National Estimates (Smith) to the Chief of Operations, Operation MONGOOSE (Lansdale), August 17, 1962," *FRUS, 1961–1963*, vol. 10, 942–43; "Memorandum from the Director of the Bureau of Intelligence and Research (Hilsman) to Acting Secretary of State Ball," August 25, 1962, ibid., 964; "Telegram from the Department of State to the Embassy in the United Kingdom," August 30, 1962, ibid., 969–70.

31. Bundy, *Danger and Survival*, 393, 413.

32. Telephone conversation between Marshall Carter and Carl Kaysen, September 1, 1962, CREST; and "Kennedy's Cuba Statement," *NYT*, September 5, 1962. Inhibitions placed on the

distribution of intelligence provide a telling measure of how the crisis was initially perceived as domestic. By late August, the CIA was not including raw intelligence about the Cuban build-up in community-wide publications unless it had been corroborated by NPIC. The president's September 1 injunction made this practice official, although Carter pretended that he, rather than "higher authority," had imposed the clampdown on this "forbidden subject." Distribution of raw intelligence was normal until October 12, when it was restricted to USIB members. Director of Central Intelligence, "Report to the President's Foreign Intelligence Advisory Board on Intelligence Community Activities Relating to the Cuban Arms Build-up: 14 April through 14 October 1962 by the Director of Central Intelligence" (hereafter USIB Report), December 26, 1963, 48–53, CREST.

33. "Memorandum from the President's Deputy Special Assistant for National Security Affairs (Kaysen) to President Kennedy," September 1, 1962, *FRUS, 1961–1963,* vol. 10, 1023–24.

34. Memorandum for Director of Central Intelligence, "Responses to DCI Questions Regarding 10 September Meeting in the White House re IDEALIST Coverage of Cuba," November 19, 1962, CREST. Refueling a U-2 in flight was difficult because the plane's frail wings could not stand much stress. Turbulence from the jet engines on the KC-135 tankers was enough to break off a U-2's wing. On the fragility of the U-2 design, see Pedlow and Welzenbach, *The CIA and the* U-2 *Program,* 47–48.

35. Pedlow and Welzenbach, *The CIA and the* U-2 *Program,* 197–99, 201.

36. Mary S. McAuliffe, ed., *CIA Documents,* 47.

37. Lehman Report, 12, CREST; Polmar and Gresham, *DEFCON-2,* 80.

38. Memorandum for the Record, "Telephone conversation with Mr. Tom Parrott on 10 September Concerning IDEALIST Operations over Cuba," September 10, 1962, CREST. According to Thomas Hughes, the INR deputy director, Bundy and Rusk "probably did not expect a useful answer and did not get one" to this question. But "simply putting the question on the record reflected the combustible atmospherics around town." Hughes, *Perilous Encounters,* 110.

39. Memorandum for the Record, "Telephone Conversation with Mr. Tom Parrott on 10 September Concerning IDEALIST Operations over Cuba," September 10, 1962, CREST.

40. Memorandum for Director of Central Intelligence, "Responses to DCI Questions Regarding 10 September Meeting in the White House Re IDEALIST Coverage of Cuba," November 19, 1962, CREST. McCone's August proposal about staging an incident at Guantánamo reflected the "invasion-minded mentalities" prevalent in intelligence and military circles. Hughes, interview.

41. Memorandum for Director of Central Intelligence, "Responses to DCI Questions Regarding 10 September Meeting in the White House Re IDEALIST Coverage of Cuba," November 19, 1962, CREST; DD/R Memo for Record, "Cuban Overflights," September 10, 1962, CREST.

42. Pfeiffer, *Official History of the Bay of Pigs Operation,* 78–79. U-2 coverage in advance of the operation would be so complete that the CIA knew the whereabouts of every serviceable airplane that might be used against the invading force. Ibid., 87.

43. "Memorandum Prepared in the Central Intelligence Agency for the Executive Director," September 10, 1962, *FRUS, 1961–1963,* vol. 10, 1054–55.

44. Brugioni, *Eyeball to Eyeball,* 137; Hughes, *Perilous Encounters,* 109–10.

45. Memorandum for Director of Central Intelligence, "Responses to DCI Questions Regarding 10 September Meeting in the White House Re IDEALIST Coverage of Cuba," November 19, 1962, CREST.

46. C. L. Sulzberger, "The Villain Becomes a Hero," *NYT,* November 12, 1962.

47. Brugioni, *Eyeball to Eyeball,* 136; Hughes, interview.

48. Lehman Report, 13, CREST; Thomas A. Parrott, Memorandum for the Special Group, "Reconnaissance of Cuba," September 11, 1962, CREST.

49. Brugioni, *Eyeball to Eyeball*, 136.

50. A total of eight officials were in attendance: Secretary of State Dean Rusk; Attorney General Robert Kennedy; McGeorge Bundy, the president's national security adviser; Lt. Gen. Pat Carter, the CIA's deputy director; Brig. Gen. Edward G. Lansdale, chief of operations for MONGOOSE; Dr. Herbert Scoville Jr., the CIA's deputy director for research; James Q. Reber, the COMOR chairman; and James A. Cunningham, deputy director of the CIA's Office of Special Activities, which ran its U-2 program.

51. Brugioni, *Eyeball to Eyeball*, 138.

52. "Memorandum Prepared in the Central Intelligence Agency for the Executive Director," September 10, 1962, *FRUS, 1961–1963*, vol. 10, 1054; Lehman Report, 13, CREST; Memorandum for Director of Central Intelligence, "Responses to DCI Questions Regarding 10 September Meeting in the White House Re IDEALIST Coverage of Cuba," November 19, 1962, CREST.

53. "Memorandum Prepared in the Central Intelligence Agency for the Executive Director," September 10, 1962, *FRUS, 1961–1963*, vol. 10, 1054.

54. Grabo, *Anticipating Surprise*, 140.

55. Memorandum for DD/R, "Status of Cuban Mission Approvals," September 11, 1962, CREST.

56. Overflights were based on weather forecasts as much as forty-eight hours in advance; the last opportunity to scrub a mission because of weather conditions was about four hours before takeoff. Missions were not flown unless the weather was forecast as good (25 percent cloud cover or less) at the time of the "Go-No Go" decision. Pedlow and Welzenbach, *The CIA and the U-2 Program*, 205. Memorandum, "Forecast Weather over Cuba and Missions Status, 5 September–14 October 1962," February 27, 1963, DCI Records (released by CIA following authors' MDR request).

57. The chief way President Kennedy imposed some discipline on the U-2 program was to always insist that the CIA complete the schedule of approved missions before requesting new overflights. Helms, *A Look over My Shoulder*, 212.

58. CIA/Office of Research and Reports, "Cuba 1962: Khrushchev's Miscalculated Risk," February 13, 1964, 2–3, 50, NSF, Country File: Cuba, box 35, LBJL.

59. Albert D. Wheelon, interview by Max Holland, May 8, 2008. John Wright, a USAF colonel and the DIA's intelligence officer on Cuba, described the same atmosphere. "Wright 1962 Diary," appendix to Elie Abel Oral History, April 10, 1970, JFKL.

60. Approximately 3,500 reports from agents and refugees were received prior to October 14, of which eight were later considered to have been valid testimony about the presence of SSMs. McAuliffe, ed., *CIA Documents*, 374.

61. The agent report that changed Wheelon's mind was not included in the 1992 compilation of CIA documents. Nonetheless, the same report was recalled by other officials during the 1992 CIA symposium on the crisis. Wheelon also noted that after McCone sidelined Kent, Ray Cline, and others for "having gotten it wrong," he ordered Wheelon's GMAIC to assume an instrumental role in evaluating photographic intelligence along with NPIC's Arthur C. Lundahl. Eric Schmitt, "Once More unto the Brink: Cuban Crisis Relived," *NYT*, October 20, 1992; Wheelon, interview.

The only other dissent from orthodoxy was voiced by the intelligence arm of the Strategic Air Command. But their concerns did not make it past the USIB. Laubenthal, "Missiles in Cuba," 12, 14.

It bears pointing out that Sherman Kent openly solicited dissenting views. Just before forwarding the SNIE to the USIB for final approval and dissemination to the administration, Kent called a meeting of his staff and all participants in the Board of National Estimates. He asked everyone in the room to express his or her view, specifically, whether they agreed with McCone and why or why not. No one agreed with the DCI, the consensus being there was not enough evidence to support the claim. As Kenneth Absher points out, however, analysts were generally unaware of just how limited U-2 coverage had become since September 10. And when Dino Brugioni personally brought up the issue to Kent, he responded "that's another ball game that we are not to get involved in." Absher, *Mind-Sets and Missiles*, 41; Brugioni, *Eyeball to Eyeball*, 144–45.

62. McAuliffe, ed., *CIA Documents*, 42. At this USIB meeting, Maj. Gen. Robert Breitweiser, the air force's chief of intelligence, wondered if a pilotless "Firefly drone" might substitute for the U-2. Someone around the table immediately suggested that "Remember the Drone" would not be as gripping a battle cry as "Remember the Maine" had been in 1898. Hughes, interview.

63. Hughes, *Perilous Encounters*, 109.

64. On September 20, Carter asked for a reconsideration of the September 10 decision, but Rusk easily deflected Carter's effort. "Thursday, 20 September [1962], Acting," CREST; Lehman Report, 17, 30, CREST.

65. Measuring the electronic reaction to reconnaissance of Cuba was one of the NSA's top priorities following the discovery of the SA-2s. On September 15 NSA collected the first signals from a SPOONREST target acquisition radar, an advanced kind associated with the SA-2. When not tied into an integrated command-and-control system, however, one SA-2 was practically incapable of shooting down a high-speed target acquired on its own radar. An integrated system was not turned on until late in October. According to General Gribkov, Soviet commanders were not allowed to activate the system earlier because the SAMs had been emplaced to defend against an air attack against the missiles, not reconnaissance aircraft. "Handwritten Draft of DIRNSA Note on Reporting Priorities," October 10, 1962, and "New Radar Deployment in Cuba," September 19, 1962, Cuban Missile Crisis Document Archive, NSA, http://www.nsa.gov/public_info/_files/cuban_missile_crisis/19_september_new_radar.pdf; CIA/Office of Research and Reports, "Cuba 1962: Khrushchev's Miscalculated Risk," February 13, 1964, 30–31, 37–38, NSF, Country File: Cuba, box 35, LBJL; Gribkov and Smith, *Operation ANADYR*, 52.

66. Unidentified officer, quoted in Brugioni, *Eyeball to Eyeball*, 139.

67. Ibid., 97.

68. As late as December 1962, the DCI remained perplexed about exactly what had happened during his absence. "I do not have an explanation of this and I'd like to know where this change in procedure came from, by whose order, and under what circumstances." McCone, "Notes for Mr. Earman," December 17, 1962, CREST.

69. Bundy, *Danger and Survival*, 419–20.

70. Richard M. Helms, interview by Mary S. McAuliffe, June 19, 1989, http://www.foia.cia.gov/helms/pdf/6_19_oral.pdf. Years later McCone said that he had "left orders to overfly Cuba every day [before leaving for his honeymoon] and the ship had hardly left the dock when my order was canceled by Rusk and McNamara [*sic*], especially Rusk, who feared a U.S. plane with a civilian pilot would be shot down and create a hell of a mess." Of course, the DCI could not unilaterally order U-2 flights. Schecter and Deriabin, *Spy Who Saved the World*, 332.

71. No minutes of the September 26 meeting are extant, but this may have been when McCone made a "strong representation to President Kennedy to remove some of the restraints on operations over Cuba," according to Richard Helms. McCone also had an unrecorded conversation with the president on October 8 and may have pressed his case then. "Memorandum for the Record," September 27, 1962, *FRUS, 1961–1963*, vol. 10, 1094–95; Helms, *A Look over My Shoulder*, 212; Giglio, "Kennedy on Tape," 749.

72. The administration's general line during this period was that the Soviet military build-up on Cuba "is under our most careful surveillance." Indeed, the opening line in President Kennedy's October 22 speech, which revealed the presence of offensive missiles, was "This

government, as promised, has maintained the closest surveillance of the Soviet military buildup on the island of Cuba." "The President's News Conference of 13 September 1962," and "Radio and Television Report to the American People on the Soviet Arms Buildup in Cuba," October 22, 1962, US President, *Public Papers: JFK, 1962*, 674, 806.

73. US Senate, *Executive Sessions*, vol. 14, 760, 765.

74. Larson, ed., *"Cuban Crisis" of 1962*, 28.

75. Walter Lippmann, "On War over Cuba," *WP*, October 9, 1962, and James Reston, "On Cuba and Pearl Harbor—the American Nightmare," *NYT*, October 12, 1962. Rusk intensely disliked both columnists, so their private source was almost certainly McGeorge Bundy, acting on President Kennedy's instructions. Hughes, interview.

76. McCone, "Notes for Mr. Earman," December 17, 1962, CREST.

77. Laubenthal, "Missiles in Cuba," 16.

78. Brugioni, *Eyeball to Eyeball*, 159.

79. "Memorandum by Director of Central Intelligence McCone," October 4, 1962, *FRUS, 1961–1963*, vol. 11, 12.

80. Pedlow and Welzenbach, *The CIA and the U-2 Program*, 206.

81. McAuliffe, ed., *CIA Documents*, 16.

82. Lehman Report, 13, CREST; McCone, "Notes for Mr. Earman," December 17, 1962, CREST.

83. "[Overflight] recommendations presented to the Special Group on behalf of the intelligence community were approved . . . without appeal to the president," Bundy would observe in February. "Every request which was presented to you was approved." Bundy to the President, February 14, 1963, Cuba, Subjects: Reconnaissance, 9/62–3/63, NSF, box 56, JFKL.

84. "Memorandum by Director of Central Intelligence McCone," October 4, 1962, *FRUS, 1961–1963*, vol. 11, 13.

85. U. Alexis Johnson, *Right Hand of Power*, 381; Pedlow and Welzenbach, *The CIA and the U-2 Program*, 206; McAuliffe, ed., *CIA Documents*, 136.

86. The flight went across the northeast coast that day. Memorandum, "Forecast Weather over Cuba . . . ," February 27, 1963, DCI Records, MDR release.

87. This meeting was also tense. McCone said that restrictions on U-2 flights "had placed the United States intelligence community in a position where it could not report with assurance the development of offensive capabilities in Cuba." Bundy took refuge in expert opinion, stating that he "felt the Soviets would not go that far." McAuliffe, ed., *CIA Documents*, 115.

88. The White House and State Department were critical of the CIA's apparent inability to collect high-value human intelligence on Cuba and its corresponding dependence on technical means such as the U-2; at the same time, however, only absolute proof was acceptable. Helms observed in 1997 that this single piece of human intelligence was the sole "positive and productive" aspect of MONGOOSE. Hughes, interview; Shackley with Finney, *Spymaster*, 63.

89. McAuliffe, ed., *CIA Documents*, 103–104, 107–109; Absher, *Mind-Sets and Missiles*, 49–51; "Chronology of Specific Events Relating to the Military Buildup in Cuba" (hereafter PFIAB Chronology), undated, 38, compiled for the President's Foreign Intelligence Advisory Board, National Security Archive, http://www.gwu.edu/~nsarchiv/nsa/cuba_mis_cri/chron.htm.

90. Samuel Halpern, interview by Max Holland, May 3, 2003; Halpern, "Revisiting the Cuban Missile Crisis," 2–3; Laubenthal, "Missiles in Cuba," 15. In 2011 DIA historian Michael B. Petersen attempted to cast doubt on Halpern's account, claiming that it rested solely on an "oral history interview conducted some forty years [*sic*] later." The 1995 oral history was recorded by Marquette University professor Ralph E. Weber, a historian of intelligence and a former scholar in residence at both the CIA and NSA. Halpern then reiterated his account in a May 3, 2003,

interview with one of the authors (Holland). Moreover, in March 1994—a year before Weber's interview—Halpern had also written a short article describing how it was agreed that DIA's Colonel Wright would take on "the task of submitting the overflight request to the COMOR." In the article Halpern desisted from referring to the tension between the CIA and the Kennedy administration but described it later. The distrust is also evident from the paper trail (e.g., Bundy's September 10 memo to Reber) as well as in the published recollections of such well-placed observers as Thomas L. Hughes, the INR deputy director. Lastly, it should noted that even in retirement, Halpern was widely known within and without the intelligence community as being an absolute stickler for accuracy. Petersen, *Legacy of Ashes*, 17, 32; Weber, *Spymasters*, 124–25; Halpern, interview; Halpern, "Revisiting the Cuban Missile Crisis," 2–3; Hughes, *Perilous Encounters*, 108–11.

91. "Wright 1962 Diary."

92. Ibid.

93. Halpern, interview; and interview of Halpern in Weber, ed., *Spymasters*, 125. The DIA's proposal formed the basis for the flurry of memos submitted to the COMOR, USIB, NRO, and, finally, the SGA in early October.

94. Hughes, "San Cristóbal Trapezoid," 59–60. For an example of the credit that accrued to the DIA, see Laubenthal, "Missiles in Cuba."

95. The October 7 peripheral overflight skirted what would turn out to be the SSM complexes in central Cuba, but photo interpreters were unable to detect any sites, presumably because of the oblique coverage. The U-2s were not allowed to fly closer than twenty-five miles from the Cuban shore.

96. *CR,* October 6, 1962, 22738. Dole inserted his remarks rather than voicing them.

97. McAuliffe, ed., *CIA Documents,* 119–22.

98. Jack C. Ledford, interview by Jeffrey T. Richelson, October 7, 1999.

99. CIA/Office of Research and Reports, "Cuba 1962: Khrushchev's Miscalculated Risk," February 13, 1964, 28, NSF, Country File: Cuba, box 35, LBJL.

100. Pedlow and Welzenbach, *The CIA and the U-2 Program,* 207. The odds cited likely pertained to an extended overflight of Cuba.

101. "I feel it would be erroneous to give the impression this [14 October] flight went where it went because we suspected [SSMs] were there. This was simply not the case," McCone would later tell CIA inspector general John Earman. McCone was apparently loathe to make missions or flight paths contingent on human intelligence reports, since he was dead set on lifting restrictions in principle. The logic behind the SGA's recommendation may have been perceived differently by others. The newly minted chairman of the Joint Chiefs of Staff, Gen. Maxwell Taylor, was acutely aware of the San Cristóbal trapezoid. Colonel Wright had briefed him by October 1. McCone, "Notes for Mr. Earman," December 17, 1962, CREST; "Briefing Paper," October 1, 1962, *FRUS, 1961–1963,* vol. 11, 1.

102. PFIAB Chronology, 39–41; Lehman Report, 30–31, CREST; USIB Report, 75–77, CREST. The pivotal COMOR memo prepared on October 5 stated that the military items "of most immediate concern are the missile installations springing up all over the island." These were identified, in order, as known and suspected SAM sites; coastal cruise missile installations; and SSM sightings that required confirmation or denial. According to Colonel Ledford, another factor that put the San Cristóbal trapezoid at the top of the list was that this area had not been overflown for too long a time. Memo for USIB, "Intelligence Justification for U-2 Overflight of Cuba," October 5, 1962, CREST; Ledford, interview.

103. Wheelon, interview. Despite the passage of years, Wheelon insisted on the clarity and accuracy of his conversations at various times with Ledford about the October 9, 1962, meeting: "I knew Jack so well. . . . we've seen a lot over the years, and I'd classify him one of my best

friends" (Ibid.)For an informal biography of Ledford, see Roadrunners Internationale, "Brig. Gen. Jack C. Ledford," http://roadrunnersinternationale.com/ledford.html.

104. Pedlow and Welzenbach, *The CIA and the* U-2 *Program,* 207; USIB Report, 32, 75–77, CREST.

105. Pedlow and Welzenbach, *The CIA and the* U-2 *Program,* 207; Memorandum for the Record, "Reconnaissance of Cuba," October 21, 1962, CREST.

106. Ledford, interview.

107. Second Conversation between General Carter and General McKee, October 12, 1962, released to Max Holland under the FOIA, December 2005; posted as "Reconnaissance Over-flights of Cuba (w/Attachments)," Electronic Reading Room, CIA, http://www.foia.cia.gov/docs/DOC_0001274180/DOC_001274180.pdf.

108. "Memorandum for the Director: Chronology of DCI's Position Re: Cuba," October 21, 1962, box 3, Rockefeller Commission, JFKARC.

109. Compilation of all of RBR's interactions with CIA, August–October 1962, based on David Barrett's examination of Russell's papers at the RBRL.

110. Ledford, interview. The switch caused some squabbling (which Bundy likened to "two quarreling children"). See Pedlow and Welzenbach, *The CIA and the* U-2 *Program,* 207–209; Bundy, *Danger and Survival,* 687n45; and Marshall Carter Memos and Transcripts, released to Max Holland under the FOIA, December 2005; posted as "Reconnaissance Overflights of Cuba (w/Attachments)," Electronic Reading Room, CIA, http://www.foia.cia.gov/docs/DOC_0001274180/DOC_001274180.pdf.

111. Pedlow and Welzenbach, *The CIA and the* U-2 *Program,* 207–209.

112. "Editorial Note," *FRUS, 1961–1963,* vol. 11, 29.

113. Brugioni, *Eyeball to Eyeball,* 200.

114. Sherman Kent, "A Crucial Estimate Relived," 115.

115. Although the CIA's NPIC claimed the right, based on its first access to the main camera film, to make the determination on what was in Cuba, the SAC's own photo interpreters, who had first access to the auxiliary or tracker camera film, were probably the first Americans to see unmistakable evidence of offensive missiles in Cuba. Laubenthal, "Missiles in Cuba," 6, 17, 21.

116. *CR,* October 8, 1962, 22841. In the Soviet Union the confrontation would be termed the "Caribbean crisis," and in Cuba it would become known as the "October crisis." Brenner, "Thirteen Months," in Nathan, ed., *Cuban Missile Crisis Revisited,* 201.

Chapter 2

1. Hughes, *Perilous Encounters,* 50, 57.

2. Ibid., 107.

3. Aside from the president, the ExComm members were Vice President Lyndon Johnson, Secretary of State Dean Rusk, Secretary of Defense Robert McNamara, Secretary of the Treasury C. Douglas Dillon, Attorney General Robert Kennedy, National Security Affairs adviser McGeorge Bundy, Chairman of the Joint Chiefs of Staff Gen. Maxwell Taylor, Director of Central Intelligence John McCone, Undersecretary of State George Ball, Deputy Secretary of Defense Roswell Gilpatric, Deputy Undersecretary of State U. Alexis Johnson, Assistant Secretary of State for Latin America Edward Martin, ambassador-at-large Llewellyn Thompson, speechwriter Theodore Sorensen, and former Truman Cabinet officers Dean Acheson and Robert Lovett.

4. The vaunted "missile gap" of the 1960 campaign, of course, had turned out to be a mirage. As Washington itself admitted publicly in October 1961, the United States was well ahead of the Soviet Union both in the number of intercontinental ballistic missiles that it had as well as in the total number of strategic nuclear weapons available in its arsenal. US emplacement of theater-

range missiles in Turkey and Italy thus only bolstered the Soviets' sense of strategic inferiority, which Moscow dared not admit. Rather, Khrushchev had apparently resolved to do something about it.

5. Bernstein, "Cuban Missile Crisis," 391.

6. Hughes, *Perilous Encounters,* 110–11. Several military leaders barely disguised their disappointment with President Kennedy's decision not to bomb Cuba immediately. One journalist, Charles W. Bailey, after interviewing Gen. Curtis LeMay, was so taken aback by LeMay's off-the-record outspokenness that he half wondered why the general had not attempted a military coup. Together with Fletcher Knebel, Bailey subsequently wrote a best-selling novel, *Seven Days in May,* about a megalomaniacal US general who plans a coup d'etat. Adam Bernstein, "Charles W. Bailey, 82: Co-Wrote Bestseller *Seven Days in May*," *WP,* January 5, 2012.

7. Technically, there were twenty-four MRBM launchers and forty-two MRBM missiles, along with sixteen IRBM launchers, but no IRBM missiles ever reached Cuba.

8. Bernstein, "Cuban Missile Crisis," 387.

9. Information provided by a CIA agent and Soviet colonel, Oleg Penkovsky, for two years prior to the missile crisis was fundamental to the intelligence community's ability to evaluate the photographs, understand the threat posed by the SSMs, and gauge their operational readiness. Penkovsky had provided the CIA with manuals for the MRBMs and IRBMs. Memorandum for Director of Central Intelligence, January 21, 1963, RIF 206-10001-10012, Mary Ferrell Foundation; Helms, *A Look over My Shoulder,* 217; Scott, "Espionage and the Cold War," 34–35; Absher, *Mind-Sets and Missiles,* 6.

10. The president later observed, "I don't think we would have chosen as prudently as we finally did" if the administration had had to act decisively within the first twenty-four hours. Schlesinger, *A Thousand Days,* 803.

11. Alexander L. George, "The Cuban Missile Crisis," in George, ed., *Avoiding War,* 225; Ulam, *Expansion and Coexistence,* 671–73.

12. Cline, *Secrets, Spies, and Scholars,* 197.

13. George and Smoke, *Deterrence,* 473.

14. "I am sure the impact on American thinking would have been shattering if we had not detected the missiles before they were deployed," former deputy director for intelligence Cline observed years later. By October 20 the CIA was estimating that the San Cristóbal MRBM site, the most advanced of several under construction, "could now have full operational readiness," although later estimates would differ somewhat. But what mattered, of course, was the perception on October 15 that there was still time, and thus the five days of ExComm deliberations in the interim were vital in helping the president achieve his preference for a limited objective, i.e., the removal of offensive weapons, rather than launch an invasion of Cuba. A later analysis on October 27 deemed twenty of the twenty-four MRBM launchers fully operational by that date, meaning they could be fired after the approximately six hours it took to fuel them; subsequently, during the February 1963 briefing by Secretary of Defense Robert McNamara and DIA officer John T. Hughes, it was stated that the San Cristóbal SSMs achieved limited capability on October 14 and were completely operational for the first time on October 28. "Commentary: The Cuban Missile Crisis," *FA* 68, no. 4 (Fall 1989): 194; McAuliffe, ed., *CIA Documents,* 228; Stern, *Averting the 'Final Failure,'* 132–37; "Extent of Cuban Missile Threat Revealed," *Aviation Week and Space Technology,* February 11, 1963, 31; Garthoff, *Intelligence Assessment and Policymaking,* 32.

15. Though the election largely went unmentioned during ExComm's deliberations, at one critical juncture, a Republican (later identified as Treasury Secretary C. Douglas Dillon) passed a frank note to special counsel Ted Sorensen. "Have you considered the very real possibility that if we allow Cuba to complete installation and operational readiness of missile bases," the note read, "the next House of Representatives is likely to have a Republican majority?" Sorensen, *Kennedy,*

688. On the interplay between domestic politics and the missile crisis, see Paterson and Brophy, "October Missiles and November Elections."

16. If direct negotiations failed to produce a settlement, the president was seemingly prepared to authorize the so-called Cordier ploy, named after Andrew Cordier, then president of Columbia University and a former United Nations parliamentarian. The scheme, first revealed by Dean Rusk during a 1987 conference in Florida on the missile crisis, envisioned a public quid pro quo ostensibly proposed by U Thant, the UN secretary-general. Cordier was to have passed the White House–authored proposal to U Thant. Blight and Welch, *On the Brink*, 83–84; Eric Pace, "Rusk Tells a Kennedy Secret: Fallback Plan in Cuba Crisis," *NYT*, August 28, 1987; Dorn and Pauk, "Unsung Mediator," 284.

17. See, for example, Hanson W. Baldwin, "An Intelligence Gap: Experts Ask If Reports on Cuba Were Poor or Adapted to Policy," *NYT*, October 31, 1962. Baldwin observed that if it turned out that estimates had been tailored, "an alleged over-centralization of intelligence was the most likely cause, because it might have created an intelligence community "unduly influenced by the knowledge of what current policy was." Ibid.

18. Helms, *A Look over My Shoulder*, 212.

19. Frankel, *High Noon in the Cold War*, 27. Robert McNamara's position vis-à-vis the collection deficit is still something of a mystery; it appears, though, that he didn't speak out against it, realizing that the curtailment came from the White House.

20. During a press conference on September 13, for example, the president had asserted, "We shall increase our surveillance of the whole Caribbean area." US President, *Public Papers: JFK, 1962*, 675.

21. Taubman, *Khrushchev*, 557. Reflecting criticism that might have become widespread, one conservative critic asked what the American public should think about a president "who, in the 59th year of the Communist enterprise, is shocked when a Communist lies to him?" James Burnham, "Intelligence on Cuba," *National Review*, November 20, 1962.

22. "The Fall Offensive of Senator Keating" in White, *Cuban Missile Crisis*, 89–114. McCone's Republican loyalties were such that "some liberal Democrats hinted darkly" that the DCI was leaking intelligence to Keating. Rowland Evans and Robert Novak, "The Cuba Expert," *WP*, July 12, 1963.

23. Keating's intelligence service was apparently drawn from the ranks of the anti-Castro *Directorio Revolucionario Estudiantil* (Students Revolutionary Directorate or DRE), which infiltrated Cuba and put out reports that were cited by influential columnists, such as the *Miami News*'s Hal Hendrix, who would win a Pulitzer Prize in 1963 for his reporting on the Soviet build-up. On Keating's sources, see Peter Kihss, "Exiles Describe 15 Missile Bases," *NYT*, October 24, 1962; Evans and Novak, "The Cuba Expert"; "Parallels to Keating Data on Cuba Noted," *WP*, August 3, 1963; Paterson, "The Historian as Detective," 67–70; and Holland, "A Luce Connection."

24. Oval Office Meeting, Tape No. 32, 11 A.M., October 22, 1962, Presidential Recordings, JFKL. President Kennedy's full statement was "Now the point of the matter is, these things [missiles] are so *mobile* that it doesn't require a helluva lot of work. You don't want them to make like there's been work for two months here that, ah, our fellas knew about. In fact, it's the *mobile* [MRBMs]—the *other* ones [IRBMs] are *not* ready, and they're the ones [that are] far more so[phisticated] . . . the[se] other ones [MRBMs] are *mobile* and can move rather quickly, so that. . . . Listen: you don't want to say the blockhouses are complete, and so on. I mean, I wouldn't . . . I'd make sure this doesn't look like it's been going on for months."

Although widely praised initially, the published transcripts on the missile crisis produced by Ernest May and Philip Zelikow are not reliable, as Stern persuasively documented in *Averting the 'Final Failure,'* 427–40. Compare the above passage, for example, to the renditions offered in May and Zelikow, eds., *The Kennedy Tapes*, 220; and, later, Zelikow and May, eds., *The Presi-*

dential Recordings, 29–30. In their first rendition (1997), May and Zelikow transcribe Kennedy as saying: "Now, the point of the matter is, these things [missiles] are so mobile that it doesn't require a hell of a lot of work just to make it look like they've been [unclear] working too much here. The other ones are not ready, and they're the ones that are [unclear] more. The other ones are mobile and can move rather quickly. So . . . We ought to take the blockhouses and so on, and make sure . . ."

In their second cut (2001) at the same conversation, Zelikow and May transcribed the president as saying: "Now, the point of the matter is, these things [missiles] are so mobile that it doesn't require a hell of a lot of work. You don't want to make it look like they've been working for two months here. Before we knew about it. The fact is the mobile [MRBMs] . . . The other ones [the IRBMs] are not ready, and they're the ones that require more [construction]. These other ones are mobile and can move rather quickly. So that the president . . . we don't want to say the blockhouses are complete and so on. And we have to make sure it doesn't look like it's been going on for months."

Clearly, scholars must listen to the original tape recordings to render accurate quotations.

25. McAuliffe, ed., *CIA Documents,* 7–8. A later CIA analysis would fix September 17–18 as the earliest date after which SSMs might have been detected had there been constant and intrusive aerial surveillance. CIA/Office of Research and Reports, "Cuba 1962: Khrushchev's Miscalculated Risk," February 13, 1964, 2–3, NSF, Country File: Cuba, box 35, LBJL.

26. Stern, *Averting the 'Final Failure,'* 143. RFK, of course, had initially opposed the September 10 decision to alter the U-2 surveillance regime. Hilsman had been one of the intelligence officials who argued against McCone's dire predictions, and had worried more about the CIA and Pentagon entrapping the president into an unnecessary confrontation with Moscow over Cuba. "Memorandum from the Director of the Bureau of Intelligence and Research (Hilsman) to Secretary of State Rusk," September 1, 1962, *FRUS, 1961–1963,* vol. 10, 1014–22.

27. Stern, *Averting the 'Final Failure,'* 143.

28. Ibid., 143–44.

29. Ibid., 152.

30. Ibid.

31. According to Amuchastegui, refugees' debriefings and correspondence between Cubans and their relatives or friends in the United States were both utilized as part of the KGB-engineered deception campaign. Amuchastegui, "Cuban Intelligence and the October Crisis," 100–101.

32. Stern, *Averting the 'Final Failure,'* 152–53.

33. Ibid., 153.

34. Ibid.; "Minutes of the 507th Meeting of the National Security Council," October 22, 1962, *FRUS, 1961–1963,* vol. 11, 154. According to the minutes from this NSC meeting, the "possibility of an attack on an overflying American plane led to a restriction on the number of U-2 flights." However, the September 10 decision was much more about flight *paths* than the *number* of flights.

35. Stern, *Averting the 'Final Failure,'* 153, 154. If not outright misleading, Kennedy's assertion was premature at best. Again, it would later be established that recognizable equipment reached the vicinity of San Cristóbal on September 17–18, and that was subsequently fixed as the earliest date after which U-2 surveillance might have gathered evidence of SSMs in Cuba. Lehman Report, 21, CREST.

36. Stern, *Averting the 'Final Failure,'* 178.

37. Ibid. Krock's column that morning had raised the question of whether the president's nationwide address was "a contrivance of political and public relations art," aimed at influencing the November election. Krock had been friends with the president's father, former ambassador Joseph P. Kennedy, since 1935 and knew the sons well. But ever since the 1960 campaign,

relations between the conservative columnist and the Kennedys had been cool. The influential Krock persisted in casting a critical eye on the administration, much to the dismay of the Kennedys. Arthur Krock, "The Preparations Anything but 'Secret,'" *NYT*, October 23, 1962; Krock, *Memoirs*, 328, 366.

38. "Memorandum of Meeting of Executive Committee of the NSC," October 23, 1962, *FRUS, 1961–1963*, vol. 11, Document 370, Microfiche Supplement.

39. When McCone briefed congressional leaders the day before, he neatly, if disingenuously, sidestepped the gap in U-2 surveillance. Aerial reconnaissance on September 5 indicated no offensive weapons, McCone stated, and the flights for September 17 and September 22 had been aborted because of adverse weather. Stern, *Averting the 'Final Failure,'* 159–60.

40. Ibid., 178. Reston was much more favorably inclined toward the administration than Arthur Krock.

41. US Senate, *Executive Sessions*, vol. 14, 689, 716.

42. Stern, *Averting the 'Final Failure,'* 161–62. In five days, on October 27, an SA-2 would down a U-2 piloted by Maj. Rudolph Anderson of the USAF.

43. In March 1963 Arthur Krock would write harshly about the administration's stance toward the media during the missile crisis. The Kennedy administration's "news management policy . . . has been enforced more cynically and boldly than by any previous administration in a period when the United States was not in a war," he wrote in *Fortune* magazine. In the modern era, however, Kennedy's attention to the press was more the rule and not the exception. One of the lasting insights that comes from listening to the secret recordings made during the Kennedy, Johnson, and Nixon administrations is the degree to which these presidents sought to influence and thwart media coverage. While such sensitivity has often been the subject of speculation and comment, the tapes provide documentation of almost ceaseless efforts to shape press coverage. Krock, "Mr. Kennedy's Management of the News"; see also Robert Hotz, "Editorial: Loud but Late," *Aviation Week and Space Technology,* February 11, 1963. For a vivid example of media management just after LBJ took power, see Holland, *The Kennedy Assassination Tapes*, 92–103.

44. In point of fact, the Republicans would desist from criticism of the president until the crisis abated. Milton Viorst, "GOP Ends the Truce on JFK's Cuba Policy," *New York Post,* October 31, 1962.

45. Stern, *Averting the 'Final Failure,'* 178.

46. Undated memorandum re "Blank Space in Overflying Cuba," Document CC03336, Cuban Missile Crisis Digital Collection, National Security Archive.

47. Stern, *Averting the 'Final Failure,'* 179.

48. The DCI had first shared his personal estimate with key members of Congress in mid-August, just after telling the president about his premonition for the first time. McCone then continued to warn Congress about the possibility of SSMs until they were actually found. It was this kind of frankness that created the impression that McCone was "always straightforward with Congress," and the DCI actively cultivated good relations with Capitol Hill. McAuliffe, ed., *CIA Documents*, 13; "Chronology of Specific Events Relating to the Military Buildup in Cuba," undated, JFKARC, 44; Brugioni, *Eyeball to Eyeball*, 66; Campbell, "John A. McCone," 53.

McCone later stated that McNamara, Rusk, and Bundy "should have been more alert to the possibility or probability that the Soviets were planning to put missiles in Cuba, but they would never accept that probability because the missiles hadn't actually arrived. . . . This was the position I took, and I preached it to everybody, but nobody listened. Although they were warned of the possibility, it was a judgment factor . . . I was dealing with intuition and judgment which you often use in business. But I was a loner." "Conversation with John McCone," 1987–1988, Conversations with History, Institute of International Studies, University of California, Berkeley, http://conversations.berkeley.edu/content/john-mccone.

49. "Memorandum of Meeting of Executive Committee of the NSC," October 23, 1962, *FRUS, 1961–1963*, vol. 11, Document 370, Microfiche Supplement.

50. Ibid.; and Stern, *Averting the 'Final Failure,'* 178–79. When Krock's name came up, several ExComm participants chuckled, prompting Kennedy to tease McCone: "Maybe you're a friend of his." Ibid.

51. Marshall Carter, "Memorandum for the Record," October 30, 1962, CREST; "NSC Executive Committee Record of Action," November 29, 1963, *FRUS, 1961–1963*, vol. 11, Document 560, Microfiche Supplement.

52. John Finney, "Questions on Lack of a Warning on Blockade Rife in the Capital," *NYT*, October 26, 1962.

53. James Reston, "Kennedy's New Diplomacy in Cuba," *NYT*, October 26, 1962.

54. "Executive Memorandum No. 64," October 29, 1962, CREST. CIA official Herbert Scoville argued that the "proposed line" would improve (and be more in accord with the facts) if it stated that the successful flights in September and October "concentrated on developing information on areas not previously covered by photography since the August build-up." Ibid.

55. Between September 10 and the October 14, there had been five days—September 17, 26, 28, 29, and October 7—during which the weather over most of Cuba had been good, and an additional ten days when the cloud cover over either the western (two days) or central regions (eight days) was light enough to permit an overflight. Memorandum, "Forecast Weather over Cuba . . . ," February 27, 1963, DCI Records, MDR release; McAuliffe, ed., *CIA Documents*, 344.

56. "Memorandum of a Meeting of Executive Committee of the NSC, October 31, 1962, *FRUS, 1961–1963*, vol. 11, Document 474, Microfiche Supplement.

57. Baldwin, "An Intelligence Gap," *NYT*, October 31, 1962. In a November 3 memorandum, CIA official Ray Cline took an early stab at explaining the seemingly abrupt discovery of SSMs. His two-page memo suggested that "positive identification of the type of MRBM sites observed in Cuba would be difficult even with good quality photography prior to the arrival of the missile trailer and launcher-erector equipment at the site." This analysis prefigured the findings of what would become known as the USIB postmortem. Memo, "Time Factors in Construction of Soviet Missile Bases in Cuba," November 3, 1963, *FRUS, 1961–1963*, vol. 11, Document 490, Microfiche Supplement.

58. Joseph Alsop, "The Real Intelligence Story," *WP*, November 2, 1962.

59. Arthur Krock, "After the Crisis," *NYT*, October 28, 1962; Memorandum, "Forecast Weather over Cuba . . . ," February 27, 1963, DCI Records, MDR release.

60. E. W. Kenworthy et al., "Cuban Crisis: A Step-By-Step Review," *NYT*, November 3, 1963; Relman Morin, "Russians Caught in the Act," *WS*, November 5, 1962.

61. Burnham, "Intelligence on Cuba," 396.

62. Ibid.

63. Martin Weil, "Columnist David Lawrence, 84, Dies," *WP*, February 12, 1973.

64. David Lawrence, "Cuban Crisis Vindicates the U-2," *WS*, October 31, 1962; David Lawrence, "Truth about the Cuban Missiles," *WS*, November 6, 1962. Lawrence was perhaps the most prominent of the president's critics, finding fault with virtually every aspect of Kennedy's policy during the crisis. He also wrote that a blockade should have been imposed long before the offensive missiles arrived—i.e., from the moment the build-up was detected—and even called for a reinvestigation of the Bay of Pigs debacle, à la conservative Senator Barry Goldwater (R-AZ). David Lawrence, "Why the Delay in Cuban Action?" *WS*, October 24, 1962; David Lawrence, "Dealing with Cuban Missiles," *WS*, October 24, 1962; David Lawrence, "'Hollow Victory' for U.S. in Cuba," *WS*, October 30, 1962; David Lawrence, "Lucky America?" *USNWR*, December 31, 1962; "U.S. and the Bay of Pigs Fiasco—Question of Military Competence or Civilian Interference Is Raised"; and "The Story of How President Kennedy Upset Cuban Invasion of April, 1961," *USNWR*, February 4, 1963.

65. "Briefing Paper for the President's Press Conference," November 20, 1962, Document CC02467, Cuban Missile Crisis Digital Collection, National Security Archive.

66. "NSC Executive Committee Record of Action," November 29, 1962, *FRUS, 1961–1963*, vol. II, Document 560, Microfiche Supplement.

67. McCone, Memorandum for the Record, November 29, 1962, *FRUS, 1961–1963*, vol. II, 543–45.

68. Ibid.

69. Warner, Memorandum for the Record, November 29, 1962, CREST. Russell indicated that he did not take charges of "poor intelligence in the Cuban crisis" seriously.

70. Alsop and Bartlett, "In Time of Crisis."

71. In early November, the president had also authorized McCone to meet with *Life*'s John Dille to discuss that magazine's coverage of the missile crisis. The *Life* article turned out to be relatively superficial. "Meeting of Executive Committee of the NSC," November 5, 1962, *FRUS, 1961–1963*, vol. II, Document 492, Microfiche Supplement.

72. A recent critique of the article is in Alterman, *When Presidents Lie*, 93–95, 118–19. The tendentious *Saturday Evening Post* article was probably a factor in Arthur Krock's *Fortune* article in March 1963, which criticized the Kennedy administration's news management policy.

73. Stevenson was the first person to raise (on October 17) the question of removing the Jupiters from Turkey as a quid pro quo; it was actually a brave thing to do because, at the time, there was a lot of posturing about not ceding an inch to the Soviets. The president basically adopted the idea during the second week of deliberations. The major difference was that Stevenson backed U Thant's plan for jointly suspending the quarantine and halting construction of the missile sites, whereas the president insisted that the Soviets immediately render the missiles inoperable. In addition, Kennedy placed a greater emphasis on appearing steely and determined and thus wanted to keep the trade of missiles secret, while the UN ambassador was open to making it public (although in the end, the president was willing to devise the Cordier ploy). It was also true that on October 20 Stevenson broached the idea of including a US evacuation of the Guantánamo naval base as part of any deal, a proposal President Kennedy sharply rejected. However, no one ever criticized Secretary of Defense Robert McNamara for having hinted, also on October 20, that it might be advisable to accept a time limit on the US occupation of Guantánamo. Alsop and Bartlett savaged Stevenson in their article because that's what Robert F. Kennedy wanted; finding a scapegoat for "appeasement" made it that much easier to conceal the truth—namely, that President Kennedy had cut a deal. Stern, *Averting the 'Final Failure,'* 93, 135; Stern e-mail to Holland, September 1, 2010; Elie Abel Oral History, April 10, 1970, JFKL, 5.

74. Bundy later opined that "Stevenson unwisely chose to take the matter seriously, and Kennedy unwisely failed to clear it up by a ringing denial of the false charge. Each man concentrated on the error of the other, and lasting damage was done." Bundy, *Danger and Survival*, 459. Stevenson's reaction to the article was described in Martin, *Adlai Stevenson and the World*, 741–47. For a contemporaneous account, see Drew Pearson, "'Inside' Story on Adlai Stevenson," *WP*, December 12, 1962; E. W. Kenworthy, "Adlai Case Aftermath," *NYT*, December 17, 1962. Aside from depicting Stevenson unfairly as an appeaser, the *Saturday Evening Post* article was also the first to propagate the Trollope Ploy fable. Stern, *Averting the 'Final Failure,'* 421–25.

75. Alsop and Bartlett, "In Time of Crisis," 20.

76. Bundy, *Danger and Survival*, 459. Bundy was probably referring to the kind of internecine feuding that absorbed the press during the administrations of Nixon (Kissinger vs. everybody), Carter (Vance vs. Brzezinski), and Reagan (Shultz vs. Weinberger).

77. "Contradictions on Cuba," *CR*, March 6, 1963.

78. Holland, "A Luce Connection," 143. During the annual Gridiron dinner in 1963, one skit would feature a "KIA" (Keating Intelligence Agency) that rivaled the CIA. Dorothy McCardle, "Old Miss, CIA, JFK In-Laws All Roast in Gridiron Pan," *WP*, March 10, 1963.

79. The best account of the unsettled aftermath is Coleman, "The Missiles of November, December, January, February."

80. Schlesinger, *A Thousand Days,* 840–41.

Chapter 3

1. In chronological order the postmortems were as follows: Memorandum for the Director of Central Intelligence, "CIA Handling of the Soviet Build-up in Cuba, 1 July–16 October 1962," November 14, 1962 (the Lehman Report), CREST; Memorandum for DCI McCone from J. S. Earman, Inspector General, "Inspector General's Survey of Handling of Intelligence Information during the Cuban Arms Build-up," November 20, 1962 (hereafter IG Survey), CREST; "Report to the President's Foreign Intelligence Advisory Board on Intelligence Community Activities Relating to the Cuban Arms Build-up (14 April through 14 October 1962) by the Director of Central Intelligence," December 26, 1963 (hereafter USIB Report), CREST; and "Report of the President's Foreign Intelligence Advisory Board on the Soviet Military Build-up in Cuba," February 4, 1963 (hereafter PFIAB Report), in McAuliffe, ed., *CIA Documents,* 361–71. McCone ordered the first two postmortems in his capacity as DCI (Lehman's on October 27 and the IG Survey in mid-November); the USIB postmortem was instigated on November 14 as the result of a PFIAB request and a request by President Kennedy; and the PFIAB commenced its postmortem upon receipt of the USIB Report. The operational deficit was addressed in each postmortem and was easily the most controversial aspect in each one. See Holland, "Politics of Intelligence Post-Mortems."

All four postmortems were released gradually following the end of the Cold War. Four pages of the Lehman Report and the entire PFIAB postmortem were excerpted in McAuliffe's 1992 volume of edited CIA documents. A sanitized version of the USIB Report first became available in 1998 under provisions of the John F. Kennedy Assassination Records Collection Act; in 2004 more complete versions of the USIB and Lehman Reports were released via CREST at NARA. The IG Survey was footnoted in an official CIA history of the U-2, published in 1998 but not released until June 2007 in a new tranche of CREST documents. Holland, "More on Post-Mortems."

2. Kovar, "Mr. Current Intelligence"; Dennis Hevesi, "Richard Lehman, 83, Creator of Crucial Intelligence Memo," *NYT,* February 24, 2007.

3. Kovar, "Mr. Current Intelligence," 57; Lehman Report, CREST. Strictly speaking, Deputy Director Pat Carter was the first official to ask for a postmortem; Carter probably anticipated that criticism for the photo gap would be directed at him since he had been acting DCI when the coverage was degraded. In response, James Reber, chairman of the COMOR, submitted a memorandum to Carter on October 24, 1962. Reber concluded that nothing had indicated "that any other approach would have served us better." Of course, Reber had some reason to be concerned, too, as the White House might well suggest (and indeed did) that the COMOR, charged with developing overflight requirements, had failed to keep the president fully apprised of the dysfunctionality of the surveillance regime after September 10. Memorandum for DDCI, "Historical Analysis of U-2 Overflights of Cuba," October 24, 1962, released under FOIA, December 2005.

4. Walter Elder, "John A. McCone: The Sixth Director of Central Intelligence," 1987, box 1, CIA Miscellaneous Files, JFKARC.

5. Portions of the Lehman Report are still classified, and the annexes are apparently unavailable. One of the senior CIA officials known to have read the report was Dr. Herbert Scoville Jr., the deputy director of research. He called it an "excellent presentation of the facts" but differed in one significant aspect. Scoville maintained that the most important objective of the October 14 mission was coverage of the co-called San Cristóbal trapezoid, while Lehman suggested

overflying an advanced SAM site in western Cuba had actually been a higher priority. McCone meanwhile insisted that it was "erroneous to give the impression [that] this flight went where it went because we suspected [offensive missiles] were there. This was simply not the case." These divergent views reflected the intense struggle that occurred in early October over resuming more intrusive overflights. Scoville was apparently more familiar than McCone with how the COMOR had fashioned its requirement, while the DCI was closer to the rationales that were argued within the Special Group Augmented and the Oval Office. Memo, DDR to CDCI, "Comments on Lehman Paper," November 7, 1962; "Notes for Mr. Earman," December 17, 1962, CREST.

6. Lehman Report, CREST.

7. Lehman, interview, April 14, 2003.

8. Lehman Report, CREST.

9. Bundy to the President, February 14, 1963, Cuba, Subjects: Reconnaissance, 9/62–3/63, NSF, box 56, JFKL.

10. Earman wrote, "On 21 November you asked me to consider two additional conclusions for my report." Memorandum for DCI, "Inspector General's Report on Handling of Intelligence Information during the Cuban Arms Build Up (Revised), dated 20 November 1962," November 26, 1962, CREST.

11. Ibid.

12. Ibid.

13. Ibid.

14. As with the Lehman Report, Scoville reviewed the IG postmortem. "From all the information available to the DD/R, it is believed that the report of the Inspector General is factually accurate," Scoville wrote. Memorandum for Deputy Director of Central Intelligence, "Handling of Intelligence Information during the Cuban Arms Build Up," December 15, 1962, CREST.

15. Memorandum for Director of Central Intelligence, "Department of State's Objections to the Report on the Cuban Arms Build Up," March 12, 1963, CREST. Simultaneously, the president asked McCone personally for the same type of report. Memorandum of the Record, "Meeting with PFIAB," December 7, 1962, CREST.

16. The PFIAB, originally called the President's Board of Consultants on Foreign Intelligence Activities, was created by Eisenhower at the recommendation of the second Hoover Commission. *The President's Foreign Intelligence Advisory Board* (Washington, DC: Hale Foundation, 1981).

17. At the time, one of the ways the DCI coordinated the intelligence effort was through the machinery of the USIB, which consisted of representatives from all the intelligence agencies— e.g., the deputy director of the CIA; the directors of INR, DIA, and NSA; the intelligence director for the Joint Chiefs of Staff; an assistant director from the FBI; and the assistant general manager for administration of the Atomic Energy Commission. The heads of army, navy, and air force intelligence also attended USIB meetings as observers. The USIB met weekly and, among other things, rendered advice on National Intelligence Objectives and the production of National Intelligence Estimates, two of the DCI's most important responsibilities. Statement for the Record, Document 21b, Central Intelligence Agency, vol. 2, box 9, NSF, Presidential Papers, LBJL; Memorandum of the Record, "Meeting with PFIAB, 7 December 1962," December 10, 1962, CREST.

18. The other working group members (as chosen by their respective agencies) were William McAfee, director of the Coordination Staff in the State Department's INR; Samuel Halpern, executive officer of the CIA's Task Force W on Cuba; a representative (name unknown) from the DIA's Office of Estimates; the chief (name unknown) of the DIA's Current Intelligence Indications Center; the deputy chief (name unknown) of the NSA's Policy Division; and the CIA's deputy assistant director (name unknown) for Central Reference.

19. DD/R Memo, "Cuban Missile Crisis," November 13, 1962, CREST.

20. Memorandum for Deputy Director (Research), "Interagency Review of Intelligence Activities Relating to the Cuba Situation," November 26, 1962, CREST.

21. The most detailed memorandum about the pivotal September 10 meeting is published in the *FRUS* volume, but it was prepared long after the fact—on February 28, 1963—by someone who was apparently not in attendance. More contemporaneously, Gen. Marshall "Pat" Carter, acting DCI, wrote only a one-paragraph summary about the unusual meeting, and the only other record is a memo written the next day, September 11, by Thomas A. Parrott, executive secretary of the NSC Special Group, who did not attend the meeting. All three memos are in agreement that Secretary of State Dean Rusk, national security adviser McGeorge Bundy, Attorney General Robert F. Kennedy, and acting DCI Pat Carter were present. The detailed *FRUS* memo also notes that Gen. Edward Lansdale, Dr. Herbert Scoville, James Reber, and James Cunningham were in attendance. Carter's contemporaneous summary states that two more principal officials, Secretary of Defense Robert McNamara and Gen. Maxwell Taylor, also attended, while Parrott's September 11 memo does not list McNamara and Taylor as among the principals at the meeting. See "Memorandum Prepared in the Central Intelligence Agency for the Executive Director," dated September 10, 1962 (but prepared February 28, 1963), *FRUS, 1961–1963*, vol. 10, 1054–55; "Acting," September 10, 1962, *FRUS, 1961–1963*, vol. 10, Document 296, Microfiche Supplement; Memorandum for the Record, "Telephone Conversation with Mr. Tom Parrott on 10 September Concerning IDEALIST Operations over Cuba," September 10, 1962, CREST; Parrott Memorandum for the Special Group, "Reconnaissance of Cuba," September 11, 1962, CREST; Memorandum for the Director, "White House Meeting on 10 September 1962 on Cuban Overflights," March 1, 1963, in McAuliffe, ed., *CIA Documents*, 61–62.

22. Roger Hilsman Oral History, August 14, 1970, JFKL, 4, 6, 15.

23. Hilsman was furious with Rusk for not consulting him beforehand, and the INR director energetically opposed the nomination of an "alley fighter" who was a "very rich . . . very militant, anti-communist Republican." Ibid., 8–9, 13, 15; Memorandum for the Record, "Telephone Conversation with Mr. Tom Parrott on 10 September Concerning IDEALIST Operations over Cuba," September 10, 1962, CREST.

24. "Conversation between General Carter and Roger Hilsman," October 16, 1962, *FRUS, 1961–1963*, vol. 11, Document 323, Microfiche Supplement.

25. Hilsman Oral History, 6, 15, 16; Elie Abel Oral History, April 10, 1970, 12.

26. Hilsman, *To Move a Nation*, 187–88.

27. Hughes, *Perilous Encounters*, 117–18.

28. USIB Report, 89, CREST. The language quoted is from what appears to be the sixth draft and uses the handwritten changes that were presumably incorporated in the seventh draft. The original language in the sixth draft stated, " . . . but this delay was not critical, because photography obtained prior to about 17 October would not have been sufficient to warrant action or to solicit support from Western Hemisphere or NATO Allies." Presumably, the wording was changed because this formulation was at odds with the facts, i.e., photo coverage from October 14 had been sufficient to "warrant action." Moreover, introducing the element of exactly when the photographs might prove persuasive to other allied countries further muddied the issue. Ibid. IG Jack Earman was apparently able to insert only one concession in the USIB Report: that despite the skimpiness of the paper trail, operational elements in charge of U-2 overflights at least "were under the impression" that restrictions had been imposed on overflying known SA-2 sites. Ibid., 74.

29. In light of what later came to be understood as an extensive "denial and deception" program by the Soviets, the USIB Report interestingly noted that "any post-mortem . . . must take into account whether there was a planned Soviet deception program to help cover their activities. There is little hard evidence on this pro or con, and may never be unless there is a knowl-

edgeable Soviet defector." Ibid., 42; Hansen, "Soviet Deception in the Cuban Missile Crisis; Amuchastegui, "Cuban Intelligence and the October Crisis."

30. The USIB Report was formally called "Report to the President's Foreign Intelligence Advisory Board . . . by the Director of Central Intelligence," in deference to McCone's role as DCI and USIB chairman. But as shown, it genuinely represented the coordinated views of the USIB principals. U. Alexis Johnson, Memorandum for the Honorable John A. McCone, "U-2 Overflights of Cuba, 29 August through 14 October 1962," March 6, 1963, CREST; Memorandum for Director of Central Intelligence, "Department of State's Objections to the Report on the Cuban Arms Build Up," March 12, 1963, CREST.

31. "McCone, Memorandum for the President," February 28, 1963, in McAuliffe, ed., *CIA Documents*, 373; Clifford, *Counsel to the President*, 357.

32. In one widely publicized clash with scientists in 1956, McCone, a Caltech trustee, had accused some Caltech scientists of being taken in by Soviet propaganda when they expressed support for a nuclear test ban. Chalmers Roberts, "McCone Selection Criticized by Some," *WP,* October 23, 1961; Guthman and Shulman, eds., *Robert Kennedy in His Own Words*, 253–54.

33. "Clifford Named to Killian Post," *NYT,* April 24, 1963. The other PFIAB members in 1962–63 were William Baker, then director of research at Bell Laboratories; Brig. Gen. (ret.) James Doolittle of the USAF; Gordon Gray, a special assistant of national security under Eisenhower; Dr. Edwin Land, an inventor and physicist; Dr. William Langer, a Harvard history professor; former ambassador Robert Murphy; and Frank Pace Jr., secretary of the army under Truman.

34. Clifford, *Counsel to the President,* 353–55; Kistiakowsky, *A Scientist at the White House,* 21; Chalmers Roberts, "McCone Selection Criticized by Some," *WP,* October 23, 1961; Guthman and Shulman, eds., *Robert Kennedy in His Own Words,* 253–54.

35. Clifford, *Counsel to the President,* 357.

36. Memorandum for the Record, "DCI Meeting with PFIAB, 7 December 1962," December 10, 1962, CREST.

37. Ibid.

38. McCone, "Notes for Mr. Earman," December 17, 1962, CREST.

39. Memorandum for the Record, "DCI Meeting with PFIAB, 7 December 1962," December 10, 1962, CREST.

40. Memorandum for the Record, "Meeting of the DCI with PFIAB," December 28, 1962, RIF 104-10302-10000, JFKARC.

41. In his memoir Clifford even intimated that McCone had put his personal life before his official duties by being absent from Washington during a crucial period. He also declared the September 19 SNIE "preposterous" because the DCI was "predicting the opposite." Clifford, *Counsel to the President,* 357–58.

42. Ibid., 358. While the Republicans' charge was wide of the mark, of course, the charge reflected widespread confusion aided and abetted by the administration.

43. Memorandum for the Record, "Meeting with the President in Palm Beach, Florida," January 7, 1963, *FRUS, 1961–1963,* vol. 11, 651–52.

44. Clifford, *Counsel to the President,* 355.

45. "PFIAB Memorandum for the President," February 4, 1963, in McAuliffe, ed., *CIA Documents,* 363–65.

46. McCone, "Memorandum for the President," February 28, 1963, in ibid., 373.

47. Memorandum for the File, "March 8 and 9, 1963 Meeting of the PFIAB," March 11, 1963, RIF 206-10001-10012, Mary Ferrell Foundation.

48. "PFIAB Memorandum for the President," February 4, 1963, in McAuliffe, ed., *CIA Documents,* 363–65.

49. Memorandum for the File, "Board Meeting with the President, 9 March 1963," March 14, 1963, RIF 206-10001-10012, Mary Ferrell Foundation.

50. The sensitivity of the DCI-PFIAB clash was such that when Bundy sent the PFIAB Report and McCone's February 28 memo to the president's secretary for filing, he noted, "These are explosive documents, and their existence is not being widely discussed." Memorandum, McGeorge Bundy to Evelyn Lincoln, March 7, 1963, Killian, James R. 2/4–3/7/63 folder, POF, Special Correspondence, box 31, JFKL.

51. McCone Memorandum for the File, "Meeting with the President, 15 April 1963," April 16, 1963, CIA FOIA Reading Room; Lyman Kirkpatrick, "Agency Policy on Dynamic Intelligence Operations," January 28, 1963, CREST.

52. Guthman and Shulman, eds., *Robert Kennedy in His Own Words,* 254; White, Diary Notes, February 21, 1963, CREST. McCone had a point, too, about the misstatement of facts. The PFIAB document scored McCone (rather than "higher authority") for imposing the limitation that "endangered the necessary flow of information" within the intelligence community." PFIAB Memorandum for the President," February 4, 1963, in McAuliffe, ed., *CIA Documents,* 367, 369.

53. "Cloudy Intelligence," *NYT,* April 29, 1963. Right after the November 1964 election, however, McGeorge Bundy would refer to Clifford's PFIAB promotion during a telephone conversation with President Johnson. When Clifford was appointed, Bundy recalled, "The *Times* . . . wrote a very disagreeable editorial saying [we] had replaced a great statesman in Dr. Killian by a Washington fixer named Clifford. Of course, there never were two sillier remarks, because a) Killian was not a great statesman, and b) Clark was just what the doctor ordered, and [did a] judicious job for JFK." Bundy was almost certainly referring to Clifford's role in the PFIAB postmortem. Telephone Conversation among Bill Moyers, McGeorge Bundy, and Lyndon Johnson, 10:34 A.M., November 4, 1964, LBJL.

Chapter 4

1. Tom Wicker, "Gain for Kennedy Program Seen in Results of Congress Election," *NYT,* November 8, 1962.

2. Stern, *Averting the 'Final Failure,'* 174. Symington to Lyndon and Lady Bird Johnson, November 1, 1962, box 292, Symington Papers.

3. James Wallace, "Soviets on Island Pose Big Strategic, Political Problems for Kennedy," *Wall Street Journal,* February 7, 1963. "Back in Congress, Republicans are still hurting from the fact that the Cuban situation which they once considered one of their best issues, turned around and bit them. They're trying to revive it—the Democrats are trying to keep it dormant." NBC Radio News, "Week-End Report," transcript, January 27, 1963, CREST.

4. United Press International, "GOP Senator Will Conduct Own Bay of Pigs Investigation," *WP,* January 23, 1963. At one point in February, Kennedy asked McGeorge Bundy why it would not be in the administration's interest to "permit and even encourage" a congressional investigation of pre-1961 policy toward Cuba. Bundy thought that it would set a bad precedent—and that there would be "the heaviest Republican pressure to extend the time-frame up through our own period." Bundy to the President, February 19, 1963, Document 2948, National Security Archive.

5. Bundy, *Danger and Survival,* 432–33. Senator Hugh Scott (R-PA) would be among those charging a "private agreement to exchange the removal of Soviet missiles from Cuba for the dismantling of United States intermediate-range missiles [*sic*] bases in the Mediterranean area." Tad Szulc, "U.S. Again Urging Soviet to Hasten Pull-Out in Cuba," *NYT,* February 11, 1963. In response, Undersecretary of State George Ball pleaded with critics to stop "hectoring" the administration on Cuba, while anonymous administration officials asserted that "there [was] absolutely no foundation . . . to speculation . . . [about] a secret deal." Associated Press, "Ball

Asks Critics Hold Off on Cuba," *WP,* February 11, 1963; and Murrey Marder, "U.S. to Take Missiles Out of Turkey," *WP,* January 24, 1963. On the administration's disingenuousness in general, see Bundy, *Danger and Survival,* 434–35.

6. In Robert Johnson's recent history, *Congress and the Cold War,* the missile crisis aftermath is not addressed at all. Similarly, in Alterman's *When Presidents Lie,* the entire focus of the missile crisis chapter is on keeping secret the quid pro quo, with no reference to the administration's other great vulnerability.

7. Alsop and Bartlett, "In Time of Crisis," 16.

8. "Leadership Meeting, 8 January 1963," January 9, 1963, *FRUS, 1961–1963,* vol. 11, Document 592, Microfiche Supplement.

9. That awkward hearings had been anticipated is evinced by a comment on the copy of the Lehman Report, originally requested by DCI McCone in October. There is a handwritten notation on the title page, "Save for the Pearl Harbor hearings—if some, or any." Lehman Report, CREST.

10. Holland, "Politics of Intelligence Post-Mortems, 428–36.

11. McCone, "Meeting with the President in Palm Beach, Florida, 5 January, 1963," January 7, 1963, *FRUS, 1961–1963,* vol. 11, 651–52. By this time, McCone had received the findings from all three of the strictly internal postmortems being conducted by the intelligence community. Holland, "Politics of Intelligence Post-Mortems," 420–21, 428.

12. McCone, "Meeting with the President in Palm Beach, Florida, 5 January, 1963," January 7, 1963.

13. Ibid., 653. Lausche, a conservative Democrat, had aligned himself with such administration critics as Goldwater, alleging that a "secret deal" over Cuba had been negotiated with Khrushchev. Laurence Stern, "Unfortunate, Bundy Says of Adlai Story," *WP,* December 17, 1962.

14. "Editorial Notes," *FRUS, 1961–1963,* vol. 11, 657–58.

15. Even before resolution of the crisis, Arthur Krock had more or less predicted that the debate over Cuba would somehow resume. Krock, "After the Crisis: Partisan Politics Are Muted Now but Cuba Debate Will Resume," *NYT,* October 28, 1962.

16. "Probe of Cuban 'Buildup' Ordered," *Miami Herald,* January 24, 1963. This probe, conducted by Senator Wayne Morse's Latin American Affairs subcommittee, was very short-lived.

17. Tad Szulc, "Soviet Intensifies Build-up of Defense Arms in Cuba," *NYT,* January 23, 1963; "Cuba," *CR,* February 11, 1963, 2123–27; Associated Press, "Kennedy-Cuba," February 6, 1963, CREST.

18. Rovere, "Letter from Washington," 125–26; Warren Weaver, "Capital Guesses at Keating's Aims," and "Well-Cast Senator," *NYT,* February 21, 1963.

19. As the president would note during a February ExComm meeting, despite his efforts and those of the State and Defense Departments, the administration "had been unsuccessful in convincing many people that we knew exactly what was going on in Cuba." "Summary Record of the 40th Meeting of the Executive Committee of the National Security Council," February 5, 1963, *FRUS, 1961–1963,* vol. 11, 690.

20. Ford, speech notes, undated (from early 1963), box D-16, GRFL; Rovere, "Letter from Washington," 125.

21. "Your Discussion before the NSC Tomorrow," January 21, 1963, *FRUS, 1961–1963,* vol. 11, Document 601, Microfiche Supplement. Alsop's follow-up was not specifically about any photo gap; it responded to Stevenson's charge that the December article had "grossly misrepresented" the UN ambassador's views. Stewart Alsop, "Footnote for the Historians," *Saturday Evening Post,* January 26, 1963, 76; "Stevenson Charges Answered by Alsop," *NYT,* January 22, 1963.

22. Memorandum for the Record, "Director's Morning Meeting of 28 January," January 28, 1963, CREST.

23. Daniel and Hubbell, "While America Slept." The article was swiftly expanded into a book, *Strike in the West*, but the authors still proved unable to penetrate the administration's cover story. Ralph de Toledano, "Cuba Story, Wraps Off," *National Review*, April 9, 1963, 288–89.

24. Jerry Landauer, "Russia Hints at New Cut in Its Cuba Force, But Kennedy's Critics Continue Attacks," *Wall Street Journal*, February 20, 1963.

25. Rusk would also experience the same kind of single-minded grilling. E. W. Kenworthy, "Senators Query Rusk about Cuba," *NYT*, January 12, 1963.

26. "Summary Record of the 40th Meeting of the Executive Committee of the National Security Council," February 5, 1963, *FRUS, 1961–1963*, vol. 11, 689.

27. US House of Representatives, Committee on Appropriations, *Department of Defense Appropriations for 1964*, February 8, 1963, and February 14, 1963, 310–11, 333–36. Taylor's testimony also occurred on February 14, 1963. Some of his testimony and apparently some of Minshall's questions and remarks remain classified. To Ford's anger, Taylor claimed "executive privilege" and refused to testify about the Bay of Pigs. See ibid., 311; Taylor to Bundy, February 18, 1963, ARC 305113, http://arcweb.archives.gov.

28. US House of Representatives, Committee on Appropriations, *Department of Defense Appropriations*, 37. Kaplan, Landa, and Drea, *History of the Office of the Secretary of Defense*, 540.

29. Statement by McNamara, January 30, 1963, Cuba, Subjects: Testimony, Secretary McNamara, NSF, box 62, JFKL.

30. McNamara press conference, February 28 1963, Digital National Security Archive, http://nsarchive.chadwyck.com.

31. US House of Representatives, Committee on Armed Services, *Hearings on Military Posture*, January 30, 1963, 259, 264. McNamara also vigorously denied any connection between the Soviet withdrawal and the decision to remove the Jupiter missiles in Turkey. See pp. 264, 274. One of the earliest mentions of the Jupiter withdrawal had occurred in Drew Pearson's syndicated column, written in mid-December as a defense of Adlai Stevenson's position during the October crisis. The actual decision leaked out in mid-January, and the official announcement of the Jupiters' withdrawal occurred on January 24. Pearson, "'Inside Story on Adlai Stevenson," *WP*, December 12, 1962; Carroll Kilpatrick, "Polaris to Replace Jupiters in Turkey," *WP*, January 19, 1963.

32. US House of Representatives, Committee on Appropriations, *Department of Defense Appropriations*, 25, 62. McNamara and Carroll also provided an overly simplistic account of how human intelligence about the San Cristóbal trapezoid influenced U-2 coverage and gave too much credit to the DIA for assembling the mosaic that led to the missiles' discovery. See pp. 44–46, 64–65, and Holland, "The 'Photo Gap,'" 24–26.

33. US House of Representatives, Committee on Appropriations, *Department of Defense Appropriations*, 36.

34. In congressional appearances in January and February 1963, McNamara was not alone in fostering the illusion of a delay caused only by bad weather; Dean Rusk also engaged in similar dissembling. See Rusk's testimony of January 11, 1963, in US Senate, Committee on Foreign Relations, *Executive Sessions*, vol. 15, 5, 26–28.

35. US House, Committee on Armed Services, *Hearings on Military Posture*, January 30, 1963, 268. At one point McNamara suggested that the committee go into closed session to discuss Osmers's allegation, but the offer was not taken up. See p. 270.

36. Osmers, an isolationist prior to Pearl Harbor, enlisted in the army two days after the attack and had risen to the rank of major before his discharge in 1946. "Former Rep. Frank Osmers, Isolationist, Military Man," *WP*, May 24, 1977.

37. Warner, Memorandum for the Record, January 17, 1963, CREST.

38. Warner, Memorandum for the Record, January 31, 1963, CREST; untitled list of the CIA's 1963 congressional appearances, CREST; McCone to Carroll and Carter, February 9, 1963, CREST; Osmers to Vinson, January 31, 1963, POF, box 72, JFKL.

39. McCone to Bundy, February 9, 1963, with Osmers to Vinson, January 31, 1963, attached, CIA 1963, POF, box 72, JFKL.

40. "Briefings of Congressional Committees, 88th Congress—1st Session," undated, and "Agenda, CIA Subcommittee of House Armed Services Committee," November 11, 1963 (including summaries of topics discussed in earlier meetings), CREST.

41. "Weekend Reading," March 29, 1963, NSF, box 318, JFKL.

42. McCone to Bundy, February 9, 1963, with Osmers to Vinson, January 31, 1963, attached. CIA 1963, POF, box 72, JFKL; Memorandum for Lawrence O'Brien, "Report on Major Legislation," February 4, 1963, White House Staff Files, O'Brien, box 23, JFKL; McCone to Carroll and Carter, February 9, 1963, CREST. *Report to the President's Foreign Intelligence Advisory Board on Intelligence Community Activities Relating to the Cuban Arms Buildup (14 April through 14 October 1962)*, 74, JFKL Papers, box 21, JFKARC; McCone to the President, March 21, 1963, CREST. The CIA declassified the latter memo in its entirety in 2003; in 2005 it rereleased it with the part of the sentence about Osmers's lack of "understanding" censored. On Osmers's eventual satisfaction, see Osmers to Vinson, March 26, 1963, CREST.

43. McCone testified before the CIA subcommittee of the House Armed Services Committee on January 17; the CIA subcommittee of the House Appropriations Committee on January 24; the American Republics subcommittee of the Senate Foreign Relations Committee on January 25; the Defense subcommittee of the House Appropriations Committee on February 4 and 5; and the House Foreign Affairs Committee on February 19. Briefings during 88th Congress, 1st Session, CREST; and E. W. Kenworthy, "Senators Report Soviet Build-up in Cuba Continues," *NYT*, January 26, 1963. McCone was far from a reluctant witness, notifying committee chairmen that a comprehensive postmortem (the USIB Report) had just been finished and that he was anxious to share its results about the intelligence community's "excellent" performance during the Cuban crisis. McCone to Vinson, January 2, 1963, CREST; John Warner, Memorandum, "Meeting with Representative Carl Vinson," January 8, 1963, CREST; Lyman Kirkpatrick, "Briefing of the Vinson Committee," January 11, 1963, CREST. None of these hearings was ever published, with the exception of McCone's appearance before the Senate subcommittee on January 25, published in 1986 as part of the Senate Foreign Relations Committee's Historical Series. The chairmen of these various committees willingly abstained from creating a public transcript. McCone to Carter, undated, Countries: Cuba, Subjects: Testimony 3/63–4/63, NSF, box 61, JFKL.

44. McCone reasserted his conviction—an erroneous one—that the SAMs had been emplaced to protect the SSM installations. As was often said about Senator Keating, McCone "was right but for the wrong reasons." Warner, Memorandum for the Record, "DCI Briefing of CIA Subcommittee of House Appropriations Committee, 24 January 1963," January 25, 1963, CREST.

45. Ibid.

46. "Extract," John McCone Testimony before House Appropriations Committee, February 5, 1963, Roger Hilsman Papers, Cuba 1963, box 1, JFKL. The Committee on Overhead Reconnaissance (COMOR) was one of about fifteen subcommittees of the USIB, McCone's principal instrument for coordinating the intelligence community. The COMOR's task was to develop objectives and requirements for overhead reconnaissance. McCone's answer came in response to questions from Representative Mahon, the subcommittee chairman, and Glenard Lipscomb (R-CA). The full transcript is apparently still classified, though a key portion about the photo gap can be found in Hilsman's papers. Interestingly, and in keeping with his apparent decision to be less candid in appearances before nonintelligence committees, in this appearance McCone

stated (in contrast to his earlier testimony) that the October 14 overflight was largely prompted by reports of offensive missiles. Ibid. On McCone and House Appropriations, see also Brugioni, *Eyeball to Eyeball*, 151.

47. US House, Committee on Appropriations, *Department of Defense Appropriations*, 1, 24–25; Scoville, "Director's Morning Meeting," February 6, 1963, CREST. The Appropriations hearings would extend into the middle of February, though most of the challenges to McNamara regarding Cuba apparently happened on February 6 and 7. Carroll, a former FBI agent, had risen up through the ranks during the 1950s as an air force intelligence officer and was the DIA's first director. William Grimes, "America, The Great Engine of War," *NYT*, June 7, 2006. Carroll was invariably accompanied by DIA officer John Hughes, Carroll's special assistant for photo analysis, who became instantly famous for conducting most of the February 7 briefing over national television. John Finney, "Briefing Officer Anonymous Again," *NYT*, February 8, 1963.

48. US House, Committee on Appropriations, *Department of Defense Appropriations*, 27–30.

49. Ibid., 62. Both Ford and Minshall had the advantage of having been briefed by McCone on January 25. Warner, "DCI Briefing of CIA Subcommittee of House Appropriations Committee," January 25, 1963, CREST.

50. Gerald Ford, untitled, undated (from February 1963) notes for speech material, box D16, and correspondence with Glenn Macauley, February 1 and 6 February 1962, folder A4-17, GRFL.

51. Associated Press, "McNamara Denies Cuba Peril to U.S.," *NYT*, February 5, 1963. This wire service story carried the allegation, leveled by Representative Donald Bruce (R-IN), that there had been eighty-eight Soviet SSMs in Cuba and that forty or more remained. The allegation was sufficiently alarming that McCone spoke directly to INR director Hilsman about how to handle it. Memorandum of Conversation, McCone and Hilsman, February 4, 1963, Cuba 1963, Hilsman Papers, box 1, JFKL.

52. "Summary Record of the 40th Meeting of the Executive Committee of the National Security Council," February 5, 1963, *FRUS, 1961–1963*, vol. 11, 689.

53. Fred Dutton to Bundy, February 4, 1963, Document 2899, National Security Archives. Dutton, a longtime Democratic Party political operative, served at the time as assistant secretary of state for congressional relations.

54. "Summary Record of NSC Executive Committee Meeting No. 40," February 5, 1963, NSF, box 316, JFKL.

55. "All Soviet Offensive Arms Removed," *WP*, February 7, 1963; Transcript, "Special Cuba Briefing by Robert McNamara," February 6, 1963, 39–40, CREST.

56. Ted Lewis, "McNamara Seeks to Allay Distrust of Statements on Cuba," *Philadelphia Inquirer*, February 7, 1963.

57. US House, Committee on Appropriations, *Department of Defense Appropriations*, 67–69.

58. The truth, of course, was that most of western Cuba and all interior portions of the island had gone without photo coverage after September 5 because of the September 10 decision. Holland, "The 'Photo Gap,'" 20–21.

59. US House, Committee on Appropriations, *Department of Defense Appropriations*, 32.

60. Ibid., 57.

61. Ibid., 363–64. Minshall vigorously pressed McNamara on the topic again on February 11, but to no avail. "Excerpts on Cuba . . . 11 Feb 1963," Cuba, Subjects: Testimony, NSF, box 62, JFKL; Geoffrey Gould, "Ford Says CIA Withheld Early Data on Cuba," *WP*, March 3, 1963. It is also possible, but unlikely given other news articles, that the AP story misstated Ford's views. A correction was not published.

62. Jules Witcover, "CIA Conceals 'Picture Gap,' Pentagon Says," *WS*, February 27, 1963. Apparently, one of the ways the Pentagon deflected reporters' questions was to point out that the CIA, rather than the air force, had been responsible for aerial surveillance of Cuba during the period in question.

63. As noted in chapter 1, the only major omission in Witcover's account was that it did not actually mention the pivotal meeting on September 10, 1962, in Bundy's office. Witcover cited a "high administration source" in the article, but he was unnamed, and forty-five years later, Witcover could not remember who that was. Jules Witcover, interview by Max Holland, January 15, 2007.

64. Jules Witcover, "'Photo Gap' on Cuba Traced to Fear of New 'U-2 Incident,'" *LAT,* March 10, 1963.

65. In addition, because he wrote for a news service, Witcover's stories were not guaranteed to appear in the same venue every time.

66. Notes on Ball-Mahon conversation, February 11, 1963, box 146, Ball Papers, Mudd Library; E. W. Kenworthy, "U.S. Admits a Gap in Watching Cuba," *NYT,* March 30, 1963.

67. As the hearings commenced, Selden claimed that it might be possible to classify missiles as "offensive" or "defensive," but there was no such thing as "defensive subversion." E. W. Kenworthy, "Goldwater, in Senate, Asks a New Blockade of Cuba," *NYT,* February 19, 1963.

68. Geoffrey Gould, "'Picture Gap' Quiz Faced by McCone," *WP,* February 21, 1963.

69. US House of Representatives, Committee on Foreign Affairs, *Castro-Communist Subversion,* 173. The give-and-take of McCone's testimony was not published, although he did testify; only his prepared statement was printed as part of the record.

70. "Rogers Charges That Weather Not the Reason for CIA Missile Photo Lag," *CR,* February 28, 1963, 3269; Memorandum, "Forecast Weather over Cuba . . . ," February 27, 1963, DCI Records, MDR release.

Chapter 5

1. The House Government Operations Committee's Special Subcommittee on Government Information also mounted an inquiry that provoked consternation in the White House because it, too, possibly threatened to expose the gap in U-2 coverage of Cuba. These hearings, on the administration's alleged management of the news, took testimony from members of the press and administration officials, but ultimately, no report was issued. "Administration Actions on Cuba Reviewed in Congress," *Congressional Quarterly Almanac 1963,* 1109.

2. William S. White, "Senate Inquiry on Cuban Arms Vital Matter for Hemisphere," *LAT,* February 5, 1963.

3. Fry, *Debating Vietnam,* 86.

4. Russell to Stennis, January 13, 1961, box 35, series 43, Stennis Collection. Fry's *Debating Vietnam,* 3–6, provides a good portrait of Stennis.

5. US Senate, Committee on Armed Services, Preparedness Investigating Subcommittee, *Military Cold War Education.*

6. Russell's deft handling of the MacArthur investigation greatly enhanced his reputation, even among liberals. Richard Henschel, "The Committee on Armed Services," *Washington World,* February 24, 1964, 14.

7. Richard Dudman, *Men of the Far Right* (New York: Pyramid Books, 1962), 40–51.

8. Hedrick Smith, "Ire over Russians in Cuba Growing," *NYT,* February 4, 1963. On October 10, well before actual missiles were detected, Stennis had taken the Senate floor to advocate a blockade or quarantine of Cuba. *CR,* October 10, 1962, 21737.

9. Stennis, Group Telegram to Stuart Symington, Leverett Saltonstall, Margaret Chase Smith, E. L. Bartlett, Henry Jackson, Barry Goldwater, October 30, 1962, box 70, series 4, Stennis Collection.

10. Saltonstall to Stennis, October 31, 1962, box 35, series 43, Stennis Collection.

11. Kendall to Stennis, "Major Matters on Agenda of Preparedness Investigating Subcommittee," January 14, 1963, box 3, series 43, Stennis Collection.

12. On Russell's extraordinary influence on the intelligence community during this period, see Barrett, *The CIA and Congress*, 203, 230–33.

13. Associated Press, "New Soviet Threats Shrugged Off by U.S.," *WS*, February 23, 1963; "A Call for Action against Reds in Cuba," *USNWR*, February 25, 1963.

14. Kendall to Taylor, March 15, 1963, and Kendall to McNamara, January 7, 1963, box 71, series 4, Stennis Collection; Stennis Interviewed on "Senator Keating Reports," February 3, 1963, CREST.

15. "News Release by Senator John Stennis," January 25, 1963, series 9, Armed Services Committee, box 128, Correspondence January–March 1963, Russell Papers, RBRL; and E. W. Kenworthy, "Senators Report Soviet Build-up in Cuba Continues," *NYT*, January 25, 1963. The CIA panel, chaired by Senator Russell, was the smallest and most secretive subcommittee of the Armed Services Committee and had virtually no staff. Two of its members (Stennis and Saltonstall) were also on the SPIS.

16. Later that same day, Rusk praised McCone's performance during an ExComm meeting with the president. "Summary Record of the 38th Meeting of the Executive Committee of the National Security Council," January 25, 1963, *FRUS, 1961–1963*, vol. 11, 683. Further illustrating the partisan nature of the debate over Cuba, Rusk and McCone "were barely out the door of the committee room," according to one news report, before senators "started leaking [their testimony] all over town." NBC Radio News, "Week-End Report," transcript, January 27, 1963, CREST.

17. E. W. Kenworthy, "Senators Report Soviet Build-up in Cuba Continues," *NYT*, January 26, 1963; Gardner Bridge, "Senators Prepare Probe of Soviet-Cuba 'Buildup,'" *WP*, February 2, 1963; US Senate, Committee on Foreign Relations, *Executive Sessions*, vol. 15; Stennis to Russell, August 5, 1963, series 9, Armed Services Committee, box 128, Correspondence April–December 1963, Russell Papers, RBRL; United Press International, "Russians in Cuba a Concern to Rusk," *NYT*, February 2, 1963.

18. News Release by Senator Stennis, January 25, 1963, box 71, series 4, Stennis Collection; Hedrick Smith, "Ire over Russians in Cuba Growing," *NYT*, February 4, 1963; Gardner Bridge, "Senators Prepare Probe of Soviet-Cuba 'Buildup,'" *WP*, February 2, 1963.

19. Russell indicated he would have undertaken the review himself, but "did not have the time." Journal, Office of Legislative Counsel, February 6, 1963, CREST.

20. NBC Radio News, "Week-End Report," transcript, January 27, 1963, CREST.

21. Russell, "White House Visit of 2 February 1963," President's File, 1960–1963, Exhibit B, series 18, Russell Papers, RBRL. Or as Walter Lippmann put it, with respect to Cuba, Keating had "won the right to be listened to." Lippmann, "On the Cuban Question Today," *WP*, February 12, 1963. Around this time, Undersecretary of State George Ball attacked critics in Congress like Keating as "voluntary intelligence gatherers who like to make speeches." Fulton Lewis, "Special Reports: Exclusive," February 13, 1963, box 71, series 4, Stennis Collection.

22. Untitled, detailed notes of conversation between Rusk and Dobrynin, February 9, 1963, Secretary and Undersecretary Memcons, State Department Records, box 25, NARA.

23. Russell, "White House Visit," RBRL. In early January Russell had indicated his willingness to be helpful after McCone notified him about the results of the USIB postmortem. The Georgia senator suggested he was willing to make a statement on the floor defending the intelligence community after a closed hearing on the USIB Report. McCone, Memorandum for the Record, "Meeting with Senator Richard B. Russell," January 9, 1963, CREST.

24. Senator Thurmond, for one, was also engaged in a running dispute with the Pentagon over the Soviet order of battle in Cuba, as was Everett Dirksen (R-IL), the minority leader. Thurmond was claiming as many as 30,000 to 40,000 Soviet troops remained in Cuba. Hedrick Smith, "Ire over Russians in Cuba Growing," *NYT*, February 4, 1963.

25. "President Meets Congress Chiefs on Foreign Policy," *NYT*, February 19, 1963.

26. Lewis, "Special Reports," February 13, 1963, box 71, series 4, Stennis Collection.

27. Hal Hendrix, "Growing Outrage over Cuba," *Miami News,* February 19, 1963. Hendrix was also suggesting that the White House was equally concerned about a set of hearings just announced by Representative Armistead Selden's Subcommittee on Inter-American Affairs, but these did not prove troublesome. Associated Press, "Latin Red Subversion to be Probed by U.S.," *LAT,* February 16, 1963. A more sanguine estimate of the SPIS inquiry was given by columnist William S. White, "Stennis Group Well Qualified," *LAT,* February 5, 1963.

28. Max Frankel, "President Hints He Prods Soviet on Cuba Forces," *NYT,* February 8, 1963; United Press International, "Stennis Warns of Build-Up," *NYT,* February 9, 1963. Goldwater, *CR,* February 18, 1963, 2410.

29. Helms, *A Look over My Shoulder,* 212.

30. One administration official particularly under attack was George Ball, the undersecretary of state. Ball had spoken of "very good and very hard" intelligence regarding Cuba as late as October 3, 1962. Ball was simply reiterating what Bundy and Rusk had been saying in different forums; because Ball said it during congressional testimony, however, some Republicans were pouncing on Ball for allegedly misleading Congress. A CIA analysis of Ball's remarks commented, "Very hard is not the terminology that we would have applied to the intelligence available on Cuba in early October." Memorandum for the Record, "Undersecretary of State Ball's Testimony," February 20, 1963, CREST.

31. Marquis Childs, "For a White Paper on Bay of Pigs," *WP,* March 6, 1963.

32. The *Times's* military correspondent, Hanson Baldwin, noticed the difference between the administration's position and McCone's in testimony before Congress. Baldwin, "Arms and Men in Cuba," *NYT,* February 8, 1963.

33. "Outline of Proposed Inquiry into Cuban Situation," February 1, 1963, box 71, series 4, Stennis Collection.

34. "Natalie" to Stennis, February 11, 1963, box 17, series 4, Stennis Collection. On the basis of interviews with refugees and/or his contacts with anti-Castro activists, Hendrix had written about the presence of Soviet missiles in Cuba about two weeks before they were photographed in mid-October. Rowland Evans and Robert Novak, "The Cuba Expert," *WP,* July 12, 1963. Hendrix also had good contacts with the CIA's JMWAVE station in Miami. Don Bohning, *The Castro Obsession,* 192.

35. "Interviews of Cuban Refugees, Miami, Florida," March 25, 1963, box 71, series 4, Stennis Collection; Cline to McCone, January 14, 1963, CREST.

36. Kendall to Stennis, "Abstracts of Senator Stennis' Public Statements on Cuba," February 13, 1963, box 3, series 43, Stennis Collection. On February 17 Stennis would also make an appearance on *Meet the Press,* the NBC Sunday-morning public affairs program, and his public remarks, insofar as they related to Cuba, would often be the topic of news stories during this period. It was an unusual amount of exposure for a senator who normally operated quietly and in the background.

37. It is possible that the military intelligence leaders briefed only the staff of SPIS in early February. In a letter to Stuart Symington, Stennis referred to the staff receiving "verbal briefings by the service intelligence agencies in describing the Cuban buildup." Whether this was in addition to testimony in an SPIS hearing, which would have covered other related Cuban topics, or instead of it is unclear. Stennis to Symington, February 8, 1963, box 67, series 43, Stennis Collection.

38. *CR,* February 7, 1963, 1974; "Arrangement for Meeting on Wednesday, February 6th," February 5, 1963, box 7, series 47, Stennis Collection.

39. "Statement on Cuba by Director of Central Intelligence," February 6, 1963, Cuba, Subjects: Testimony, Director McCone, 2/6/63–2/26/63, NSF, box 63, JFKL. McCone also wanted it shared with the chairmen of the CIA oversight committees.

40. Excerpts from McCone testimony, SPIS, February 6–7, 1963, NLJ-04-122, LBJL; untitled excerpts, McCone testimony, SPIS, February 6–7, Cuba, Subjects: Testimony, Director McCone, 2/6/63–2/26/63, NSF, box 63, JFKL.

41. Excerpts from McCone testimony, SPIS, February 6–7, 1963, NLJ-04-122, LBJL; Stennis Committee Hearings, Cuba, Subjects: Testimony, Director McCone, 2/6/63–2/26/63, 62, NSF, box 63, JFKL. McCone's refreshing performance did not go unnoticed by the senators. At one point (p. 96), Senator Symington even noted, "I would hope we don't quote [McCone] in any way which might hurt [him], do you see what I'm getting at?" See also "Statement by John McCone to the House of Representatives Committee on Foreign Affairs," February 19, 1963, CREST.

42. Regarding Stennis and McNamara, see "Kennedy Sees No Cuba Threat," *NYT,* February 7, 1963, and United Press International, untitled news report, February 7, 1963, CREST. Robert Allen and Paul Scott, "Cuba Arms, Money Are Behind Increase Red Guerrilla Threat," February 18, 1963, CREST. Testimony excerpts show McCone referring to "some 1000 to 1500 that were in training there at the present time." He seems to be summarizing a previous statement to SPIS on the topic. Stennis Committee Hearings, Cuba, Subjects: Testimony, Director McCone, 2/6/63–2/26/63, NSF, box 63, JFKL.

43. The chiefs reported that every country in the hemisphere had a Communist apparatus to some extent, and there was no doubt that every one was or would be linked to Havana, and through Havana to Moscow. Thus, Cuba represented unequivocally the "bridgehead of [Soviet] communism" into the hemisphere. The chiefs also felt that the decline in Castro's hemispheric stature owing to the missile crisis was only a momentary dip, McCone added.

44. Untitled excerpts, McCone testimony, SPIS, February 6–7, 1963, Cuba, Subjects, NSF, box 63, JFKL. However, McCone admitted, "We haven't found a single instance where appreciable quantities of arms have been exported into any Latin American country."

45. Excerpts from McCone testimony, SPIS, February 6–7, 1963, NLJ-04-122, LBJL; SPIS, February 6–7, 1963, Cuba, Subjects: Testimony Director McCone, NSF, box 63, JFKL.

46. Untitled excerpts, McCone testimony, SPIS, February 6–7, 1963, Cuba, Subjects, NSF, box 63, JFKL. Senator Margaret Chase Smith even expressed the desire to quote McCone's estimate, as presented to the SPIS, of the threat posed by Cuba—something that would have been certain to irritate the White House.

47. McCone, Memorandum for the President, February 7, 1963, NSF, box 63, JFKL.

48. "Memorandum for the Record," February 6, 1963, *FRUS, 1961–1963,* vol. 11, 694. Notes by Lawrence Legere, February 7, 1963, Chairman's Staff Group, February 1963, Taylor Papers.

49. The administration's line, which McNamara accurately reflected, was that Cuba represented a lessening military threat, while McCone was inclined to describe it as looming, if not imminent. A year later, Bundy remarked to a different president, "John McCone especially has a way of saving his skin." Telephone Conversation between Bundy and President Johnson, March 4, 1964, Presidential Recordings, LBJL.

50. Marshall Carter, Memorandum for the Record, April 2, 1963, CREST; McCone, Memorandum, "Disclosure of U.S. Intelligence Methodology," March 29, 1963, CREST. After reading what McCone called an "intelligence 'damage' assessment," which was completed in late March, NSC secretary Bromley Smith informed DDCI Carter that if the president read the paper, he "might get the feeling that Mr. McCone was taking off after Mr. McNamara, and the paper might create the wrong impression." It had been decided, therefore, not to show the study to the president, although Bundy had read it.

51. *CR,* February 7, 1963, 1976–77; "McNamara Sends Aerial Photos to Reassure Keating," *Philadelphia Inquirer,* February 8, 1963.

52. "Cuba—Still a Soviet Fortress," *St. Louis Globe-Democrat*, February 8, 1963.

53. Stennis to McCone, February 16, 1963, box 70, series 4, Stennis Collection. The CIA did

so on a country-by-country basis, to the satisfaction of the SPIS. One year later Stennis reiterated the request for information on the "subversive, revolutionary and agitational activities" emanating from Cuba and directed at other Latin American countries.

54. Whereas McCone vividly depicted Cuba as a wellspring for hemispheric subversion, McNamara testified he did "not believe [Cuba] is being used as a base for the export of communism in a substantial degree today, certainly not in any effective way today." *Facts on File,* March 7–13, 1963, 114.

55. A full transcript is apparently not extant. McCone was well aware that the secret testimony was being reviewed at the White House. Lawrence Houston, Memorandum for the Record, "Stennis Transcript," March 25, 1963, CREST.

56. "Transcript of Telephone Conversation between Hilsman and Ball, 20 February 1963," *FRUS, 1961–1963,* vol. 11, Document 620, Microfiche Supplement. Dean Rusk, of course, was among those McCone warned. The two officials also complained about what they considered McCone's selective memory. "The next time I tell [McCone] anything," said Ball, "I'm going to get it signed in writing and notarized." Ball was also upset with the DCI because prior to testifying before Congress the previous October, Hilsman had checked some of the facts (on Ball's behalf) with McCone directly, and now McCone was saying he was not familiar with Ball's testimony. Memorandum, "Apparent Conflict in Testimony Regarding Cuba," February 17, 1963, Document 2937, National Security Archive. The CIA's view was that there was no formal intelligence community document on inventories of Soviet military equipment at that time and that Ball, in his actual testimony, presented the intelligence available in a way calculated to dispel any concerns. Memorandum, "Undersecretary of State Ball's Testimony," February 20, 1963, CREST.

57. Taylor Schedule, February 14, 1963, Taylor Papers.

58. Sorensen, "Memorandum for the Attorney General," February 13, 1963, Document 2944, National Security Archive. Knoche, Memorandum for the Record, February 14, 1963, CREST.

59. Geoffrey Gould, "'Picture Gap' Quiz Faced by McCone," *WP,* February 21, 1963.

60. Bundy to the President, February 14, 1963, NSF, box 56, JFKL.

61. Lippmann, "On the Cuban Question Today," *WP,* February 12, 1963. Hanson Baldwin, the *Times*'s military correspondent who had been the first reporter to raise the issue of the "intelligence gap," also observed in mid-February that the administration's had still not dispelled questions about whether it "withheld, minimized, or 'managed'" some of the facts about Cuba last fall." Baldwin, "Arms and Men in Cuba," *NYT,* February 8, 1963.

62. "Telcon Summaries," February 12, 1963, box 146, Ball Papers.

63. It is not clear who prepared one such explanation, found in the Hilsman papers and dated February 13. It may have been formulated but never made public, or prepared for Secretary McNamara, who testified before Representative Mahon's House Subcommittee on Defense Appropriations. "Question," February 13, 1963, Cuba 1963, Hilsman Papers, box 1, JFKL.

64. "Intelligent Intelligence," *NYT,* February 25, 1963.

65. "Memo to Defense Appropriations Subcommittee Staff from George Mahon," February 16, 1963, Mahon Papers. John Warner, CIA legislative counsel, recommended to McCone that Mahon's request that two of his staffers "review aerial photography during the period 5 September through 14 October" be approved. "Mr. Mahon would like this done some time this week." Warner to McCone, February 18, 1963, CREST. The document states that the recommendation was approved, but it is not entirely clear if that is the case.

66. Baldwin, "Arms and Men in Cuba," *NYT,* February 8, 1963. On February 18 Ambassador Anatoly Dobrynin informed the White House that Soviet forces on the island would be substantially reduced by March 15. Tom Wicker, "Soviet Promises to Cut Cuba Units before March 15," *NYT,* February 20, 1963. Stennis's response to this development was typically cautious, but it effectively diminished the "order of battle" issue that had been the original reason for the SPIS

probe. A thoughtful *Wall Street Journal* article about the difficulties of intelligence gathering appeared around this time, but was not enough to quell the controversy. See Philip Geyelin, "Intelligence Gathering: In Cuba or Elsewhere, Imprecision Is Hard to Avoid," *WSJ,* February 11, 1963.

67. "JFK's McGeorge Bundy—Cool Head for Any Crisis," *Newsweek,* March 4, 1963; Tad Szulc, "New Issues Fan Debates on Cuba," *NYT,* February 27, 1963. The supposed dispute was a nonissue, in terms of causing the photo gap. Charles Corddry, "Shift to SAC in Cuba Air Photos Told," *WP,* February 27, 1963; Holland, "The 'Photo Gap,'" 26; and Memorandum, "The Chronology of Events Leading to the Transfer of Cuban Overflight Responsibility," February 28, 1963, CREST. The switch to a USAF pilot occurred because the administration was anxious to preserve a modicum of "plausible deniability" if a U-2 were to be shot down. A cover story involving an air force pilot was deemed to be marginally more credible—this, despite the fact that the CIA's role in the overflight program was to lend an "unaggressive and unmilitaristic nature to overflights." Holland, "The 'Photo Gap,'" 26, and Memo, "CIA's Role in National Reconnaissance Programs," October 9, 1963, CREST.

68. Warner, "Meeting with Senator Richard B. Russell," February 28, 1963, CREST.

69. Warner, "Meeting with Senator John Stennis," February 28, 1963, CREST.

70. Warner extended an identical offer to Representative Mahon. "Meeting with Representative George H. Mahon," February 28, 1963, CREST.

71. Witcover, "CIA Conceals 'Picture Gap,' Pentagon Says," *WS,* February 27, 1963. Warner, "Meeting with Senator John Stennis," February 28, 1963, CREST.

Chapter 6

1. Walter Lippmann, "On the Cuban Question Today," *WP,* February 12, 1963. Some critics of the administration claimed that it had reserved for itself the right to manipulate and manage the news in the nuclear age, pointing to Arthur Sylvester's statement on December 6. The assistant secretary of defense for public affairs had asserted "the inherent right of the government to lie—to lie to save itself when faced with nuclear disaster—is basic." "U.S. Aide Defends Lying to Nation," *NYT,* December 7, 1962.

2. Robert Kennedy Oral History, April 30, 1964, JFKL, 224.

3. Initially this was done by NSC staffer Michael Forrestal. "Hearings on Cuba before Congressional Committees," February–March 1963, Cuba, Testimony, Hearings & Trawler Testimony, NSF, box 61, JFKL. One contribution to the effort came from David McGiffert at the Defense Department; a memo simply titled "Cuba" has twelve attachments relating to congressional testimony relative to Cuba. McGiffert to Bromley Smith, February 15, 1963, NSF, box 61, JFKL.

4. "I rather think they are going to centralize all testimony over in Bundy's shop," Ball told Hilsman. "Telcon, Hilsman, Ball," February 20, 1963, *FRUS, 1961–1963,* vol. 11, Document 620, Microfiche Supplement. Bundy was apparently worried by what not only McCone might say but also the military chiefs of intelligence. He asked McNamara's staff to send officials to monitor the chiefs' testimony before the SPIS, but Stennis rebuffed the request. "This being an investigative committee, and this Cuban matter being a special investigation . . . the witness will have with him only such persons as may be actually needed by him in presenting his testimony." McNamara's staff observed to Bundy, "We think we can live with it so long as we get the transcripts directly or under the table." Yarmolinsky to Bundy, February 26, 1963, Countries, Cuba, Subjects, Testimony, 5/7/62–2/27/63, NSF, box 61, JFKL. "Memorandum from the President's Special Assistant for National Security Affairs to Secretary of State Rusk," February 19, 1963, *FRUS, 1961–1963,* vol. 11, 702; Memorandum for McGeorge Bundy, "Congressional Testimony re Cuba," February 18, 1963, ARC 305113, http://arcweb.archives.gov.

5. Notes on Ball-Bundy conversation, February 14, 1963, box 146, Ball Papers. "Memorandum from the President's Special Assistant . . . ," February 19, 1963, *FRUS, 1961–1963*, vol. II, 703. Holland, "The 'Photo Gap.'"

6. "Memorandum from the President's Special Assistant . . . ," February 19, 1963, *FRUS, 1961–1963*, vol. II, 704.

7. Rusk said the guidelines were "O.K. with him," but apparently the comments from McNamara and McCone were sufficiently divergent that Bundy realized the effort was hopeless and might even backfire. Ibid., 702; Bundy to Secretary of State, Secretary of Defense, Director of Central Intelligence, February 25, 1963, CREST.

8. "U-2 Overflights of Cuba, 29 August through 14 October 1962," February 27, 1963, in McAuliffe, ed., *CIA Documents*, 127–37. (In 2005 the CIA released a substantially censored version of the same document in CREST.)

9. Memo, "U-2 Overflights of Cuba, 29 August through 14 October," March 6, 1963, *FRUS, 1961–1963*, vol. II, Document 626, Microfiche Supplement.

10. In this same memo, Johnson, without a hint of embarrassment, took issue with the claim that the USIB Report was a coordinated postmortem. The USIB Report had been McCone's "personal report" to the PFIAB because the DCI had not accepted a "number of suggestions and amendments" offered by the State Department, observed the undersecretary. In response, McCone reminded Johnson that USIB's representative from the State Department (Hilsman) was present when the board met on January 3 and that the USIB had unanimously agreed on the version to be submitted to the PFIAB. It had also been represented to PFIAB as a coordinated analysis, and not the product of the "DCI alone or CIA." Marshall Carter to USIB Members, January 7, 1963, CREST; McCone to Johnson, March 7, 1963, *FRUS, 1961–1963*, vol. II, Document 627, Microfiche Supplement. Jack Earman, the CIA inspector general who led the interagency group that produced the USIB analysis, protested Johnson's characterization of the USIB Report as "inconceivable" in a memo to McCone. Memorandum for Director of Central Intelligence, "Department of State's Objections to the Report on the Cuban Arms Build Up," March 12, 1963, CREST.

11. McCone to Johnson, March 7, 1963, *FRUS, 1961–1963*, vol. II, Document 627, Microfiche Supplement.

12. Marshall Carter to USIB Members, January 7, 1963, CREST; Memorandum, McCone to Johnson, March 7, 1963, *FRUS, 1961–1963*, vol. II, Document 627, Microfiche Supplement; Memorandum for the U. S. Intelligence Board, "U-2 Overflights of Cuba, 29 August through 14 October 1962," March 7, 1963, CREST; Memorandum for the Record, "Meeting with the President's Foreign Intelligence Advisory Board," December 10, 1962, CREST.

13. This possibility is underscored by the cover sheet to the memo, which read (even before Johnson's protest), "The attached paper and its enclosure is for background use only. It will not be used as a verbatim briefing paper." McCone to Johnson, March 7, 1963, *FRUS, 1961–1963*, vol. II, Document 627, Microfiche Supplement.

14. McCone, "Memorandum of Discussion with Mr. Bundy, 28 February," March 1, 1963, *FRUS, 1961–1963*, vol. II, Document 625, Microfiche Supplement.

15. McCone to Carter, Re: Congressional Transcripts, undated, Cuba, Testimony 3/63–4/63, NSF, box 61, JFKL.

16. Stennis to Mansfield, June 16, 1961, box 78, series 43, Stennis Collection.

17. Kraft, "Confusion over the Cuban Affair," *WP*, March 1, 1963. Kraft added that "wrong areas were covered," which was true enough, but deceptive if Kraft was not going to mention the conscious degradation of U-2 coverage.

18. Stennis to Symington, February 8, 1963, box 67, series 43, Stennis Collection.

19. McNamara to Stennis, April 26, 1963, Cuba, Main File 1, Cuba & Miscellaneous, 1956–1965, box 71, series 4, Stennis Collection.

20. Yarmolinsky to Bundy, February 26, 1963, Countries: Cuba, Subjects, Testimony 5/7/62–2/27/63, NSF, box 61, JFKL. Yarmolinsky was a special assistant to McNamara.

21. McGiffert to Lawrence O'Brien, "White House Memorandum of 23 February 1961," March 4, 1963, Cong. Liaison: O'Brien, box 23, JFKL.

22. John Warner, "Meeting with John Stennis, February 28, 1963, CREST.

23. "Opening Statement by Senator John Stennis," February 27, 1963, CREST.

24. "Statement by RADM Vernon L. Lowrance before the Subcommittee on Preparedness Investigation Concerning Cuba," February 28, 1963, box 89, series 43, Stennis Collection.

25. John Goldsmith, "AF Intelligence Chief Denies Rift with CIA," *WP,* February 28, 1963.

26. Ibid. and "Natural Transfer Mission, Says Senator Stennis," *Baltimore Sun,* February 28, 1963, clipping file of same date, box 93, series 43, Stennis Collection.

27. Kendall to McGiffert, March 2, 1963, Cuba, General, 3/63, NSF, box 38, JFKL.

28. Ibid.

29. One example of this was a March 15 letter from Kendall to Maxwell Taylor, asking for the JCS's appraisal of the Soviet and Cuban order of battle and related questions. Copies of Kendall's letter and the draft response were located at the JFKL. Kendall to Taylor, March 15, 1963, and Taylor to Kendall, undated (but apparently March 20, 1963), Cuba, General, 3/63, NSF, box 38, JFKL. Taylor's actual letter, which was also sent to McCone for approval before being transmitted, was sent to the SPIS on March 23. Taylor to Stennis, March 23, 1963, CREST.

30. Jack Raymond, "C.I.A. Head Finds Cuba Is Training Latin Saboteurs," *NYT,* March 2, 1963.

31. Coincidentally, in early March GOP leader Senator Everett Dirksen renewed his call for an investigation of the Bay of Pigs because of new revelations involving the deaths of four Americans during the invasion. Cabell Phillips, "Dirksen to Push Senate Study of 1961 Bay of Pigs Invasion," *NYT,* February 28, 1963; Associated Press, "Mystery Pensions Go to Widows of 4 U.S. Airmen Killed in Cuba," *NYT,* March 4, 1963.

32. While the SPIS was undertaking its investigation, the Senate Internal Security Subcommittee got into the fray by printing an OAS document originally published in Spanish only. See US Senate, Committee on the Judiciary, *Cuba as a Base for Subversion in America.*

33. Marquis Childs, "Blank Spot in Cuban Picture," *WP,* March 4, 1963.

34. Alsop and Bartlett, "In Time of Crisis."

35. Childs, "Blank Spot in Cuban Picture," *WP,* March 4, 1963.

36. Bundy, "Memorandum for the Record," March 11, 1963 (but reporting events of a week earlier), Bundy Personal Papers, box 32, JFKL.

37. Conversation between John F. Kennedy and Robert F. Kennedy, Item 9A.6, March 4, 1963, Transcript and Recording of Cassette C (side 2), Presidential Recordings, JFKL. See also "President's Foreign Intelligence Advisory Board, Meeting of March 8–9, 1963," Mary Ferrell Foundation. Raymond, "C.I.A. Head Finds Cuba Is Training Latin Saboteurs," *NYT,* March 2, 1963.

38. Conversation between John F. Kennedy and Bundy, Item 9B.2, March 4, 1963, Presidential Recordings, JFKL. "Facts for John McCone to Emphasize from President's Standpoint," Cuba Testimony, Director McCone, 2/28–3/28/63, NSF, box 63, JFKL.

39. McCone, "Meeting with the President, 4:30 P.M.," March 4, 1963, *FRUS, 1961–1963,* vol. 11, 713–14.

40. "Meeting with the President in Palm Beach, Florida, 5 January 1963," January 7, 1963, *FRUS, 1961–1963,* vol. 11, 651–52.

41. Bundy, "Memorandum for the Record," February 28, 1963, Daily Memoranda, Personal Files, box 32, JFKL.

42. Transcript of Conversation, President Kennedy with McGeorge Bundy, March 4, 1963, Dictabelt Item 9B2, Telephone Recordings, Presidential Recordings, POF, JFKL.

43. "The President's News Conference of 6 March 1963," US President, *Public Papers: JFK, 1963*, 239–40.

44. *Facts on File*, March 7–13, 1963, 85.

45. Such issues were the subject of several presidential conversations with key advisers in early March. See Transcripts of Conversation, President Kennedy with Robert McNamara, March 2, 1963, Dictabelt Items 8A4, 8B1, 8B3, and 8B4; with McGeorge Bundy, March 2, 1963, Dictabelt Items 8B2 and 8B3; with Robert Kennedy, March 2, 1963, Dictabelt Items 8B4 and 8B5; with Bundy, March 6, 1963, Dictabelt Items 10A2 and 10A3; and with Richard Helms, March 6, 1963, Dictabelt Item 10A4; all in Telephone Recordings, Presidential Recordings, POF, JFKL.

46. Helms, *A Look over My Shoulder*, 212. Gen. Maxwell Taylor seems to have been the only ExComm member whose memoir explicitly referred to the administration's problem vis-à-vis the photo gap. See the historiography in the appendix.

47. Transcript of Conversation, President Kennedy with Robert McNamara, March 2, 1963, Dictabelt Items 8A4 and 8B1, and with McGeorge Bundy, Dictabelt Item 8B2, Telephone Recordings, Presidential Recordings, POF, JFKL. Meanwhile, as the president acknowledged in these conversations, the putative Republican nominee in 1964, Senator Barry Goldwater—a reserve USAF general—was becoming vocal about the need for continuous, intrusive surveillance.

48. Joseph Sterne, "McCone Gets Full Report by Senator," *Baltimore Sun*, February 8, 1963. Keating "had no intention of telling McCone the sources of his information in Cuba." The SPIS had also asked Keating for his cooperation, but to no avail, since the subcommittee made it clear that the source of the information would have to be revealed, at least in the privacy of the hearing room.

49. Joseph Sterne, "Keating Defends CIA for Cuba Crisis Role," *Baltimore Sun*, March 4, 1963. Memo for Deputy Director (Plans), April 26, 1963, CREST. Stennis to Keating, February 11, 1963, box 71, series 4, Stennis Collection. Stennis also made the same request of others who claimed special knowledge about Cuba, including Senators Thurmond and Dirksen and Representatives Donald Bruce (R-IN) and William Cramer (R-FL).

50. E. W. Kenworthy, "Keating Sees Misuse of Reports on Cuba," *NYT*, March 5, 1963.

51. Sterne, "Keating Defends CIA for Cuba Crisis Role," *Baltimore Sun*, March 4, 1963.

52. Geoffrey Gould, "Ford Says CIA Withheld Early Data on Cuba," *WP*, March 3, 1963.

53. Hanson Baldwin, "Again the Cuba Problem," *NYT*, March 11, 1963.

54. In early March, Ford's story prompted Mahon to ask more questions about the photo gap in the apparent belief that it was a false issue. "Ask McCone about Ford *Washington Post* story," Mahon scrawled on a piece of paper. "Can CIA lay to rest the Picture Gap by showing. . . . I want CIA to find all testimony on the Photo Gap." Handwritten notes, undated, early March 1963, Mahon Papers.

55. Transcript of Conversation, President Kennedy with Mahon, March 7, 1963, Dictabelt Item 11B3, Telephone Recordings, Presidential Recordings, POF, JFKL.

56. Bundy also wrote Mahon, "I think your statement will make it very much easier for all those who prefer to keep their mouth shut, and that much harder for people with an opposite interest, and I quite agree with you that this is not a matter in which any branch or party has been perfect." Bundy to Mahon, March 11, 1963, Mahon Papers.

57. Stennis to Symington, February 28, 1963, box 71, series 4, Stennis Collection.

58. Both McCone and Undersecretary Johnson would dispute the impression that the October 14 flight went where it did primarily because SSMs were suspected in that area. Holland, "The 'Photo Gap,'" 26, and Memo, "U-2 Overflights of Cuba, 29 August through 14 October," March 6, 1963, *FRUS, 1961–1963*, vol. 11, Document 626, Microfiche Supplement. Yet that was precisely the false impression the DIA director sought to foster in his testimony before the SPIS. A more accurate depiction would have been to state that the suspect area was to be overflown

if the prohibition against overflights of known SAM sites was lifted. Statement by Lieutenant General Joseph Carroll, "The Military Buildup in Cuba," Cuba, Testimony, 2/25/63–3/8/63, 8a, 13–15, NSF, box 62, JFKL. There is no extant transcript of the rest of Carroll's testimony.

59. French to Saltonstall, "Visit with Mr. McCone on the Cuban Matter," May 25, 1963, box 51, Saltonstall Papers. The transcript of his testimony was treated like those of previous witnesses: after the hearing was finished, the classified transcript was kept in the office of the subcommittee, Room 224 of the Old (Russell) Senate Office Building, where it could be examined by members of the subcommittee and designated staff.

60. "McCone's Report on Cuban Intelligence Prior to the October Crisis," March 13, 1963, *FRUS, 1961–1963*, vol. 11, Document 632, Microfiche Supplement.

61. Ibid.

62. Holland, "The 'Photo Gap,'" 29.

63. Testimony of John McCone before the Preparedness Investigating Subcommittee, March 12, 1963, CREST.

64. Warner to Bundy, with transcript pages attached, March 28, 1963, Cuba, Testimony, McCone, 2/28/63–3/28/63, NSF, box 63, JFKL.

65. As Richard Lehman, who conducted the first postmortem for McCone, had written, the four U-2 missions "did not—and since they were designed to avoid SAM-defended areas, could not—detect the ballistic missile deployments then under way." Lehman Report, CREST.

66. "Meeting with the Stennis Preparedness Investigating Subcommittee, 12 March 1963," March 14, 1963, CREST. Transcript of Russell-JFK conversation, November 9, 1961, Special Presidential File, 1941–1967, RBRL.

67. Stennis, "Conference with Senator Thurmond . . . February 25, 1963," March 4, 1963, box 37, series 46, Stennis Collection. Thurmond claimed to have received thousands of letters supporting his critical stance toward JFK on Cuba and only three in opposition. Frank van der Linden, "Cuban Inquiry," undated (from February 1963) syndicated column, CREST.

68. "Meeting with the Stennis Preparedness Investigating Subcommittee, 12 March 1963," March 14, 1963, CREST.

69. Memo, "Discussion with the President Today at 4:15 p.m.," March 13, 1963, *FRUS, 1961–1963*, vol. 11, Document 631, Microfiche Supplement.

70. Ibid.; "Weekend Reading," March 29, 1963, NSF, box 318, JFKL.

71. "Summary Record of the 509th National Security Council Meeting," March 13, 1963, *FRUS, 1961–1963*, vol. 11, 715–18.

72. Ibid.

73. Holland, "Politics of Intelligence Post-Mortems," 425–26. Houston to Elder, March 19, 1963, CREST; "Meeting with the Stennis Preparedness Investigating Subcommittee, 12 March 1963," March 14, 1963, CREST; "Stennis Transcript," March 25, 1963, CREST.

Chapter 7

1. Stennis to Jackson, March 29, 1963, box 67, series 43, Stennis Collection.

2. Stennis to Symington, April 4, 1963, box 71, series 4, Stennis Collection. The draft was classified as secret because it was prepared without regard to the nature or source of the information acquired during the inquiry. Any public release would have to be submitted to the appropriate agencies for security screening and deletion of classified information. The exact practice was that prepared statements were put through the DOD's Directorate for Security Review, which could include a referral to other agencies of the government with an equity. The statements were also sent to the general counsel of the Department of Defense for comment and to the White House for information. McGiffert to Kendall, March 6, 1963, and Kendall to McGiffert, March 2, 1963, box 71, series 4, Stennis Collection.

3. E-mail message from Richard McCulley, Center for Legislative Archives, NARA, July 10, 2006.

4. Stennis to Symington, May 8, 1963, box 67, series 43, Stennis Collection.

5. Stennis to McNamara, April 10, 1963, box 71, series 4, Stennis Collection.

6. Stennis to Thurmond, April 23, 1963, and Stennis to McNamara, April 25, 1963, box 71, series 4, Stennis Collection. The Thurmond staff member who conducted the review of the hearing transcripts was Fred Buzhardt. James Gehrig conducted the review for Senator Symington; Stuart French and John Jackson did the same for Senator Saltonstall.

7. McNamara to Stennis, April 26, 1963, box 71, series 4, Stennis Collection.

8. David Barnett, North American Newspaper Alliance, untitled, undated article on Smith, 1963 scrapbook, M. C. Smith Papers.

9. Smith, "Congressional Report," February 10, 1963, M. C. Smith Papers.

10. Pearson, undated article in 1962 scrapbook, M. C. Smith Papers.

11. As Smith well knew, the two subcommittees met and functioned jointly. Russell later told President Lyndon Johnson, "I've been very careful. I've even kept Margaret Chase Smith off that [sub]committee . . . even though I've got a lot of faith in her." United Press International news article, January 25, 1962, CREST; "Telephone Conversation between the President and Sen. Richard Russell," November 29, 1963, LBJL.

12. John Warner, journal entry, April 1, 1963, CREST.

13. *CR*, May 1, 1963, 7106. Lewis's "Anatomy of Decision" was never published. The unmarried Smith and Lewis were much talked about in Washington and in Maine, as they lived for years in the same home, with bedrooms on different floors, in the suburbs of Washington. Sherman, *No Place for a Woman*, 97. Russell invited Smith to join the CIA subcommittee a few years later.

14. Front Office Notes, March 21, 1963, April 10, 1936, and April 17, 1963, M. C. Smith Papers.

15. Interview transcript, dated April 21, 1963 (but recorded four days earlier), Statements and Speeches series, M. C. Smith Papers.

16. Notes by Smith, April 24, 1963, box 71, series 4, Stennis Collection. Another copy of this document (in Foreign Relations: Cuban, General, M. C. Smith Papers) has handwritten notations by Smith, suggesting that she used the notes in an SPIS session.

17. Front Office Notes, April 25, April 30, and May 2, 1963, M. C. Smith Papers.

18. Warner, journal entry, May 3, 1963, CREST.

19. Goldwater to Stennis, April 8, 1963, Folder: 1965, Symington Papers.

20. Stennis to Symington, May 8, 1963, box 67, series 43, Stennis Collection.

21. Robert Allen and Paul Scott, "President's Staff Blamed for U.S. Fiasco on Cuba," *Washington World,* April 26, 1963. Fred Hurst to Stennis, April 18, 1963, box 3, series 43, Stennis Collection.

22. Stennis to McCone, April 23, 1963, box 71, series 4, Stennis Collection. Stennis to Houston, April 25, 1963, CREST. The CIA and the DIA promptly arranged to coordinate their reviews so that they would request "deletion of the same material."

23. One example of a requested deletion that was not made concerned the frequency of U-2 overflights. "Notes on Stennis Subcommittee Interim Report," May 10, 1963, CREST.

24. Drew Pearson, "Reactor Case News Suppressed," *WP,* April 22, 1963; Robert Healy, "Cuba Critics Losing Steam," *Boston Globe,* April 19, 1963.

25. "3 in CIA among 21 Released by Cuba," *NYT,* April 25, 1963. Bundy to the President, February 19, 1963, Document 2948, National Security Archive.

26. Healy, "Cuba Critics Losing Steam," *Boston Globe,* April 19, 1963.

27. Robert Allen and Paul Scott, "JFK's Cuba Policy Bars Checkup on Red Forces," *Long Island Press,* May 9, 1963.

28. *CR*, May 9, 1963, 7731–33.

29. US Senate, Committee on Armed Services, Preparedness Investigating Subcommittee,

Interim *Report on the Cuban Military Buildup*, (hereafter SPIS Report), 3. "Forecast Weather over Cuba . . . ," February 27, 1963, DCI Records, MDR release. The chief of the weather staff of the Office of Special Activities thought this was the best characterization of weather over Cuba: "Between 5 September and 14 October, poor to bad weather prevailed over specific target areas in Cuba for thirty of the forty days. Poor to bad weather prevailed over all of Cuba, thereby nullifying any possibility of photo coverage for nine of the forty days." "Forecast Weather over Cuba . . . 5 September–14 October 1962," March 1, 1963, CREST.

30. *CR*, May 9, 1963, 7733; Warner, journal entry, and memo to McCone, May 9, 1963, CREST; untitled, undated deleted section of SPIS Report draft, box 74, series 43, Stennis Collection.

31. *CR*, May 9, 1963, 7733.

32. Transcript, ABC Radio News, May 20, 1963, CREST.

33. *CR*, May 9, 1963, 7733.

34. At 12:15, one of her aides made this note: "Senate floor phoned and said please tell the Senator that Sen. Stennis has the floor now, talking on Cuba." Why Smith waited to speak is unknown. Front Office Notes, May 9, 1963, M. C. Smith Papers.

35. *CR*, May 9, 1963, 7776–79. Though Stennis was not there, Smith praised his "truly magnificent judicial temperament." Stennis had already written her, "Your counsel and suggestions were so sound and helpful that I wanted to send you this special word of deepest thanks for the splendid work you did and for your fine attitude as to the Report as a whole." Stennis to Smith, May 3, 1963, box 35, series 43, Stennis Collection.

36. Kendall to Forbes, June 19, 1964, box 70, series 4, Stennis Collection.

37. William Saltonstall to Leverett Saltonstall, May 21, 1963, box 274, Saltonstall Papers.

38. *CR*, May 16, 1963, 8286–88. Stratton to McCone, May 20, 1963, CREST. An aide who summarized Stratton's "purported" analysis for Stennis advised that it probably was not worth dignifying Stratton's rather transparent effort. Shaw to Stennis, "Comment on Cuba Military Buildup Report," May 18, 1963, Cuban Main File 3—July, Stennis Collection.

39. "An Interim Report of the Special Subcommittee on Cuba and Subversion in the Western Hemisphere," *CR*, May 20, 1963, 8969–71.

40. Max Freedman, "President's Cuba Responsibility," *WS*, May 13, 1963.

41. "'62 Discord on Cuba Denied by Sorensen," *NYT*, May 10, 1963.

42. Shaw to Stennis, "Comment on Cuba Military Buildup Report," May 18, 1963, Cuban Main File 3—July, Stennis Collection.

43. "Weekend Reading, May 17, 1963," NSF, Bundy Correspondence Chron file, box 403, JFKL.

44. Congressional Mail, May 20, 1963, Cong. Liaison: O'Brien, box 25, JFKL.

45. "G.O.P. Chief Asks Facts about Cuba," *NYT*, May 20, 1963.

46. President Kennedy to McCone, May 13, 1963, CREST; "pay" to Bromley Smith, May 12, 1963, JFKL.

47. McCone to the President, May 14, 1963, CREST.

48. *CR*, June 4, 1963, 10041, and July 18, 1963, 12174.

49. "Special Memorandum for Kendall from Stennis (given by telephone today)," February 12, 1963, box 7, series 47, Stennis Collection.

50. Smith remarks, reprinted in *CR*, February 18, 1963, 2298. Coincidentally, James Reston had just written that critics of the president were implying what they had not proved—that JFK had made a deal with Khrushchev to scrap the missile bases in Turkey. Reston, "How to Turn Victory into Defeat," *NYT*, February 11, 1963.

51. Kendall, interview.

52. French to Saltonstall, "Visit with Mr. McCone on the Cuban Matter," May 25, 1963, box 51, Saltonstall Papers.

53. Ibid.

54. Stennis to Ross, April 13, 1967, box 70, series 4, Stennis Collection. There was also said to be a "secret" or classified version of the report. Stennis to Senator Harry Flood Byrd, May 9, 1963, box 71, series 4, Stennis Collection. If there was such a version, it has never seen the light of day. Though no "final" SPIS report on Cuba would ever be issued, on June 28, 1963, after receiving the latest intelligence on Cuba from CIA's Lawrence Houston, Kendall told Houston that SPIS "would now be undertaking the final report on Cuba." [Name deleted], Memorandum for the Record, June 28, 1963, CREST.

Chapter 8

1. Smith, typescript, with handwritten editing and notations for March 12, 1963, hearing with McCone, Foreign Relations Committee [*sic*], Cuba: General, M. C. Smith Papers.

2. Mary Robinson to Ford, April 9, 1963, Folder A6–9, and Ford, speech text, April 26, 1963, box D16, GRFL. Emphasis in the original text.

3. Eric Alterman has argued, for example, that the degree of force Lyndon Johnson sought to calibrate during the Vietnam War was based on his misunderstanding of how the Kennedy administration had managed the missile crisis. Alterman, *When Presidents Lie*, 145–51.

4. Bundy, *Danger and Survival*, 459.

5. Kennedy, Commencement Address, Yale University, June 11, 1962, US President, *Public Papers: JFK, 1962*, 470–75.

6. Secretary of Defense McNamara stated categorically on February 6, 1961, "There is no missile gap." His deputy, Roswell Gilpatric, stated more comprehensively in October of that year that the United States had nuclear war-fighting superiority over the USSR. See, for example, Cimbala, *Nuclear Strategy*, 48.

7. Bundy, *Danger and Survival*, 459.

8. May and Zelikow, *The Kennedy Tapes*, 696, cited in Rabe, "After the Missiles of October," 716.

9. Bundy, *Danger and Survival*, 420.

10. Garthoff, "US Intelligence in the Cuban Missile Crisis," 53–55; Wirtz, "Organizing for Crisis Intelligence," 139, 142–45; Blight and Welch, "The Cuban Missile Crisis and Intelligence Performance," 199.

11. Garthoff, "US Intelligence in the Cuban Missile Crisis," 24.

12. McCone's standing in the Kennedy administration is sometimes overestimated in the literature. See, for example Michael A. Turner's generally impressive examination of US intelligence, which nonetheless describes McCone as having been "a close friend of President John F. Kennedy." Turner, *Why Secret Intelligence Fails*, 117.

13. Hughes, *Fate of Facts*, 27.

Appendix

1. Jules Witcover, "Cuban 'Photo Gap' Tied to Fear of U-2 Ruckus," *WS*, March 6, 1963. Witcover could not recall his source, although it seems likely it was someone in the Pentagon, probably the DIA, familiar with the pattern of U-2 coverage. Witcover, interview.

2. Ten months later, syndicated columnists Allen and Scott would also hint at what really happened, though with less detail. Robert S. Allen and Paul Scott, "Cuba Surveillance Again CIA Job," *LAT*, October 21, 1963.

3. US Senate, Committee on Armed Services, Preparedness Investigating Subcommittee, *Interim Report*.

4. George and Smoke, *Deterrence in American Foreign Policy*, 473.

5. Pachter, *Collision Course*, v, viii, 8–9.

6. Ibid., 8.

7. Ibid., 8–9.

8. Knorr, "Failures in National Intelligence Estimates."

9. Horelick, "Cuban Missile Crisis," 381.

10. Munson and Southard, "Two Witnesses for the Defense."

11. Kent, "A Crucial Estimate Relived," 115; Absher, *Mind-Sets and Missiles*, 41–43.

12. Wohlstetter, *Pearl Harbor*. Wohlstetter argued that the "signal-to-noise" ratio was such that pregnant indicators of a sneak attack were lost in the din.

13. Wohlstetter, "Cuba and Pearl Harbor," 693.

14. Ibid., 697.

15. Ibid., 697–98, 705.

16. Schlesinger, *A Thousand Days*, 799–800.

17. Sorensen, *Kennedy*, 672.

18. Abel, *The Missile Crisis,* 3rd ed., v, x. This paperback edition also listed, in alphabetical order, everyone interviewed by Abel. The list included Bundy, Rusk, Hilsman, and McCone, meaning that Abel interviewed most of the members of ExComm.

19. Abel, *The Missile Crisis,* 3rd ed., vi.

20. Abel, *The Missile Crisis,* 11, 14.

21. Helms, *A Look over My Shoulder*, 212.

22. Weintal and Bartlett, *Facing the Brink*, 62. An interesting claim, asserted with no foundation, was that Senator Keating had "had access to ground intelligence [CIA] reports which were not being forwarded to the president." Ibid., 61.

23. Hilsman was one of the first officials that Lyndon Johnson forced out of the State Department once he became president. As assistant secretary of state for Far Eastern affairs, Hilsman had been a major proponent of US support for the November 1963 military coup against South Vietnamese president Ngo Dinh Diem, a decision that Johnson had strongly opposed.

24. Hilsman, *To Move a Nation*, 182–93.

25. Ibid., 196. Such an assertion was not compatible with the CIA's analysis that IRBM construction began as early as September 1–5 at the Guanajay IRBM site and September 15–20 at the San Cristóbal and Remedios MRBM sites. McAuliffe, ed., *CIA Documents*, 7–8.

26. Hilsman, *To Move a Nation*, 189.

27. Hilsman chided the intelligence community for missing other signs of the missile deployment, such as the fact that two Soviet freighters, the *Omsk* and the *Poltava,* had exceptionally large hatches and rode "high in the water" because they were carrying a bulky but relatively light load. "It is difficult to understand why the professional intelligence technicians down the line failed to see enough significance in these facts to bring them to the attention of the top levels." He also deceptively asserted a U-2 could have been dispatched sooner and guided over suspected sites if the CIA had had "a better network of traditional agents." The "intelligence community should have . . . turned their attention to the western end of the island some ten days to two weeks sooner than it did," Hilsman wrote—thereby leaving the inference, for anyone who insisted there was a photo gap, that any delay was primarily the CIA's fault. Ibid., 186–87, 189, 191.

28. Hilsman's account was not footnoted. As described in a prefatory note in his book, however, he clearly used classified documents, which he had probably taken with him when he left the State Department. Ibid., xv, xviii.

29. Krock, *Memoirs*, 378.

30. Kennedy, *Thirteen Days*, 27.

31. Ibid., 29.

32. Steel, "Endgame."

33. Hilsman and Steel, "An Exchange on the Missile Crisis."

34. Thomas, *Cuba*, 1398.

35. For a critique of Allison's *Essence of Decision* as originally published and later revised, see Bernstein, "Understanding Decisionmaking." One measure of *Essence of Decision*'s influence: it was cited more than 1,100 times in the Social Sciences Citation Index between 1971 and 1991. Alterman, *When Presidents Lie*, 138.

36. Allison, *Essence of Decision*, 121, 191, 306.

37. Taylor, *Swords and Plowshares*, 263.

38. Krasner wrote that the decision reflected the COMOR's "sensitivity to the needs and policies of the president rather than the parochial concerns of the permanent government." Krasner, "Are Bureaucracies Important?," 172–73.

39. Chayes, *The Cuban Missile Crisis*, 12.

40. George and Smoke, *Deterrence in American Foreign Policy*, 474. Although the book was coauthored with Smoke, George was identified as the primary author of the missile crisis chapter.

41. George and Smoke, *Deterrence in American Foreign Policy*, 473, 485, 496.

42. Alexander L. George, "The Cuban Missile Crisis," in George, ed., *Avoiding War*, 222–68.

43. Dinerstein, *The Making of a Missile Crisis*.

44. Moser, "The Time of the Angel."

45. Schlesinger, *Robert Kennedy and His Times*, 506, 523.

46. Ibid.

47. Gleichauf, "Red Presence in Cuba," 38; Gleichauf, "A Listening Post in Miami," 52–53.

48. Detzer, *The Brink*, 58.

49. Ibid., 70.

50. Arnold, "Omens and Oracles," 52.

51. Ball, *The Past Has Another Pattern*, 287.

52. Prados, *The Soviet Estimate*, 146; Pollard, "Cuban Missile Crisis," 150.

53. "The Lessons of the Cuban Missile Crisis," *Time*, September 27, 1982; B. Drummond Ayres Jr., "The Cuba Missile Showdown: Kennedy Aides Note Lessons," *NYT*, September 20, 1982.

54. Laubenthal, "The Missiles in Cuba, 1962," 6, 7–8, 14, 16–17. Laubenthal's study was declassified in October 1999.

55. U. Alexis Johnson, *The Right Hand of Power*, 381.

56. Ibid.

57. Laqueur, *A World of Secrets*, 161–70.

58. Ranelagh, *The Agency*, 396.

59. Usowski, "John McCone and the Cuban Missile Crisis."

60. Bundy, *Danger and Survival*, 432, 687.

61. Newhouse, *War and Peace in the Nuclear Age*, 166.

62. Altogether, five major international conferences would be held from 1987 to 1992 under various auspices. Scott and Smith, "Lessons of October," 662.

63. Blight and Welch, *On the Brink*.

64. Rusk, *As I Saw It*, 230.

65. Brugioni, *Eyeball to Eyeball*. Brugioni published an article about the missile crisis as early as 1972, but it appeared in a classified publication. Brugioni, "The Cuban Missile Crisis."

66. For example, according to Brugioni, Bundy posed three questions regarding U-2 overflights to acting DCI Marshall Carter on the afternoon of September 10. In fact, the questions had been posed at 10:00 A.M. Brugioni, *Eyeball to Eyeball*, 138–39.

67. Ibid., 164.

68. Beschloss, *The Crisis Years*, 423–25.

69. Clifford, *Counsel to the President*, 429–36.

70. McAuliffe, ed., *CIA Documents*, 1–4, 13–17, 39–44, 61–62, 99–102, 127–37, 361–76.

71. Walter Pincus, "CIA Records Offer Behind-the-Scenes Look at Cuban Missile Crisis," *WP*, October 19, 1992; Eric Schmitt, "Once More unto the Brink: Cuban Crisis Relived," *NYT*, October 20, 1992.

72. Chang and Kornbluh, *The Cuban Missile Crisis*, 355.

73. Nathan, ed., *Cuban Missile Crisis Revisited*.

74. Thompson, *The Missiles of October*.

75. Schecter and Deriabin, *The Spy Who Saved the World*, 332.

76. Ibid., 333.

77. McAuliffe, "Return to the Brink," 4–5, 10–11.

78. Halpern, "Revisiting the Cuban Missile Crisis," 2–3.

79. Blight, Allyn, and Welch, eds., *Cuba on the Brink*, 86.

80. Lebow and Stein, *We All Lost the Cold War*, 1994.

81. Scott and Smith, "Lessons of October," 675.

82. Gribkov and Smith, *Operation ANADYR*, 16, 28, 40, 51–52, 102, 117.

83. *FRUS, 1961–1963*, vol. 11, 1, 12–13, 689, 694, 698, 702–706, 710, 713–16, and vol. 10, 1054. Several key documents are to be found in the microfiche supplements to these FRUS volumes.

84. Hilsman, *Cuban Missile Crisis*, 55; Hilsman, *To Move a Nation*, 187.

85. Hilsman, *Cuban Missile Crisis*, 53, 65. This argument was disingenuous, as surveillance had never been based on starting from one end of the island and working slowly toward the other.

86. White, *Cuban Missile Crisis*.

87. Fursenko and Naftali, *"One Hell of a Gamble,"* 214, 220.

88. McAuliffe, ed., *CIA Documents*, 2.

89. May and Zelikow, *The Kennedy Tapes*.

90. More than fifteen hours (68 percent) of the ExComm recordings were not released until October 1996, and two hours (9 percent) were not released until February 1997. Yet the volume was published in October 1997. Stern and Holland, "Presidential Tapes and Transcripts."

91. May and Zelikow, *The Kennedy Tapes*, xiii; Stern, *Averting the 'Final Failure,'* 427–40.

92. Pedlow and Welzenbach, *The CIA and the U-2 Program*, 205.

93. "Intelligence and the Cuban Missile Crisis," special issue, *I&NS* 13, no. 3 (Autumn 1998); Blight and Welch, eds., *Intelligence and the Cuban Missile Crisis*.

94. Garthoff, "US Intelligence in the Cuban Missile Crisis," 24.

95. Kennedy, *Thirteen Days*, 29.

96. Wirtz, "Organizing for Crisis Intelligence."

97. Blight and Welch, "What Can Intelligence Tell Us?," 6. The authors' explanatory footnote to the phrase "sordid Camelot sub-plots" noted that "Chroniclers of Camelot closest to the president—most notably, Robert F. Kennedy, Theodore Sorensen, and Arthur Schlesinger—have repeatedly characterized Rusk and Bundy as overly timid, indecisive, ineffective, and obstacles to crisis management. Rusk appears to have been the target of deliberate character assassination." Ibid., 16n24.

98. Blight and Welch, "The Cuban Missile Crisis and Intelligence Performance," 180.

99. Merom, "The 1962 Cuban Intelligence Estimate," 52, 56, 74n21, 75–76n30. In a footnote Merom did note that the September flight paths had been altered.

100. Allison and Zelikow, *Essence of Decision*, 2nd ed., 338, 370–71.

101. Freedman, *Kennedy's War*, 167–69.

102. Zelikow and May, *The Presidential Recordings*.

103. Richelson, *The Wizards of Langley*, 52.

104. Weisbrot, *Maximum Danger*.

105. Helms, *A Look over My Shoulder*, 212–13.

106. Stern, *Averting the 'Final Failure,'* 142–44, 152–54.

107. Taubman, *Khrushchev*, 551.

108. Frankel, *High Noon in the Cold War*, 17.

109. Grabo, *Anticipating Surprise*, 140.

110. Holland, "The 'Photo Gap'"; Holland, "Politics of Intelligence Post-Mortems"; Holland, "More on Post-Mortems."

111. Polmar and Gresham, *DEFCON-2*, 85–86.

112. Johnson, *Congress and the Cold War*.

113. Kaplan, Landa, and Drea, *History of the Office of the Secretary of Defense*, 201–203.

114. Weiner, *Legacy of Ashes*, 194–97.

115. Munton and Welch, *The Cuban Missile Crisis*, 41, 47.

116. Dobbs, *One Minute to Midnight*.

117. Renshon, "Mirroring Risk," 331.

118. Absher, *Mind-Sets and Missiles*, 41–43.

Bibliography

Abbreviations

AG: Attorney General of the United States
CIA: Central Intelligence Agency
COMOR: Committee on Overhead Reconnaissance
CR: Congressional Record
CREST: CIA Records Research Tool, NARA
CWIHP: Cold War International History Project
DCI: Director of Central Intelligence
DDCI: Deputy Director of Central Intelligence
DH: Diplomatic History
DIA: Defense Intelligence Agency
DOD: Department of Defense
DOJ: Department of Justice
DOS: Department of State
ExComm: Executive Committee of the National Security Council
FA: Foreign Affairs
FBI: Federal Bureau of Investigation
FOIA: Freedom of Information Act
FP: Foreign Policy
FRUS: Foreign Relations of the United States, DOS
GMAIC: Guided Missile and Astronautics Intelligence Committee
GPO: Government Printing Office
GRFL: Gerald R. Ford Library
HASC: House Armed Services Committee
ICBM: Intercontinental Ballistic Missile
IJICI: International Journal of Intelligence and CounterIntelligence
IG: Inspector General
INR: Bureau of Intelligence and Research, DOS
I&NS: Intelligence and National Security
IRBM: Intermediate-Range Ballistic Missile

IS: International Security
JCS: Joint Chiefs of Staff, DOD
JCWS: Journal of Cold War Studies
JFKARC: John F. Kennedy Assassination Records Collection, NARA
JFKL: John F. Kennedy Library
LAT: Los Angeles Times
LBJL: Lyndon B. Johnson Library
MDR: Mandatory Declassification Review
MRBM: Medium-Range Ballistic Missile
NARA: National Archives and Records Administration
NIE: National Intelligence Estimate
NPIC: National Photographic Interpretation Center
NRO: National Reconnaissance Office
NSA: National Security Agency
NSC: National Security Council
NSF: National Security File
NYRB: New York Review of Books
NYT: New York Times
OSA: Office of Special Activities
PFIAB: President's Foreign Intelligence Advisory Board
POF: President's Office Files
RBRL: Richard B. Russell Library
RMNL: Richard M. Nixon Library
SAC: Strategic Air Command
SAM: Surface-to-Air Missile
SASC: Senate Armed Services Committee
SG: Special Group, NSC subcommittee
SGA: Special Group Augmented, NSC subcommittee with AG
SII: Studies in Intelligence
SNIE: Special National Intelligence Estimate
SPIS: Senate Preparedness Investigating Subcommittee
TFW: Task Force W, CIA
SSM: Surface-to-Surface Missile
USAF: United States Air Force
USIB: United States Intelligence Board
USNWR: U.S. News & World Report
WP: Washington Post
WS: Washington Star

Archives

Dwight D. Eisenhower Library, Abilene, KN
Gerald R. Ford Library, Ann Arbor, MI

Lyndon B. Johnson Library, Austin, TX
John F. Kennedy Library, Boston, MA
Seeley G. Mudd Manuscript Library, Princeton University, Princeton, NJ
National Archives, College Park, MD
Richard M. Nixon Library, Yorba Linda, CA
Richard B. Russell Library, University of Georgia, Athens
Margaret Chase Smith Library, Skowhegan, Maine
Marquis Childs Papers, Wisconsin Historical Society, Madison
George H. Mahon Papers, Texas Tech University, Lubbock
Leverett Saltonstall Papers, Massachusetts Historical Society, Boston
George A. Smathers Papers, University of Florida, Gainesville
John C. Stennis Papers, Mississippi State University, Starkville
Stuart Symington Papers, Western Historical Manuscript Collection, Columbia, MO
Maxwell C. Taylor Papers, National Defense University Library, Washington, DC

Archives Online

Central Intelligence Agency
    Electronic Reading Room
      Studies in Intelligence
CWIHP
    Bulletin
    Digital Archive: Cuban Missile Crisis
Department of State
    Foreign Relations of the United States (*FRUS*)
Mary Ferrell Foundation (by subscription)
National Archives
    CIA Records Search Tool (CREST)
National Security Agency
    Cuban Missile Crisis
National Security Archive
    Cuban Missile Crisis, 1962: 40th Anniversary
    Digital National Security Archive, Cuban Missile Crisis, 1962 (by subscription)

Correspondence and Interviews

Barton J. Bernstein, June 22, 2005
Edward T. "Ned" Dolan, July 8, 2005
Harold P. Ford, July 2, 2005
Alexander L. George, April 1, 2006
Samuel Halpern, May 3, 2003
Thomas L. Hughes, July 2, 2005
James Kendall, April 18, 2003
Jack C. Ledford, October 7, 1999 (courtesy of Jeffrey T. Richelson)

Richard Lehman, April 14 and June 3, 2003
Albert D. Wheelon, May 8, 2008
Jules Witcover, January 15, 2007

Periodicals

Aviation Week and Space Technology
Baltimore Sun
Boston Globe
Congressional Record
Foreign Affairs
Foreign Policy
Los Angeles Times
Miami Herald
Miami News
National Review
New York Times
New Yorker
Newsweek
Philadelphia Inquirer
Time
U.S. News & World Report
Wall Street Journal
Washington Post
Washington Star

Scholarly Journals

Cold War History
CWIHP *Bulletin*
Diplomatic History
Intelligence and National Security
The Intelligencer
International Journal of Intelligence and CounterIntelligence
International Security
Journal of Intelligence History
Journal of Cold War Studies
Studies in Intelligence

US Government Documents, Books, and Monographs

Bird, Joan, and John Bird, eds. *Resolving the Missile Gap with Technology*. Washington, DC: CIA, 2011.
Kaplan, Lawrence, Ronald Landa, and Edward Drea. *History of the Office of the Sec-*

retary of Defense. Vol. 5, *The McNamara Ascendancy, 1961–1965.* Washington, DC: GPO, 2006.

Laubenthal, Sanders A. "The Missiles in Cuba, 1962: The Role of SAC Intelligence." *SAC Intelligence Quarterly,* May 1984.

McAuliffe, Mary S., ed. *CIA Documents on the Cuban Missile Crisis.* Washington, DC: CIA, 1992.

Pedlow, Gregory W., and Donald E. Welzenbach. *The CIA and the U-2 Program, 1954–1974.* Washington, DC: CIA, 1998.

Petersen, Michael B. *Legacy of Ashes, Trial by Fire: The Origins of the Defense Intelligence Agency and the Cuban Missile Crisis Crucible.* Washington, DC: Defense Intelligence Agency, 2011.

Pfeiffer, Jack B. *Official History of the Bay of Pigs Operation.* Vols. 1–4. Washington, DC: CIA History Staff, 1979, 1984; http://www.foia.cia.gov/.

US Department of Defense, *Special Cuba Briefing, 6 February 1963.* Washington, DC: GPO, 1963.

US Department of State. *Foreign Relations of the United States, 1961–1963.* Vol. 10, *Cuba 1961–1962.* Washington, DC: GPO, 1997.

——. *Foreign Relations of the United States, 1961–1963.* Vol. 11, *Cuban Missile Crisis and Aftermath.* Washington, DC: GPO, 1996.

US House of Representatives, Committee on Appropriations. *Department of Defense Appropriations for 1964,* 88th Cong., 1st Sess., part 1. Washington, DC: GPO, 1963.

——, Committee on Armed Services. *Hearings on Military Posture,* 88th Cong., 1st Sess. Washington, DC: GPO, 1963.

——, Committee on Foreign Affairs. *Castro-Communist Subversion in the Western Hemisphere.* Washington, DC: GPO, 1963.

US President. *Public Papers of the Presidents of the United States: John F. Kennedy, January 1 to December 31, 1962.* Washington, DC: GPO, 1963.

——. *Public Papers of the Presidents of the United States: John F. Kennedy, January 1 to November 22, 1963.* Washington, DC: GPO, 1964.

US Senate, Committee on Armed Services, Preparedness Investigating Subcommittee. *Interim Report on the Cuban Military Buildup,* 88th Cong., 1st Sess. Washington, DC: GPO, 1963.

——. *Military Cold War Education and Speech Review Policies,* 87th Cong., 2nd Sess. Washington, DC: GPO, 1962.

——, Committee on the Judiciary. *Cuba as a Base for Subversion in America,* 88th Cong., 1st Sess. Washington, DC: GPO, 1963.

——, Select Committee to Study Government Operations with Respect to Intelligence Activities. *Alleged Assassination Plots Involving Foreign Leaders,* 94th Cong., 1st Sess. Washington, DC: GPO, 1975.

——, Committee on Foreign Relations. *Executive Sessions of the Senate Foreign Relations Committee Together with Joint Sessions with the Senate Armed Services Committee.* Vol. 14, 87th Cong., 2nd Sess. Washington, DC: GPO, 1986.

———. *Executive Sessions of the Senate Foreign Relations Committee.* Vol. 15, 88th Cong., 1st Sess. Washington, DC: GPO, 1987.

Articles

Allyn, Bruce J., James G. Blight, and David A. Welch. "Essence of Revision: Moscow, Havana, and the Cuban Missile Crisis." *IS* 14, no. 3 (Winter 1989/90): 136–72.

Alsop, Stewart, and Charles Bartlett. "In Time of Crisis." *Saturday Evening Post,* December 8, 1962, 15–21.

Amuchastegui, Domingo. "Cuban Intelligence and the October Crisis." *I&NS* 13, no. 3 (Autumn 1998): 88–119.

Arnold, Joseph C. "Omens and Oracles." *U.S. Naval Institute Proceedings* 106 (August 1980): 48–53.

Bernstein, Barton J. "Bombers, Inspection and the No Invasion Pledge." *Foreign Service Journal* 56, no. 7 (July 1979): 8–12.

———. "Cuban Missile Crisis." In *Encyclopedia of U.S. Foreign Relations,* edited by Bruce W. Jentleson and Thomas G. Paterson, 1:387–96. New York: Oxford University Press, 1997.

———. "The Cuban Missile Crisis: Trading the Jupiters in Turkey?" *Political Science Quarterly* 95, no. 1 (Spring 1980): 97–125.

———. "Reconsidering Khrushchev's Gambit—Defending the Soviet Union and Cuba." *DH* 14, no. 2 (Spring 1990): 231–40.

———. "Understanding Decisionmaking, U.S. Foreign Policy, and the Cuban Missile Crisis: A Review Essay." *IS* 25, no. 1 (Summer 2000): 134–64.

———. "The Week We Almost Went to War." *Bulletin of the Atomic Scientists* 32, no. 2 (February 1976): 13–21.

Blight, James G., Bruce J. Allyn, and David A. Welch, "Kramer vs. Kramer: Or, How Can You Have Revisionism in the Absence of Orthodoxy?" CWIHP *Bulletin,* no. 3 (Fall 1993): 41, 47–50.

———, Joseph S. Nye Jr., and David A. Welch. "The Cuban Missile Crisis Revisited." *FA* 66, no. 1 (Fall 1987): 170–88.

———, and David A. Welch. "What Can Intelligence Tell Us about the Cuban Missile Crisis, and What Can the Cuban Missile Crisis Tell Us about Intelligence?" *I&NS* 13, no. 3 (Autumn 1998): 1–17.

———. "The Cuban Missile Crisis and Intelligence Performance," *I&NS* 13 no. 3, (Autumn 1998): 173–217.

Brugioni, Dino A. "The Cuban Missile Crisis: Phase One." *SII* 16, no. 3 (Fall 1972): 1–52.

Burr, William, and Thomas Blanton, eds. "The Submarines of October: U.S. and Soviet Naval Encounters during the Cuban Missile Crisis." National Security Archive Electronic Briefing Book, no. 75 (October 31, 2002), http://www.gwu.edu/~nsarchiv/NSAEBB/NSAEBB75/.

Campbell, Kenneth J. "John A. McCone: An Outsider Becomes DCI," *SII* 32, no. 2 (Summer 1988): 49–60.

Cline, Ray. "Commentary: The Cuban Missile Crisis." *FA* 68, no. 4 (Fall 1989): 190–96.

Coleman, David G. "The Missiles of November, December, January, February . . . : The Problem of Acceptable Risk in the Cuban Missile Crisis Settlement." *JCWS* 9, no. 3 (Summer 2007): 5–48.

Cooper, Chester L. "The CIA and Decision-Making." *FA* 50, no. 2 (January 1972): 223–36.

Davis, Jack. "Sherman Kent's Final Thoughts on Analyst-Policymaker Relations." Sherman Kent Center for Intelligence Analysis, Occasional Papers 2, no. 3 (June 2003), www.cia.gov/library/kent-center-occasional-papers/vo12no3.htm.

Domínguez, Jorge I. "The @#$%& Missile Crisis: (Or, What Was "Cuban" about U.S. Decisions during the Cuban Missile Crisis?" *DH* 24, no. 2 (Spring 2000): 305–15.

Dorn, A. Walter, and Robert Pauk. "Unsung Mediator: U Thant and the Cuban Missile Crisis." *DH* 33, no. 2 (April 2009): 261–92.

Fischer, Beth A. "Perception, Intelligence Errors, and the Cuban Missile Crisis." *I&NS* 13, no. 3 (Autumn 1998): 150–72.

Fursenko, Alexandr, and Tim Naftali. "Soviet Intelligence and the Cuban Missile Crisis." *I&NS* 13, no. 3 (Autumn 1998): 64–87.

Garthoff, Raymond L. "Cuban Missile Crisis: The Soviet Story." *FP*, no. 72 (Fall 1988): 61–80.

———. "Documenting the Cuban Missile Crisis." *DH* 24, no. 2 (Spring 2000): 297–303.

———. "Evaluating and Using Historical Hearsay." *DH*, 14, no. 2 (Spring 1990): 223–30.

———. "The Havana Conference on the Cuban Missile Crisis." CWIHP *Bulletin*, no. 1 (Spring 1992): 2–4.

———. "New Evidence on the Cuban Missile Crisis: Khrushchev, Nuclear Weapons, and the Cuban Missile Crisis." CWIHP *Bulletin*, no. 11 (Winter 1998): 251–62.

———. "US Intelligence in the Cuban Missile Crisis." *I&NS* 13, no. 3 (Autumn 1998): 18–63.

Giglio, James. "Kennedy on Tape." *DH* 27, no. 5 (November 2003): 747–50.

Gleichauf, Justin F. "A Listening Post in Miami." *SII* 45, no. 1 (Spring 2001): 33–38.

———. "Red Presence in Cuba: The Genesis of a Crisis." *Army* 29 (November 1979): 34–38.

Goodell, Thaxter L. "Cratology Pays Off," *SII* 8, no. 4 (Fall 1964): 1–10.

Greiner, Bernd. "The Soviet View: An Interview with Sergo Mikoyan." *DH* 14, no. 2 (Spring 1990): 205–22.

Haight, David. "Ike and His Spies in the Sky." *Prologue* 41, no. 4 (Winter 2009): 14–22.

Halpern, Samuel. "Revisiting the Cuban Missile Crisis." Society for Historians of American Foreign Relations *Newsletter* 25, no. 1 (March 1994): 1–9.

Hansen, James H. "Soviet Deception in the Cuban Missile Crisis." *SII* 46, no. 1 (2002): 49–58.

Hanyok, Robert J. "A Reconsideration of the Role of SIGINT during the Cuban Missile Crisis, October 1962 (Part 1 of 4)," *Cryptologic Almanac*, 2002, http://www.nsa.gov/public_info/_files/crypto_almanac_50th/reconsideration_of_the_role_of_sigint_part_2.pdf.

Hershberg, James G. "Anatomy of a Controversy: Anatoly F. Dobrynin's Meeting with Robert F. Kennedy, Saturday, 27 October 1962," CWIHP *Bulletin*, no. 5 (Spring 1995): : 75–80.

———. "Before 'The Missiles of October': Did Kennedy Plan a Military Strike against Cuba?" *DH* 14, no. 2 (Spring 1990): 163–98.

Hilsman, Roger, and Ronald Steel. "An Exchange on the Missile Crisis." *NYRB* 12, no. 9 (May 8, 1969): 36–38.

Holland, Max. "A Luce Connection: Senator Keating, William Pawley, and the Cuban Missile Crisis," *JCWS* 1, no. 3 (Fall 1999): 139–67.

———. "More on Post-Mortems." *IJICI* 21, no. 1 (2008): 188–89.

———. "The 'Photo Gap' That Delayed Discovery of Missiles in Cuba," *SII* 49, no. 4 (2005): 15–30.

———. "The Politics of Intelligence Post-Mortems, Cuba 1962–1963," *IJICI* 20, no. 3 (2007): 415–52.

———, with Tara Egan. "What Did LBJ Know about the Cuban Missile Crisis? And When Did He Know It?" *Washington Decoded*, October 19, 2007, www.washingtondecoded.com/site/2007/10/what-did-lbj-kn.html.

Horelick, Arnold L. "The Cuban Missile Crisis: An Analysis of Soviet Calculations and Behavior." *World Politics* 16, no. 3 (April 1964): 363–89.

Hughes, John T., with A. Denis Clift. "The San Cristóbal Trapezoid." *SII* 36, no. 5 (1992): 55–71.

Husain, Aiyaz. "Covert Action and US Cold War Strategy in Cuba, 1961–62." *Cold War History* 5, no. 1 (February 2005): 23–53.

James, Daniel, and John Hubbell. "While America Slept," *Reader's Digest*, March 1963, 60–66, 239–86.

Judt, Tony. "On the Brink." *NYRB* 24, no. 1 (January 15, 1998): 52–59.

Kent, Sherman. "A Crucial Estimate Relived." *SII* 36, no. 5 (1992): 111–19.

———. "The Cuban Missile Crisis of 1962: Presenting the Photographic Evidence Abroad." *SII* 16, no. 2 (Spring 1972): 19–42.

Knorr, Klaus. "Failures in National Intelligence Estimates: The Case of the Cuban Missiles." *World Politics* 16, no. 3 (April 1964).

Kovar, Richard. "Mr. Current Intelligence: An Interview with Richard Lehman." *SII* 43, no. 2 (Summer 1999): 51–63.

Kramer, Mark. "The Cuban Missile Crisis and Nuclear Proliferation." *Security Studies* 5, no. 1 (Autumn 1995): 171–79.

———. "Remembering the Cuban Missile Crisis: Should We Swallow Oral History?" *IS* 15, no. 1 (Summer 1990): 212–18.

———. "Tactical Nuclear Weapons, Soviet Command Authority, and the Cuban Missile Crisis." CWIHP *Bulletin*, no. 3 (Fall 1993): 40, 42–46.

Krasner, Stephen D. "Are Bureaucracies Important? (Or Allison Wonderland)." *FP*, no. 7 (Summer 1972): 159–79.

Krock, Arthur. "Mr. Kennedy's Management of the News." *Fortune*, March 1963, 199–202.

Laffey, Mark, and Jutta Weldes. "Decolonizing the Cuban Missile Crisis." *International Security Quarterly* 52 (2008): 555–77.

Lukas, J. Anthony. "Class Reunion: Kennedy's Men Relive the Cuban Missile Crisis." *NYT Magazine*, August 30, 1987, 22–27, 51, 58, 61.

McAuliffe, Mary S. "Return to the Brink: Intelligence Perspectives on the Cuban Missile Crisis." Society for Historians of American Foreign Relations *Newsletter* 24, no. 2 (June 1993): 4–18.

Merom, Gil. "The 1962 Cuban Intelligence Estimate: A Methodological Perspective." *I&NS* 14, no. 3 (Autumn 1999): 48–80.

Moser, Don. "The Time of the Angel: The U-2, Cuba and the CIA." *American Heritage*. 28, no. 6 (October 1977): 4–15.

Munson, Harlow T., and W. P. Southard. "Two Witnesses for the Defense." *SII* 8, no. 4 (Fall 1964): 93–98.

Nathan, James A. "The Missile Crisis: His Finest Hour Now." *World Politics* 27, no. 2 (January 1975): 256–81.

Nolan, Cynthia M. "The PFIAB Personality: Presidents and Their Foreign Intelligence Boards." *IJICI* 23, no. 1 (December 2009): 27–60.

Orlov, Alexander. "The U-2 Program: A Russian Officer Remembers." *SII*, Winter 1998–99, 5–14.

Parkinson, Len. "Penkovskiy's Legacy and Strategic Research." *SII* 16, no. 2 (Spring 1972): 1–18.

Paterson, Thomas G. "The Defense-of-Cuba Theme and the Missile Crisis." *DH* 14, no. 2 (Spring 1990): 249–56.

———. "The Historian as Detective: Senator Kenneth Keating, the Missiles in Cuba, and His Mysterious Sources." *DH* 11, no. 1 (Winter 1987): 67–71.

———, and William J. Brophy. "October Missiles and November Elections: The Cuban Missile Crisis and American Politics, 1962." *Journal of American History* 73, no. 1 (June 1986): 87–119.

Pious, Richard M. "The Cuban Missile Crisis and the Limits of Crisis Management." *Political Science Quarterly* 116, no. 1 (2001): 81–105.

Pollard, Robert A. "The Cuban Missile Crisis: Legacies and Lessons." *Wilson Quarterly*, Autumn 1982, 148–58.

Pressman, Jeremy. "September Statements, October Missiles, November Elections: Domestic Politics, Foreign Policy Making, and the Cuban Missile Crisis." *Security Studies* 10, no. 3 (Spring 2001): 80–114.

Rabe, Stephen. "After the Missiles of October: John F. Kennedy and Cuba, November 1962 to November 1963." *Presidential Studies Quarterly* 30, no. 4 (December 2000): 714–26.

———. "John F. Kennedy and Latin America: The 'Thorough, Accurate, and Reliable Record' (Almost)." *DH* 23, no. 3 (Summer 1999): 539–52.

Renshon, Jonathan. "Mirroring Risk: The Cuban Missile Estimation." *I&NS* 24, no. 3 (June 2009): 315–38.

Rovere, Richard. "Letter from Washington." *New Yorker,* March 2, 1963, 125–31.

Rumpelmayer, J. J. "The Missiles in Cuba." *SII* 8, no. 4 (Fall 1964): 87–92.

Savaranskaya, Svetlana. "Tactical Nuclear Weapons in Cuba: New Evidence." CWIHP *Bulletin,* nos. 14/15 (Winter 2003/Spring 2004): 385–98.

Scott, Len. "Espionage and the Cold War: Oleg Penkovsky and the Cuban Missile Crisis." *I&NS* 14, no. 3 (Autumn 1999): 23–47.

———, and Steve Smith. "Lessons of October: Historians, Political Scientists, Policy-Makers and the Cuban Missile Crisis." *International Affairs* 70, no. 4 (1994): 659–84.

Scott, William F. "The Face of Moscow in the Missile Crisis." *SII* 10, no. 2 (Spring 1966): 29–36.

Shryock, Richard. "The Intelligence Community Post-Mortem Program, 1973–1975." *SII* 21, no. 3 (Fall 1977): 15–28.

Smith, Michael Douglas. "Revisiting Sherman Kent's Defense of SNIE 85-3-62." *SII* 51, no. 3 (September 2007): 29–32.

Steel, Ronald. "Endgame." *NYRB* 12, no. 5 (March 13, 1969): 15–22.

Stern, Sheldon M., and Max Holland. "Presidential Tapes and Transcripts: Crafting a New Historical Genre." History News Network, February 21, 2005, http://hnn.us/node/10256.

Stone, I. F. "The Brink." *NYRB* 6, no. 6 (April 14, 1966): 12–16.

Tierney, Dominic. "'Pearl Harbor in Reverse': Moral Analogies in the Cuba Missile Crisis." *JCWS* 9, no. 3 (Summer 2007): 49–77.

Trachtenberg, Marc. "The Influence of Nuclear Weapons in the Cuban Missile Crisis." *IS* 10, no. 1 (Summer 1985): 137–63.

———. "New Light on the Cuban Missile Crisis?" *DH* 14, no. 2 (Spring 1990): 241–48.

Usowski, Peter S. "John McCone and the Cuban Missile Crisis: A Persistent Approach to the Intelligence-Policy Relationship." *IJICI* 2, no. 4 (Winter 1988): 547–76.

White, Mark J. "New Scholarship on the Cuban Missile Crisis." *DH* 26, no. 1 (Winter 2002): 147–53.

Wirtz, James J. "Organizing for Crisis Intelligence: Lessons from the Cuban Missile Crisis." *I&NS* 13, no. 3 (Autumn 1998): 120–49.

Wohlstetter, Roberta. "Cuba and Pearl Harbor: Hindsight and Foresight." *FA* 43, no. 4 (July 1965): 691–707.

Books and Monographs

Abel, Elie. *The Missile Crisis*. Philadelphia, PA: J.B. Lippincott, 1966.

——. *The Missile Crisis*. 3rd ed. New York: Bantam Books, 1968.

Absher, Kenneth M. *Mind-Sets and Missiles: A First-Hand Account of the Cuban Missile Crisis*. Carlisle, PA: Strategic Studies Institute, U.S. Army War College, 2009.

——, Michal Desch, and Roman Popadiuk. *Confidential and Privileged: The President's Foreign Intelligence Advisory Board*. Washington, DC: Richard Lounsberry Foundation, 2008.

Acacia, John. *Clark Clifford: The Wise Man of Washington*. Lexington: University Press of Kentucky, 2009.

Allison, Graham T. *Essence of Decision: Explaining the Cuban Missile Crisis*. Boston: Little, Brown, 1971.

——, and Philip Zelikow. *Essence of Decision: Explaining the Cuban Missile Crisis*. 2nd ed. New York: Longman, 1999.

Allyn, Bruce J., James G. Blight, and David A. Welch, eds. *Back to the Brink: Proceedings of the Moscow Conference on the Cuban Missile Crisis, January 27–28, 1989*. Lanham, MD: University Press of America, 1992.

Alterman, Eric. *When Presidents Lie: A History of Official Deception and Its Consequences*. New York: Viking, 2004.

Ball, George W. *The Past Has Another Pattern: Memoirs*. New York: W. W. Norton, 1982.

Barrett, David M. *The CIA and Congress: The Untold Story from Truman to Kennedy*. Lawrence: University of Kansas Press, 2005.

Beschloss, Michael R. *The Crisis Years: Kennedy and Khrushchev, 1960–1963*. New York: Edward Burlingame Books, 1991.

Blight, James G., Bruce J. Allyn, and David A. Welch, eds. *Cuba on the Brink: Castro, the Missile Crisis, and the Soviet Collapse*. New York: Pantheon Books, 1993.

——, and Philip Brenner. *Sad and Luminous Days: Cuba's Struggle with the Superpowers after the Missile Crisis*. Lanham, MD: Rowman & Littlefield, 2002.

——, and David A. Welch, eds. *Intelligence and the Cuban Missile Crisis*. Portland, OR: Frank Cass, 1998.

——, and David A. Welch. *On the Brink: Americans and Soviets Reexamine the Cuban Missile Crisis*. New York: Hill and Wang, 1989.

Bohning, Don. *The Castro Obsession: U.S. Covert Operations against Cuba, 1959–1965*. Washington, DC: Potomac Books, 2005.

Brune, Lester H. *The Missile Crisis of October 1962: A Review of Issues and References*. Claremont, CA: Regina Books, 1985.

Brugioni, Dino A. *Eyeball to Eyeball: The Inside Story of the Cuban Missile Crisis*. Edited by Robert F. McCort. New York: Random House, 1990.

——. *Eyes in the Sky: Eisenhower, the CIA, and Cold War Aerial Espionage*. Annapolis, MD: Naval Institute Press, 2010.

Bundy, McGeorge. *Danger and Survival: Choices about the Bomb in the First Fifty Years.* New York: Random House, 1988.

Chang, Laurence, and Peter Kornbluh. *The Cuban Missile Crisis, 1962: A National Security Archive Documents Reader.* New York: The New Press, 1992.

Chayes, Abram. *The Cuban Missile Crisis: International Crises and the Role of Law.* New York: Oxford University Press, 1974.

Childs, Marquis W. *Witness to Power.* New York: McGraw Hill, 1975.

Cimbala, Stephen J. *Nuclear Strategy in the Twenty-First Century.* Westport, CT: Praeger, 2000.

Clifford, Clark, with Richard Holbrooke. *Counsel to the President.* New York: Random House, 1991.

Cline, Ray S. *Secrets, Spies, and Scholars: Blueprint of the Essential CIA.* Washington, DC: Acropolis Books, 1976.

Detzer, David, *The Brink: Cuban Missile Crisis, 1962.* New York: Crowell, 1979.

Dinerstein, Herbert S. *The Making of a Missile Crisis: October 1962.* Baltimore: Johns Hopkins University Press, 1976.

Divine, Robert A., ed. *The Cuban Missile Crisis.* 2nd ed. New York: Markus Wiener Publishing, 1988.

Dobbs, Michael. *One Minute to Midnight: Kennedy, Khrushchev, and Castro on the Brink of Nuclear War.* New York: Alfred A. Knopf, 2008.

Dobrynin, Anatoly. *In Confidence: Moscow's Ambassador to America's Six Cold War Presidents, 1962–1986.* New York: Times Books, 1995.

FitzSimons, Louise. *The Kennedy Doctrine.* New York: Random House, 1972.

Frankel, Max. *High Noon in the Cold War: Kennedy, Khrushchev, and the Missile Crisis.* New York: Ballantine Books, 2004.

Freedman, Lawrence. *Kennedy's Wars: Berlin, Cuba, Laos, and Vietnam.* New York: Oxford University Press, 2000.

Fry, Joseph A. *Debating Vietnam: Fulbright, Stennis and Their Senate Hearings.* Lanham, MD: Rowman and Littlefield, 2006.

Fursenko, Aleksandr, and Tim Naftali. *"One Hell of a Gamble": Khrushchev, Castro and Kennedy, 1958–1964.* New York: W. W Norton, 1997.

Garthoff, Raymond L. *Intelligence Assessment and Policymaking: A Decision Point in the Kennedy Administration.* Washington, DC: Brookings Institution, 1984.

———. *Reflections on the Cuban Missile Crisis.* Rev. ed. Washington, DC: Brookings Institution, 1989.

George, Alexander, L., ed. *Avoiding War: Problems of Crisis Management.* Boulder, CO: Westview Press, 1991.

———, and Richard Smoke. *Deterrence in American Foreign Policy: Theory and Practice.* New York: Columbia University Press, 1974.

Grabo, Cynthia M. *Anticipating Surprise: Analysis for Strategic Warning.* Lanham, MD: University Press of America, 2004.

Greene, Benjamin P. *Eisenhower, Science Advice, and the Nuclear Test-Ban Debate, 1945–1963.* Stanford, CA: Stanford University Press, 2007.

Gribkov, Anatoli I., and William Y. Smith. *Operation ANADYR: U.S. and Soviet Generals Recount the Cuban Missile Crisis.* Chicago: Edition q, 1994.

Guthman, Edwin O., and Jeffrey Shulman, eds. *Robert Kennedy in His Own Words: The Unpublished Recollections of the Kennedy Years.* New York: Bantam Press, 1988.

Helms, Richard, with William Hood. *A Look over My Shoulder: A Life in the Central Intelligence Agency.* New York: Random House, 2003.

Hilsman, Roger. *The Cuban Missile Crisis: The Struggle over Policy.* Westport, CT: Praeger, 1996.

———. *To Move a Nation: The Politics of Foreign Policy in the Administration of John F. Kennedy.* Garden City, NY: Doubleday & Company, 1967.

Holland, Max. *The Kennedy Assassination Tapes: The White House Conversations of Lyndon B. Johnson Regarding the Assassination, the Warren Commission and the Aftermath.* New York: Alfred A. Knopf, 2004.

Hughes, Thomas L. *The Fate of Facts in a World of Men: Foreign Policy and Intelligence-Making.* New York: Foreign Policy Association, 1976.

———. *Perilous Encounters: The Cold War Collisions of Domestic and World Politics.* Bloomington, IN: Xlibris, 2011.

James, Daniel, and John Hubbell. *Strike in the West: The Complete Story of the Cuban Crisis.* New York: Holt, Rinehart & Winston, 1964.

Johns, Andrew L. *Vietnam's Second Front: Domestic Politics, the Republican Party, and the War.* Lexington: University Press of Kentucky, 2010.

Johnson, Loch K. *A Season of Inquiry: The Senate Intelligence Investigation.* Lexington: University Press of Kentucky, 1985.

Johnson, Robert. *Congress and the Cold War.* New York: Cambridge University Press, 2006.

Johnson, U. Alexis, with Jef Olivarius McAllister. *The Right Hand of Power: The Memoirs of an American Diplomat.* Englewood Cliffs, NJ: Prentice-Hall, 1984.

Katz, Amrom. *The Soviets and the U-2 Photos—A Heuristic Argument.* Santa Monica, CA: RAND Corporation, 1963.

Kennedy, Robert F. *Thirteen Days: A Memoir of the Cuban Missile Crisis.* New York: W. W. Norton, 1969.

Khrushchev, Nikita S. *Khrushchev Remembers: The Glasnost Tapes.* Translated and edited by Jerrold L. Schecter with Vyacheslav V. Luchkov. Boston: Little, Brown, 1990.

———. *Khrushchev Remembers: The Last Testament.* Translated and edited by Strobe Talbott. Boston: Little, Brown, 1974.

Khrushchev, Sergei, ed. *Memoirs of Nikita Khrushchev: Statesman, 1953–1964.* University Park: Pennsylvania State University Press, 2007.

Kistiakowsky, George. *A Scientist at the White House: The Private Diary of President*

Eisenhower's Special Assistant for Science and Technology. Cambridge, MA: Harvard University Press, 1976.

Kitts, Kenneth. *Presidential Commissions and National Security: The Politics of Damage Control*. Boulder, CO: Lynne Rienner, 2006.

Krock, Arthur. *Memoirs: Sixty Years on the Firing Line*. New York: Funk & Wagnalls, 1968.

Laquer, Walter. *A World of Secrets: The Uses and Limits of Intelligence*. New York: Basic Books, 1985.

Larson, David, ed. *The "Cuban Crisis" of 1962*. Boston: Houghton Mifflin, 1963.

Lebow, Richard Ned, and Janice Gross Stein. *We All Lost the Cold War*. Princeton, NJ: Princeton University Press, 1994.

McNamara, Robert, and Brian Van DeMark. *In Retrospect: The Tragedy and Lessons of Vietnam*. New York: Times Books, 1995.

Martin, John Bartlow. *Adlai Stevenson and the World: The Life of Adlai E. Stevenson*. Garden City, NY: Anchor Books, 1978.

May, Ernest, and Philip Zelikow. *The Kennedy Tapes: Inside the White House during the Cuban Missile Crisis*. Cambridge, MA: Belknap Press, 1997.

Mearsheimer, John J. *Why Leaders Lie: The Truth about Lying in International Politics*. New York: Oxford University Press, 2011.

Medland, William J. *The Cuban Missile Crisis of 1962: Needless or Necessary*. New York: Praeger, 1988.

Munton, Don, and David A. Welch. *The Cuban Missile Crisis: A Concise History*. New York: Oxford University Press, 2007.

Naftali, Tim, and Philip Zelikow, eds. *The Presidential Recordings, John F. Kennedy: The Great Crises*. Vol. 2, *September 4–October 21, 1962*. New York: W. W. Norton, 2001.

Nash, Philip. *The Other Missiles of October: Eisenhower, Kennedy, and the Jupiters, 1957–1963*. Chapel Hill: University of North Carolina Press, 1997.

Nathan, James A., ed. *The Cuban Missile Crisis Revisited*. New York: St. Martin's Press, 1992.

Newhouse, John. *War and Peace in the Nuclear Age*. New York: Alfred A. Knopf, 1989.

Ogul, Morris S. *Congress Oversees the Bureaucracy: Studies in Legislative Supervision*. Pittsburgh, PA: University of Pittsburgh Press, 1976.

Pachter, Henry M. *Collision Course: The Cuban Missile Crisis and Coexistence*. New York: Praeger, 1963.

Paterson, Thomas G. *Contesting Castro: The United States and the Triumph of the Cuban Revolution*. New York: Oxford University Press, 1994.

Penkovsky, Oleg. *The Penkovsky Papers*. Garden City, NY: Doubleday, 1965.

Polmar, Norman, and John D. Gresham. *DEFCON-2: Standing on the Brink of Nuclear War during the Cuban Missile Crisis*. Hoboken, NJ: John Wiley & Sons, 2006.

Pope, Ronald R. *Soviet Views on the Cuban Missile Crisis: Myth and Reality in Foreign Policy Analysis*. Washington, DC: University Press of America, 1982.

Power, Thomas S. *Design for Survival*. New York: Coward-McCann, 1965.

Prados, John. *The Soviet Estimate: U.S. Intelligence Analysis and Russian Military Strength*. New York: Dial Press, 1982.

Preble, Christopher A. *John F. Kennedy and the Missile Gap*. DeKalb: Northern Illinois University Press, 2004.

Ranelagh, John. *The Agency: The Rise and Decline of the CIA*. New York: Simon & Schuster, 1986.

Richelson, Jeffrey T. *The Wizards of Langley: Inside the CIA's Directorate of Science and Technology*. Boulder, CO: Westview Press, 2001.

Rovner, Joshua. *Fixing the Facts: National Security and the Politics of Intelligence*. Ithaca, NY: Cornell University Press, 2011.

Rusk, Dean, as told to Richard Rusk. *As I Saw It*. New York: W. W. Norton, 1990.

Schecter, Jerrold L., and Peter S. Deriabin. *The Spy Who Saved the World: How a Soviet Colonel Changed the Course of the Cold War*. New York: Charles Scribner's Sons, 1992.

Schlesinger, Arthur M., Jr. *Robert Kennedy and His Times*. Boston: Houghton Mifflin, 1978.

———. *A Thousand Days: John F. Kennedy in the White House*. Boston: Houghton Mifflin, 1965.

Schoultz, Lars. *That Infernal Little Cuban Republic: The United States and the Cuban Revolution*. Chapel Hill: University of North Carolina Press, 2009.

Shackley, Ted, with Richard A. Finney. *Spymaster: My Life in the CIA*. Dulles, VA: Potomac Books, 2005.

Sherman, Janann. *No Place for a Woman: A Life of Senator Margaret Chase Smith*. New Brunswick, NJ: Rutgers University Press, 2000.

Sorensen, Theodore C. *Kennedy*. New York: Harper & Row, 1965.

Stern, Sheldon M. *Averting the 'Final Failure': John F. Kennedy and the Secret Cuban Missile Crisis Meetings*. Stanford, CA: Stanford University Press, 2003.

Taubman, William. *Khrushchev: The Man and His Era*. New York: W. W. Norton, 2003.

Taylor, Maxwell D. *Swords and Plowshares*. New York: W. W. Norton, 1972.

Thomas, Hugh. *Cuba: The Pursuit of Freedom*. New York: Harper & Row, 1971.

Thompson, Robert S. *The Missiles of October: The Declassified Story of John F. Kennedy and the Cuban Missile Crisis*. New York: Simon & Schuster, 1992.

Turner, Michael A. *Why Secret Intelligence Fails*. Rev. ed. Washington, DC: Potomac Books, 2006.

Ulam, Adam B. *Expansion and Coexistence: The History of Soviet Foreign Policy, 1917–1967*. New York: Praeger, 1968.

Weintal, Edward, and Charles Bartlett. *Facing the Brink: An Intimate Study of Crisis Diplomacy*. New York: Charles Scribner's Sons, 1967.

Weber, Ralph E., ed. *Spymasters: Ten CIA Officers in Their Own Words*. Wilmington, DE: Scholarly Resources, 1999.

Weiner, Tim. *Legacy of Ashes: The History of the CIA*. New York: Doubleday, 2007.

Weldes, Jutta. *Constructing National Interests: The United States and the Cuban Missile Crisis*. Minneapolis: University of Minnesota Press, 1999.

Weisbrot, Robert. *Maximum Danger: Kennedy, the Missiles, and the Crisis of American Confidence*. Chicago: Ivan R. Dee, 2001.

White, Mark J. *The Cuban Missile Crisis*. Basingstoke, Hampshire, UK: Macmillan, 1996.

Witcover, Jules. *The Making of an Ink-Stained Wretch: Half a Century Pounding the Political Beat*. Baltimore: Johns Hopkins University Press, 2005.

Wohlstetter, Roberta. *Pearl Harbor: Warning and Decision*. Stanford, CA: Stanford University Press, 1962.

Zelikow, Philip, and Ernest May, eds. *The Presidential Recordings, John F. Kennedy: The Great Crises*. Vol. 3, *October 22–28, 1962*. New York: W. W. Norton, 2001.

Zelizer, Julian E. *Arsenal of Democracy: The Politics of National Security from World War II to the War on Terrorism*. New York: Basic Books, 2010.

Zubok, Vladislav M. *A Failed Empire: The Soviet Union in the Cold War from Stalin to Gorbachev*. Chapel Hill: University of North Carolina Press, 2007.

Index

Abel, Elie, 70, 121–22, 124–27
Absher, Kenneth M., 119, 142
Acheson, Dean, 121
Air Force, 18–20, 80, 86, 100, 106, 125;
  competition with the CIA over piloting
  of U-2s, 154n111, 175n67
Allen, Robert, 74, 103–104
Allison, Graham, 25, 125–27, 129, 138, 184n35
al-Qai'da, 116
Alsop, Joseph, 34–35
Alsop, Stewart, 34, 38, 55, 57
Alterman, Eric, 140, 182n3
American Heritage, 127
Anticipating Surprise (Grabo), 140
Appropriations Committee, House, 64–67,
  77, 93; CIA Subcommittee, 18, 62;
  Defense Subcommittee, 58, 62, 80,
  93
Appropriations Committee, Senate, 103;
  CIA Subcommittee, 101, 180n11
Arends, Les, 60
Argentina, 74
Armed Services Committee, House, 59–61;
  CIA Subcommittee, 61
Armed Services Committee, Senate, 12,
  32, 68, 80, 100–101, 103; CIA Sub-
  committee, 19, 70, 100–101, 180n11;
  Preparedness Investigating Subcom-
  mittee (SPIS), 71, 92; as viewed by the
  administration, 85, 109; hearings held
  by, 72–74, 86, 95–98, 101–104, 106, 111,

112; history of, 68–69; investigation by,
  72–75, 80–81, 101; Interim Report of,
  97, 99, 102–12, 114, 117, 182n54; staff of,
  82–85, 96, 101–102, 108, 110–11
Army, 94
Army magazine, 74
Arnold, Joseph C., 128
Artime, Manuel, 72
Associated Press, 35, 66
Atomic Energy Commission, 2, 3, 47

Baldwin, Hanson, 33, 35, 79, 93
Ball, George, 4, 67, 77, 79, 82, 84, 109, 121,
  128–29, 131, 146n5, 172n30
Bartlett, Charles, 38, 55, 122
Bay of Pigs, 1–3, 8, 14, 22–23, 47, 55, 58, 72,
  87, 104, 112, 113, 177n31
Berlin, 1, 4, 23, 24, 30
Bernstein, Barton J., 27, 184n35
Beschloss, Michael, 132
Blight, James, 131, 134, 137
Board of National Estimates, 5, 150n61
Bohlen, Charles, 5
Bolton, Frances, 77
bomber aircraft, Soviet (IL-28s), 18, 26,
  31, 56
Bowles, Chester, 22–23
Breitweiser, Robert, 86–87
Bridges, Styles, 100–101
Brink, The (Detzer), 128
Brugioni, Dino, 132, 134, 139–41